T0330002

Purchasing Identity in
the Atlantic World

Purchasing Identity in the Atlantic World

MASSACHUSETTS MERCHANTS, 1670–1780

Phyllis Whitman Hunter

CORNELL UNIVERSITY PRESS
ITHACA AND LONDON

First published 2001 by Cornell University Press

Printed in the United States of America

Library of Congress Cataloging-in-Publication Data

Hunter, Phyllis Whitman, 1943-
    Purchasing identity in the Atlantic world : Massachusetts merchants,
1670-1780 / Phyllis Whitman Hunter.
        p. cm.
    Includes bibliographical references and index.
    ISBN 0-8014-3855-1 (alk. paper)
        1. Massachusetts—Economic conditions. 2. Merchants—Massachusetts.
3. Consumption (Economics)—Social aspects—Massachusetts. 4. Massachusetts—Commerce—Europe. 5. Europe—Commerce—Massachusetts.
6. Massachusetts—Social life and customs. 7. Massachusetts—History—
Colonial period, ca. 1600-1775. 8. Massachusetts—History—Revolution,
1775-1783. I. Title.
    HC107.M4 H86 2001
    381'.09744'09032—dc21
                                                    00-012709

Cornell University Press strives to use environmentally responsible suppliers and materials to the fullest extent possible in the publishing of its books. Such materials include vegetable-based, low-VOC inks and acid-free papers that are recycled, totally chlorine-free, or partly composed of nonwood fibers. Books that bear the logo of the FSC (Forest Stewardship Council) use paper taken from forests that have been inspect-ed and certified as meeting the highest standards for environmental and social responsi-bility. For further information, visit our website at www.cornellpress.cornell.edu.

Cloth printing   10 9 8 7 6 5 4 3 2 1

FRONTISPIECE: Bristol, England by Robert Salmon, 1828. Courtesy of the Peabody Essex Museum, Salem, Massachusetts.

In memory of Dorothy and Newton
and
In gratitude for Kim and Zac

Contents

viii   Contents

Illustrations, Maps, and Tables

Acknowledgments

I BROUGHT A MIXED background of experience and interest to the research and conceptualization of this book. I had developed a strong sense of identification with seventeenth-century New Englanders, honed by restoring and researching a house built between 1654 and 1680 in Rowley, Massachusetts. A subsequent career in business produced questions about our ability to understand capitalism and its consequences in late twentieth-century America. It is not surprising, then, that I produced a book whose leading cast of characters is seventeenth- and eighteenth-century merchants, the leading capitalists of their era; nor that I undertook a study of the impact of capitalism on the material and social landscape. This work is not an effort to celebrate or denigrate individual enterprise but to explore connections between economic decisions and cultural production. Perhaps if we understand more clearly how those connections worked at a crucial moment in the past, then we will be able to demystify the specter of global capitalism and understand that it is a product of human decisions and values and therefore can be modified.

This book is the product of many people making the decision to extend a helping hand to a "young" scholar. Beginning work on an M.A. at the University of South Florida, I had the good fortune to be taken in hand by Nancy Hewitt and Steven Lawson who remain mentors and friends. In addition, Ray Arsenault encouraged me, and all his students, to aspire to fine writing as well as good history.

Purchasing Identity in the Atlantic World has been supported by fellowships from the University of North Carolina at Greensboro, the College of William and Mary, the American Antiquarian Society, Massachusetts Historical Society, and the Peabody Essex Museum. Particular thanks go to Nancy Burkett, Joanne Chaison, John Hench, Caroline Sloat and all my other friends at the American Antiquarian Society, to Peter Drummey, Conrad Wright, and the staff of the Massachusetts Historical Society, and to Will La Moy, Jane Ward, and their staff at the Phillips Library of the Peabody Essex Museum.

First among those who have contributed to this book is Robert Gross. Since our first meeting, Bob has applied his extraordinary intensity, brilliance, and commitment to this project and to the making of this historian. At William and Mary, Mike McGiffert read and edited several drafts of my dissertation and always offered a receptive but questioning audience for new ideas. Margaretta Lovell and Barbara Carson introduced me to material culture studies and the exciting debates about the complex relations between objects and people. Richard Bushman's perceptive comments as outside reader of my dissertation continued to influence the scope and direction of further research and subsequent conclusions. Others have read and offered caring and insightful comments on parts or all of this study, including Christopher Clark, Clyde Haulman, Adam Potkay, Caroline Sloat, Conrad Wright, Sharon Zuber, and my extraordinarily generous colleagues at the University of North Carolina at Greensboro—Robert Calhoon, Bill Link, and Nan Enstad. They, and commentators at a wide variety of conferences, offer ample evidence that history is a collaborative venture. Because our work ultimately finds expression in a single voice, however, the faults are my own.

Purchasing Identity in the Atlantic World

Introduction
"Emporium for the World"

The different progress of opulence in different ages and nations, has given occasion to two different systems of political oeconomy, with regard to enriching the people. . . . I shall endeavour to explain both as fully and distinctly as I can, and shall begin with the system of commerce. It is the modern system, and is best understood in our own country and in our own times.

ADAM SMITH, *The Wealth of Nations*, 1776

DURING A VISIT TO Bristol in 1739, Alexander Pope marveled at the sight of a river flowing through the center of the city flanked by a wide quay lined with shops and warehouses. Pope described the busy scene: "you come to a key [quay] along the old wall with houses on both sides, and in the middle of the street, as far as you can see, hundreds of ships, their masts as thick as they can stand by one another." He pronounced it "the oddest and most surprising sight imaginable."[1] Other visitors to eighteenth-century ports often remarked in letters and travel accounts on harbors crowded with ships from all over the Atlantic world. In completing *A Tour Through the Whole Island of Great Britain*, Daniel Defoe despaired of rendering an adequate account of the Pool, the part of the River Thames that served as the port of London. He asked his readers, "In what manner can any writer go about it, to bring [it] into any reasonable compass? The thing is a kind of infinite, and the parts . . . are so many, that it is hard to know where to begin." Defoe's efforts to capture the infinite prompted him "to count the ships as well as I could"; he "found above 2,000 sail of all sorts . . . that really go to sea."[2]

While not sporting as many as the two thousand ships crowding the Thames, ports of colonial America could compare in traffic and size with Bristol and other provincial British harbor towns.[3] Visitors called Boston, whose curving shore was lined with docks and wharves, a "large & Comodious" seaport.[4] Its Long Wharf, built in 1711–13, extended well into the bay, providing deep-water mooring that sheltered vessels "in

1

great Safety." A gentlemanly traveler sojourning there during wartime (1744) observed that even during periods of slack trade there "were above 100 ships in the harbor besides a great number of small craft." In time of peace, Dr. Alexander Hamilton noted, Boston was "a considerable place for shipping" and the merchants there carried on "a great trade." As early as 1700, a resident of Salem described a "large" trade whose "principle commodities are dry merchandise cod-fish fit for the markets of Spain [and] Portugal" and "also refuse dry fish, mackerel, lumber, horses and provision for the West Indies." When asked "whether Salem or Boston be the best place for trade?" he equivocated, indicating that both ports carried on significant business. A decade later, a seafaring captain who left an account of his voyages noted of Salem that "the Inhabitants are very industrious and carry on a very considerable Trade to the Southern Plantations." He went on to describe "a very good Trade to the Isles of Azores and Madera," as well as taking off "great Quantities of the British Manufactures and in return build us Ships."[5]

England's overseas exports expanded rapidly between 1720 and 1745; goods shipped to the East Indies increased sevenfold while shipments to the West Indies doubled.[6] The growth in trade with the American colonies invigorated westward-facing British ports including Bristol, Liverpool, and Glasgow, and colonial demand boosted British industry. Wrought iron and iron nail exports, for example, tripled during the same decades, with much of the output headed for North America. Throughout most of the eighteenth century an increasing proportion of the country's trade involved exchange of goods between the colonies and Britain. Before and after 1760, a natural connection developed between "the newest and most dynamic manufactures and the newest and most dynamic markets." And the volume of trade with the Americas grew two to three times as fast as commerce with other parts of the globe.[7]

Long-distance trade stimulated the growth and spread of capitalism. To satisfy growing demand traders sent ships sailing along the European, African, and American coasts and back and forth across the Atlantic. Commodities (fur, timber, produce, and fish), slaves, and newly abundant consumer goods (tobacco, tea, coffee, sugar, silk, calico, and porcelain) arrived from Africa, the Americas, and the Far East to slake the markets of Britain and Europe.[8] Economic expansion during this period is often characterized as "mercantilism" or "mercantile capitalism," a term that emphasizes state control over the flow of trade and competition for resources among European powers.[9] But studies of individual merchants trading overseas indicate that mercantilism operated more effectively in theory than practice.[10] What did characterize capitalist merchants during this era was an aggressive pursuit of products to ship, a search for market correspondents to sell them in distant locations, an effort to build regularity and predictability into an inherently risky business, and a desire to invest in the goods and knowledge necessary to enter the genteel ranks in their local society—a local society much like those developing in other provincial seaports on both sides of the North Atlantic.[11]

Capitalism not only changed the ocean from a vast barrier to an open channel for foreign goods and people but also produced and responded to profound cultural changes in the lives of those touched by the Atlantic economy. During the seventeenth and eighteenth centuries, Europeans in England and on the Continent struggled to understand and incorporate stories and goods from recently "discovered" lands in the Western Hemisphere and products from newly exploited peoples of Asia. European beliefs and values, challenged by knowledge of other cultures and unsettled by changes at home, altered to accommodate new ideas and practices born from a heady mix of cultural differences and growing evidence of human control over the world.

How can we bring into concrete form and particular detail the sweeping changes sketched above? How can we begin to understand the power of capitalism to produce not only economic results but cultural transformations? For example, Philip English, a trader raised in the French culture of the island of Jersey, met with a mixed and often hostile reception in seventeenth-century Salem in spite of becoming a successful merchant in a town run by wealthy merchants. Yet by the eighteenth century, another Jersey family, the Cabots, easily joined Salem's local elite, and by the nineteenth century, the Cabot family reigned as leaders of Boston society. Likewise, the Faneuils, a French Huguenot family, were able to overcome ethnic and religious differences and rise to the highest social as well as economic ranks in mid-eighteenth-century Boston. What had changed? And why?

One way to understand the sweeping changes brought about by capitalism is to study the lives of overseas merchants—the preeminent capitalists of their era. (Throughout this work, I reserve the term "merchant" for those involved in initiating and directing overseas trade. I am not including retailers, shopkeepers, middlemen working within a regional market area, or passive investors in ships and cargoes.) Merchants led the way in many facets of economic and cultural change. In concert with other influential groups, they used their economic resources to reshape social and cultural life. Prosperous merchants acquired extensive contacts overseas, abundant disposable income, recent knowledge of the latest fashions, easy access to foreign goods, and, most importantly, a growing sense of confidence in human ability to shape the present and predict the future.[12] Prompted by a constant need for up-to-date information from around the world to govern business decisions, overseas traders fostered a growing demand for public print. In pursuit of profits, merchants brought cultural diversity to Anglo-American ports—a diversity that unsettled existing social categories. Eventually individual and group choices produced a new culture that enhanced the position and power of the mercantile elite.

The cultural response to an economy fueled by the exchange of goods appeared most concretely in the material culture of port towns and their leading citizens. Often, the effects of capitalism in the age of long-distance trade are studied with attention to production, exports, and finance. Analyses concentrate on the growing volume of goods shipped from the colonies to the mother country and the alleged debt of colonial merchants to British firms.[13] But they tell us little about the cultural effects on merchants and citizens of daily exposure to the processes of gathering, packing, valuing, loading, unloading, buying, selling, and accounting for vast quantities of goods, from piles of rough timber to well-fashioned chests of drawers, from barrels of molasses to pints of rum, from chests of tea to porcelain cups. Theirs was a world financed and supported by moving goods. It is no wonder, then, that the leading figures of this society responded by developing a culture that emphasized the value of material objects in defining self and creating community. As leading capitalists in a growing economy, merchants played a significant role in shaping the urban landscape of port cities throughout Anglo-America. Operating with extensive funds, they also reconfigured the definition of a gentleman, previously associated with family origins, inherited income, extensive land holdings, and an important country seat. In market towns, and especially in London, where the exchange of goods accounted for a great deal of the business and life of the town, landed property and a country seat were no longer the essential requirements for elite status.[14] In England and in British North America, the urban elite, wealthy merchants at the fore, developed a particular culture, borrowing from aristocratic customs and developing their own forms of housing and sociability.[15] In the process they became the exemplars of "a polite and commercial people." It was not just through production (in the form of trade) and involvement in assessing, moving, and inscribing material goods that merchants reformed society, but also through their consumption of high-style possessions deployed to reshape social class and individual identity. Both practices advanced a growing emphasis on finding value in the material characteristics of objects and persons.

This cultural process developed in different ways and at a different pace throughout Anglo-America during the seventeenth and eighteenth centuries. The transformation took on a particular intensity in Puritan New England. Puritan colonists found their "ground of being" in a complex of Calvinist beliefs—predestination, free grace, and a providential interpretation of worldly events. In constructing their new Zion, they espoused a narrow, highly spiritual definition of community along with an expansive economic policy.[16] These two goals brought about opposing consequences but few Puritans were willing to acknowledge the built-in contradiction. They continued to believe that piety could tame the potentially divisive effects of profits. But the increasing influence of cultural diversity and a growing interest in consumer culture made the shift to new values later in the century inevitable yet painful. From a committed belief in the primacy of the unseen spiritual world of God and the Devil, some New Englanders traveled to a functional outlook that through science and commerce man had shed light on nature and made value visible. Others found their voices increasingly muffled by new families with conflicting values. Urban Anglo-Americans enmeshed in a world of goods found meaning and identity in the material world. Possessions, or lack thereof, mediated their relations to others. Fashionable clothes, for example, not only marked worldly affluence but also signaled new modes of experiencing and thinking about self-in-the-world. Ships transported not only profitable commodities but also the novel conception that the good of humankind could be found, not in the providence of God, but in the goods of men and women.[17]

In tracing the cultural transformations explored here, I have transgressed disciplinary boundaries by drawing on methods and interpretations from cultural anthropology, social history, the study of material culture, and cultural studies. Various approaches have shaped the questions I have asked and made possible the answers. Building this interdisciplinary work required interlacing several strands of historical scholarship. Two of the most significant interpretative conversations can be summarized in the phrases "transition to capitalism" and "the consumer revolution."

This book joins an ongoing enterprise of constructing an international history of the growth of capitalism. Any study of capitalism and cultural change in early New England engages the seminal work of German sociologist Max Weber, *The Protestant Ethic and the Spirit of Capitalism*, published at the beginning of the twentieth century.[18] In that essay, Weber concludes that a particular religious outlook created in its followers a devotion to rational and incessant striving, which Weber denotes as the "spirit of capitalism." This spirit continued to flourish in the West even after the religious beliefs that engendered it changed or died out. Beginning with a comparative perspective, Weber observes that pietist sects in England, France, and North America, most notably the Puritans, adopted a "doctrine of the calling" that encouraged believers to be diligent and please God by their "active performance of His will in a calling." A believer's daily work was to be pursued through a methodical, rational striving, accompanied by what Weber names "worldly asceticism," which "turned with all its force against one thing: the spontaneous enjoyment of life" and also "restricted consumption, especially of luxuries." Emphasis on the calling was intensified by Calvinist belief in predestination—a conviction that God had preselected those who would join him in Heaven and those who would go to Hell. While good deeds on earth could not determine one's ultimate fate, the elect were expected to behave as if they had been chosen. This dilemma created what Weber terms "strong 'psychological sanctions' " brought forth by the "necessity of proving one's faith in worldly activity." Weber suggests that by faithfully following a particular calling and practicing "worldly asceticism," Puritans came to valorize work yet eschew the wasteful consumption that often accompanied wealth. Thus, they not only built up capital to reinvest in productive activities but also developed the spirit of capitalism—the incessant seeking of profit through disciplined work and rational calculation.[19]

If Weber's theory is correct, we should find it operating in Puritan Massachusetts, as in fact we do, in the lives of leading merchants such as John Hull. Arriving in New England with his family, Hull trained as a goldsmith and, through his work as mint master for the Bay Colony, quickly rose to prominence as a trader and as treasurer of the colony. He and other merchants followed a path of worldly asceticism and a devotion to their "particular calling" (in Puritan terms the "general calling" was to love and obey God). Puritan believers were expected to "devote themselves to making profits without succumbing to the temptations of profit."[20] Richard Mather, aging patriarch of an important ministerial family, expressed the difficulty of following this injunction in his farewell sermon, delivered in 1657 to his church in Dorchester. Mather knew and "experience show[ed] that it is an easy thing in the midst of worldly business to lose the life and power of Religion." If that happened, he continued, "nothing thereof should be left but only the external form, as it were the carcass or shell, worldliness having eaten out the kernel, and having consumed the very soul and life of godliness." Mather's fears were not unfounded. Other seventeenth-century New England merchants such as Boston traders Henry and Samuel Shrimpton and Salemite Philip English pursued a lifestyle that seemed anything but ascetic. In mid-seventeenth-century Boston, not the most promising site for lavish consumption, the Shrimptons surrounded themselves with sumptuous textiles of matched colors following the latest Continental fashions, apparently indifferent to Puritanism's "fundamental antagonism to sensuous culture of all kinds."[21]

The Bay colonists did not long maintain the hoped-for balance between profits and piety. For New Englanders, profiting handsomely from selling fish to the West Indies and southern Europe, "the 'sacred cod' became a competing symbol to the Bible." By the last quarter of the seventeenth century, according to historian Perry Miller, "even the upper class of inherited position . . . became less the dedicated leaders of a religious movement and more a closed corporation of monopolists."[22]

The ministers responded by developing a genre of sermons called "jeremiads," designed to recall the people to the founders' goals. John Higginson, Salem's second-generation minister, whose sons traveled the globe in search of riches, reminded his listeners that "New England was originally a plantation not of trade but of religion—'Let merchants and such as are increasing Cent per Cent remember this.' " Jeremiads also chronicled the long list of sins the colonists had fallen into, sins that were not those typical of depraved persons but were "such as were bound to increase among good men" and were incurable. "What they gained of elegance or luxury was the just reward of blessed diligence, yet business and riches meant devotion to the world, and luxury meant pride." Miller maintained that the jeremiads "constitute[d] a chapter in the emergence of the capitalist mentality" by showing how "intelligence copes with . . . a change it simultaneously desires and abhors." Condemning these sins prepared society to "march into the future."[23]

What kind of future would it be? Miller saw the changes in the last decades of the seventeenth and the first decades of the eighteenth centuries not merely as a growth of toleration but as "a shedding of the religious conception of the universe." Religion no longer supported a communal vision; instead "Christian Liberty" was transformed into a foundation for the ownership of private property. "Soon afterward, the philosophy of social status yielded to the ethic of success, and merchants who took advantage of the market learned to control congregations despite the clerics." Even ministers closely associated with the Congregational way, like Cotton Mather, took part in the new ethos. In 1692, Mather penned a series of allegories called *Political Fables*. They aimed not only to skewer his opponents but also, said Miller, to bring the wit, urbanity, and manners of London "to solid Boston;" their "spirit is . . . worldly." Cotton Mather was well on the way to becoming a Georgian gentleman.[24]

Perry Miller described the historical trajectory of New England society as a decline into capitalism and secularism. What he failed to take into account in his emplotment was the extent to which capitalism was present from the very beginning of the Puritan errand. Miller associated the decline of communal feeling and spiritual intensity with the expansion of capitalism. But if Puritans were capitalists as Weber and his recent disciples have shown, the developments that Miller viewed as the onset of capitalism are more aptly understood as a gradually developing cultural response to the consequences of capitalism. In early New England, economic growth required the penetration of Puritan society by exotic goods and foreign others. Everyone, ministers included, accepted the necessity for the "New Zion" to be on a strong economic footing. What they never quite recognized was the extent to which economic success would depend on non-Puritan settlers arriving from all corners of the Atlantic world. To adapt to an influx of foreign goods and foreign peoples required Puritans to take on new values, new social practices, and new ideas about whom to include in the "the circle of the we."[25]

John McCusker and Russell Menard's *The Economy of British America*, published in 1985, forced colonial historians to "think seriously about the significance of an expanding Atlantic market for the development of colonial society and culture in the eighteenth century."[26] McCusker and Menard observed that studies abounded on the growth of production in British America but few works dealt with consumption. Fortunately that is no longer true. A number of English and American scholars such as John Brewer, Neil McKendrick, T. H. Breen, Richard Bushman, and Cary Carson have produced excellent studies of Anglo-American consumption. I draw on their work throughout this volume as I explore how vital participants in the distribution of commodities and consumer goods transformed economic power into cultural capital. The leading merchants in Boston and Salem, joined by professionals and provincial officials, adopted and developed social forms and shared values that supported a growing consumer culture and defined themselves as members of an Anglo-American polite and commercial culture.

Drawing on a wealth of new work and expanded perspectives, it is time to revisit New England merchants and rethink the transition from "Puritan" to "Yankee" laid out by Richard Bushman in 1967. Bushman studied the transformation in Connecticut, a colony characterized by small towns and an agrarian economy where "the most common economic ambition was the desire to produce an agricultural surplus for market." He found that colonists moved from being Puritans to being Yankees as a result of changes in religion and law, and of involvement in market exchange—key factors in colonial development. If families in small-town Connecticut became Yankees, what can we say about the leading merchants in Boston and Salem whose economic and social connections stretched broadly throughout the Atlantic world and whose cultural ties reached ever more firmly to Britain? I believe the evidence indicates that Massachusetts's mercantile elite identified itself more closely with British provincial gentry than with Yankee yeomen of inland villages. While T. H. Breen names the 1740s as the key decade for the integration of America "into the British consumer economy," the process began much earlier in Atlantic ports; by 1740, much of the lingering Puritan opposition to lavish display and genteel social gatherings had figuratively and literally died out in Boston and Salem.[27] Certainly Connecticut Yankees and Massachusetts commercial gentry shared some attributes—shrewdness in searching out profit for one, but when seen in transatlantic context, the differences outweigh the similarities. The leading merchants of Boston and Salem, members of the polite and commercial culture of eighteenth-century Anglo-America, saw themselves as Georgian gentlemen, not Yankee traders.

The fate of the New London Society for Trade and Commerce, Connecticut's most ambitious shipping project, indicates the limited scope of overseas trade in that colony. Founded in 1732 by Connecticut dealers and farmers tired of their dependence on Boston and Newport for access to transatlantic markets, the society enlisted eighty subscribers but still could not raise enough capital to purchase a ship and cargo. By establishing a land bank and issuing paper money the organization finally raised sufficient funds to charter and launch two vessels. When the governor, objecting to paper money, suspended the society's charter just as one schooner was shipwrecked and Spanish privateers captured the other, the whole venture collapsed.

The figures for shipbuilding and merchant shipping show the difference in scope of overseas trade between Connecticut and Massachusetts. Between 1678 and 1714, Connecticut shipwrights built 25 vessels in the small harbors dotting the coastline; during a similar period Massachusetts launched 1,257 ships. In the 1730s, the New London Society for Trade and Commerce, Connecticut's most ambitious shipping project, had the greatest difficulty in raising the funds to build and lade two schooners;

in the early decades of the eighteenth century, the Massachusetts fleet numbered over 1,100 vessels, including 124 ships larger than one-hundred tons. Over 400 ocean-going vessels entered Boston Harbor annually during this era, from ports throughout the Atlantic world (see table 2, p. 79). Exposure to international commerce produced a cosmopolitan culture in Boston and Salem that differed substantially from the society in Connecticut's small ports and market towns.[28]

While we cannot draw sharp boundaries between urban and rural, or between elite and middling, we certainly can demonstrate a dramatic difference in the mental or imagined world of a wealthy urban merchant dealing directly in transatlantic commerce, and the world of a substantial farmer growing crops for family and market, and directing local affairs in a relatively isolated community. If such a New England farmer is a Yankee, surely the merchant families profiled in this study—Belchers, Stoddards, Faneuils, and Ornes—are something else again. As Georgian gentry, they belong to an urban elite emerging in provincial towns such as Bristol, Liverpool, or Chester. Leading Boston and Salem merchants, comparable to the London merchants trading with America whom David Hancock portrays in his aptly named *Citizens of the World*, became full-fledged members of an Anglo-American class of "polite and commercial people."[29]

In Bushman's more recent book, *The Refinement of America*, he explores the coming of gentility and consumer culture to colonial gentry in the mid-Atlantic region and studies the spread of genteel ideals to the nineteenth-century middle class. His book has done a great deal to introduce the work of material culture historians and those charting the "Consumer Revolution" to a broader historical audience. However, Bushman does not provide a detailed exploration of the interplay between capitalism and a consumer culture. While admitting that the relationship between capitalism and refinement "receives less attention in this[his] book than it deserves," he does acknowledge that "capitalism and gentility were allies in forming the modern economy" and, I would add, in transforming culture. He asserts that gentility created demand and capitalism manufactured supply; I contend that capitalism and merchant-capitalists created demand by transforming urban life and changing ideas about value and identity. Our understanding of how cultural change is produced differs as well. Bushman emphasizes emulation as the most significant engine of change; I propose the need to reshape identity and meaning in a world of mobile property and people as the primary force for transformation. One vital point on which we both agree is that objects and behavior serve as essential historical evidence.[30]

Max Weber believed that even in the twentieth century, successful entrepreneurs followed "a manner of life . . . distinguished by a certain ascetic tendency . . . a sort of modesty." In his view, after the influence of religion declined in the eighteenth century, the "spirit of capitalism" continued in secular utilitarianism. He claims that the capitalist entrepreneur "avoids ostentation and unnecessary expenditure, as well as conscious enjoyment of his power, and is embarrassed by the outward signs of the social recognition which he receives."[31] My study demonstrates otherwise. Mid-eighteenth-century Boston and Salem merchants invested time and money in displaying their wealth to members of their own class through opulent furnishings and serving utensils from around the world. They spoke to townsmen of all classes by constructing elegant mansions in the latest English design, traveling through the streets in large coaches emblazoned with their coats of arms, and donating valuable objects and buildings to churches and towns. Peter Faneuil, scion of a Huguenot trading family that fled France and established a trading network in Boston, New York, and Amsterdam, enhanced this mercantile fortune while he simultaneously claimed his status as a provincial "English" gentleman through careful attention to consumer goods.[32] In a letter to a London merchant containing an order for silver knives and forks from England, he explained precisely the intricacies of an engraved design he requested on the handle.[33] Timothy Orne, an eighteenth-century Salem merchant who figured among the town's "codfish aristocracy," contracted with a local artisan, detailing the exact paint colors for walls and trim in each room in his new house.[34] Both of these documents and many others demonstrate an attention to fashionable details that belies any notion of worldly asceticism. Instead, merchants affirmed their identity by owning and displaying luxury goods as proof of their growing ability to master the complex details of overseas trade. In eighteenth-century port towns, capitalism was about both getting and spending.

Merchants stood at the center of the social and economic transformation of eighteenth-century New England. This study brings to light the key role they played not only as agents of capitalism but also as proponents of the new polite and commercial culture. I chose the merchants spotlighted in the following case studies after a review of primary sources in New England archives, selecting individuals or families with the largest caches of extant papers whose documents held out the hope of revealing material about their personal lives and social interactions. I also insisted on some evidence of their material possessions as part of the selection process. With the exception of John Hull, the merchants studied gave few overt clues to their inner life—to their emotions or self-images. Their self-reflective moments seemed rare or have not survived the passage of time. In spite of this lacuna, the material was richer and more extensive than I had anticipated. By assessing the choices the merchants and their families made in purchasing and displaying possessions and the social, political, and cultural practices they favored, I constructed an interpretation of colonial self-fashioning for merchant elites. I then used town records, local histories, diaries, newspapers, maps, prints, paintings, and secondary sources to situate commercial families in their local and transatlantic context and explore community responses to Puritan authority and the emergence of a polite and commercial culture.

While not denying the heuristic power of large-scale structural concepts like "commodification," "the market," "rationalization," and "the logic of capitalism," I believe it is important to understand that large forces are made up of numerous individual decisions. While these choices are constrained by or take place within situations shaped and limited by large structures, each personal action, in turn, moves or changes capitalism or the market in minute incremental fashion, resulting in a continual recursive movement between the particular and the general. It is this oscillation, between personal and impersonal, and the significance of individuals in shaping culture, that this book explores.

Studying the cultural response to capitalism implies that capitalism can be separated from culture, an artificial separation to be sure. For the purpose of demonstrating the mutual interaction of economic, social, and personal transformations, I have chosen to explore capitalism and culture as if they were two different variables. More accurately, I have attempted to separate out capitalism from an anthropological view of culture, meaning the practices and beliefs by which people order and interpret their world. Yet, as the evidence so compellingly indicates and I so firmly believe, capitalism and culture are intricately bound. By attempting to prise them apart we can see more clearly the sinews that hold them together moment by moment.

The book begins by introducing seventeenth-century Boston and Salem. The Boston merchant John Hull demonstrates the successful melding of piety and profits. Endorsing godliness and marrying into the well-connected Sewall family, he emerged as a leading figure in the Bay Colony. In contrast, Hull's fellow Bostonian Henry Shrimpton, although exceeding most townsmen in his collection of fashionable goods and leaving perhaps the largest estate of the 1660s, was never numbered among the Puritan elite. In early Boston, money could buy little in the way of intangible benefits. The career of the wealthy "French" merchant Philip English in Salem, on the other hand, exposes the contradiction built into the Puritan experiment of a godly community sustained by economic expansion via transatlantic trade. Cultural outsiders such as English continually challenged the effort of Puritans to impose a single definition of community and confirmed the difficulties faced by those from different ethnic and/or religious backgrounds.

The rest of the book follows the rise and fall of the polite and commercial culture in the two cities and the dissenting voices and the approving chorus that negotiated cultural transformation in Boston and Salem. During the years between 1700 and 1730, Massachusetts urbanites renegotiated the relationship between spiritual and commercial values as economic and social changes, initiated and fostered by leading merchants, produced a cultural shift in how people made sense of their world. Cotton Mather, the famous Puritan preacher, inveighed against toleration as a young man yet later in life he ordained a Baptist minister, took up genteel fashions, and sought advice on marketing his books. Samuel Sewall, son-in-law of the Puritan merchant John Hull, like Mather and many others, both embraced and questioned the new culture that merchant families like the Shrimptons and Belchers brought to the docks, streets, parlors, and churches of Boston and Salem. This cultural transformation culminated in the adoption of an Anglo-American version of Georgian gentility that reshaped the social and urban landscape and smoothed over ethnic and religious differences. As a result, wealthy traders of French heritage such as Boston's Peter Faneuil, Dutchman Jacob Wendell, and the Cabot family of Salem took their place among the mercantile elite. Finally we turn to the era of "Homespun," when the polite and commercial culture of mid-eighteenth-century Massachusetts was overturned by revolutionary politics. Urban patriots boycotted British finery and redefined the meaning of goods, thereby creating a new American identity. Those among the merchant gentry who remained in Massachusetts and refashioned themselves from Georgian gentlemen into Sons of Liberty could now rightly be called American.

1

Piety and Profit in Puritan Boston

Oct. 30 [1666], I sent to England a considerable adventure in sundry ships, Master Clark, Master Peirce, &c. And it pleased the Lord all that I sent arrived safe, and came to a good market. The Lord make me thankful!

JOHN HULL in "Some Passages of God's Providence"

THE MIX OF PIETY AND PROFIT melded into plans for the Bay Colony proved to be a volatile one.[1] The contradictions built into Puritan communities created an impulse for cultural change that made many in Boston and Salem receptive to the new polite and commercial culture spreading through Anglo-America during the late seventeenth and early eighteenth centuries. To fully understand the momentous impact of that transformation on Puritan Massachusetts, we must first enter into the mental and material world of early and mid-seventeenth-century Boston. John Winthrop, leader of the Puritan migration to New England in the 1630s and governor of the Bay Colony for most of two decades, fled from an England "Groaninge for Reformation." There, "so many wandering ghosts in shape of men, so many spectacles of misery in all our streets," witnessed to pervasive economic deprivation and sinful corruption.[2] Winthrop's quintessential vision of a new land free "from the Common corruptions of this evil world" has until recently shaped our understanding of early New England settlement.[3] In Winthrop's new city, Puritans "must be willing to abridge our selves of our superfluities, for the supply of others necessities," and be governed by "brotherly Affection." Winthrop cautioned his followers against worshiping other Gods—"our pleasures, and profits"—or "wee shall surely perish out of the good Land."[4]

But other, more optimistic views of commercial change in England inspired alternative visions for New England towns. The enthusiasm for entrepreneurial ventures "abroad in the realm" during the first half of the seventeenth century is captured by English historian Joan Thirsk in her study *Economic Policy and Projects*: "Everyone with a scheme, whether to make money, to employ the poor, or to explore the far corners of the earth had a 'project.' " A project, she continues, "was a practical scheme for exploiting material things; it was capable of being realized through industry and ingenuity."[5]

For many founders, Massachusetts Bay was an economic project on a grand scale. One early settler, Richard Saltonstall, son of an English knight and heir to a long line of entrepreneurial gentlemen, exhibited industry and ingenuity in his designs for colonial settlement. Young Saltonstall, writing from Massachusetts in 1631, spoke confidently of the multitude of ventures possible in the new settlements. "I doubt not but wee shall rayse good profit not only by our fishing trade . . . but by Hempe, flaxe, pitch, tarr, pottashes, sope ashes, masts, pipe staves, clapboards (and Iron as wee hope)."[6] Weighted heavily in favor of business interests, Saltonstall's vision portrayed the Puritan errand with an economic emphasis. Saltonstall's plans did not exclude religion. He envisioned "Propagating the gospel to these poor barbarous people" as the other important project of colonial New England. Men "might improve their talents and times" by both bringing Christianity to the Indians and advancing their own estates. He understood that the effort of redemption would crown England with glory while "pottashes" would produce profit and advantage for "gentlemen of abillitie."[7] In his view, both projects were important and both could be pursued simultaneously. Saltonstall's conception, grounded in English experience, formed the basis for a community fostering both Puritan orthodoxy and business enterprise—a community that thrived as a viable alternative to Winthrop's utopian dream.

Since 1970, a literature shaped by social historians has portrayed early New England as an egalitarian, communal, precapitalist society where settlers sought only a "competence."[8] According to this interpretation, colonists who were concerned more with establishing family security and less with earning profits attempted to limit and contain their involvement with markets. This outlook of restraint is clearly at odds with Saltonstall's expansive plans.

Recently, social historians have contested the precapitalist label with assertions that the Puritans were capitalists from the start. Foremost among these is Stephen Innes whose latest work, *Creating the Commonwealth: The Economic Culture of Puritan New England*, published in 1995, is a rich study of Puritanism and capitalism in early Massachusetts. Innes agrees that "much appears to support a 'pre-capitalist' portrayal of early

New England," he insists that "the weight of the evidence . . . stands squarely on the capitalist rather than pre-capitalist side of the ledger." In his view, the Puritan colonists were not "modern in any meaningful use of that term" but had, he argues, "clearly crossed the threshold that separates a pre-capitalist from a capitalist society."[9] The founders of the Massachusetts Bay Colony, he notes, "were bearers of a culture that was already capitalist when they arrived in the New World."[10] Innes, adopting a view of capitalism that stresses private property, the division of labor, and a wage labor force free of restrictions by guilds and states, all legitimated by the state, argues that a distinctive "civic ecology" based on representative government and private property developed in the Bay Colony. Following the lead of German sociologist Max Weber, Innes argues that "Puritanism played a key role in the transition to capitalism by channeling and legitimating the striving behavior increasingly common among seventeenth-century Englishmen of all religious persuasions." Furthermore, he concludes that in "seeking to establish a pure social order" based on church membership, the Bay colonists demonstrated that Puritanism both "fostered economic development" and mitigated the "socially destructive consequences" of capitalism.[11]

But the very civic ecology that Innes sees as the source of Massachusetts's splendid success contained a fundamental contradiction that would necessitate cultural change in the coming decades. Innes disregards his own evidence about the challenge that unruly Saugus ironworkers from Wales and Ireland raised for Puritans. He acknowledges that the ironworks embodied the "tension between two apparently irreconcilable goals: industrial development and the [Puritan inspired] culture of discipline." Choosing to downplay the contradiction, Innes situates the metal workers as part of the "human capital" that created the rise of maritime New England. While Innes and I agree wholeheartedly about the presence of capitalism and capitalists in early New England, we disagree fundamentally on the social and cultural consequences of capitalism. An individual could follow Puritan beliefs and strive for economic achievement—for profits—as Saltonstall and merchant John Hull demonstrate. When raised to the larger province of community, economic expansion and Puritan communal ideals opposed rather than reinforced each other as the growing cultural tensions in Boston and Salem confirmed. Studying closely the experiences of the leading Boston capitalists John Hull and Henry Shrimpton demonstrates that although striving for riches was acceptable, riches did not open the door to social or civic leadership. The careers of these two men and that of Philip English in Salem highlight the profound contradiction inherent in a desire for a homogeneous community supported by an expanding economy based on long-distance trade.[12]

A focus on two of early Massachusetts's leading merchants, John Hull and Henry Shrimpton, highlights the relationship between capitalism and Puritanism in the thriving colonial port of Boston. By delving into the diaries and letterbook of the Puritan goldsmith and trader John Hull and by "reading" the house and possessions of the wealthy brazier and merchant Henry Shrimpton, we can bring into view the spiritual and cultural practices inspired by a seventeenth-century worldview and its particular Puritan inflection.

Both Hull and Shrimpton were successful artisans turned merchants, but each arrived at a very different position in relation to the Puritan elite directing affairs in Boston. Hull maintained an obvious commitment to Puritan piety, married into a well-connected family with English gentry background, and rose to a position of social and political prominence. Shrimpton joined the church in conjunction with his admittance as a town inhabitant but rarely appeared in the town records, holding no major civic offices nor associating with any of the leading families such as the Winthrops, Bradstreets, or Dudleys. Yet in his private domain, Shrimpton built up one of the largest fortunes in town and surrounded himself and his family with opulent materials, adopting new fashions that were just coming into use in English gentry homes. Each man followed a different approach to self-fashioning. Their heirs, Hull's son-in-law Samuel Sewall and Shrimpton's eldest son Samuel, would continue to follow different cultural styles—Sewall clinging to Puritan ideals and Shrimpton Jr. adopting the new polite and commercial culture just emerging in Anglo-America. The sons' diverging paths point toward the complex negotiations that remade Boston and Salem in the eighteenth century. The fathers enshrined the cultural values of an earlier time. In mid-seventeenth-century Massachusetts, Henry Shrimpton and others not connected to Puritan leaders barely appeared in the social and political annals of the town no matter how successful their commercial ventures. In early Boston, townspeople still favored piety over possessions in awarding social and political acclaim; money could buy little in the way of intangible benefits. God's Providence bestowed all.

The Puritan world of seventeenth-century New England was fashioned around a contest between the need for an open, expansive economic life and the desire for a closed, defined social order. Early Bostonians, lacking agreed-upon "scientific" explanations for even common natural phenomena, resorted to beliefs in the supernatural, whether in the form of God's providence or the devil's work. Having survived the dislocation of a transatlantic migration and reestablished themselves in a new land, the early generations of New Englanders were acutely aware of the unpredictability of life. To cope with uncertainty, they engaged in material and spiritual practices designed to control and contain body and soul, and protect them from unknown threats and unfamiliar strangers. Material life in early New England expressed this contradiction by confining goods within movable chests and boxes that were arranged in changing locations in rooms designed for many uses. The structures themselves, framed with massive oak beams, confined and shielded families from the dangers of a New World. The need to contain and protect coupled with a desire for economic expansion created a cultural contradiction that was especially intense for committed Puritans. As Puritan colonists sought to build a city of "visible saints" on a site necessitating dependence on foreign trade and the fishing industry, they constructed a society of opposing values. Joining communal ideals and commercial practices posed a dilemma not solved until the next century. These incongruities can be seen in Boston's urban geography, in the inventoried property of one Boston merchant, and in the spiritual landscape of another.

Boston goldsmith turned merchant John Hull lived in an age of wonders. For Hull and his fellow Bostonians many events were unpredictable. No laws of nature and physics explained the movement of stars and planets. No abstract theory of social compact directed the formation of new societies or reshaped existing governments. No "invisible hand" guided merchants in understanding market behavior. Order and meaning lay in a Christian covenant with God, a system of obligations and rewards that depended ultimately on God's will. Magic and religion provided explanations for most occurrences. Comets, earthquakes, deformed animals, and infants' sudden deaths, all became portents of mysterious forces.[13] In his diary, Hull chronicled sightings of comets, "blazing stars," several earthquakes, and the birth of Quaker Mary Dyer's deformed child. Some of his fabulous stories included tales of two suns observed by men in New Haven for half an hour and "a strange mortality of fishes in a pond near Cambridge, the manner whereof was wonderful." On Long Island one clear summer morning, several towns reported seeing "many companies of armed men in the air" accompanied by sounds of drumming and "great guns."[14]

Devastating losses or safe returns of seagoing vessels posed equal mysteries. Uncertainty prevailed for Hull and other Puritan merchants because "such is man's infermyty wee know not whether wee move tow fast or to slow or whether it bee better to sit still or to go."[15] At times Hull evinced true puzzlement regarding the source of good or ill fortune. One year after losing shipments of beaver and other furs aboard two ships seized by the Dutch, he observed, "the Lord made up my lost goods in the two vessels last year by his own secret blessing, though I know not which way." In Boston one cold Sabbath morning, ice cut through the cables of four ships about to set sail for England. Hull recorded that "all [were] forced on shore; and get off they could not until . . . three days after the spring-tides." Hull concluded, "God, having tried them, set them again at liberty."[16]

God's providence explained both bad and good. In the winter of 1676–77 several fires started in Boston. One blaze "consumed about fifty dwelling-houses and the North Meeting house," but "the Lord sent much rain, moderated the spreading of it." Later that winter, a rooftop candle started a fire "yet was prevented spreading through the wonderful providence of God." Hull related the winter's events to a friend in London. "Since our Town was fired in November Last, it hath been three times (in plain evident reason) on purpose endeavored to be fired," but "the Lord hath in a very wonderful manner prevented it." Reason provided evidence for Hull to suspect arson, but reason could not explain why only one attempt succeeded. Hull invoked man's intellect in one sentence and God's mystery in the next. An oscillation between rational and spiritual and a reluctance to attribute human evil to God, or Satan, created fissures in the explanatory power of providential discourse. It was within these spaces that men's choices operated to influence God's work. God remained paramount, however, and Hull daily acknowledged "the Lord most wise & Sovereign government of the world."[17]

A system of providential thinking developed whereby natural disasters related to God's purposes for men on earth. The Connecticut sighting of armies in the air was followed by "flying caterpillars," which "arose out of the ground and from roots of corn," and by wheat blast, which "took hold of Connecticut and New Haven," destroying the crop. During the winter of 1665–66, colonists experienced "an extraordinary tempest of wind" and "very unsettled weather" in November and December. The Charles River froze solid three times that winter, and the channel beyond Castle Island, twice. Two women died in childbirth, and "several miscarried, some hardly escaping with life." This was not an unusual group of events for the seventeenth century in itself, but the key to their interpretation lay in the sequence of events—first bad weather, and then death. At the end of this section of his diary Hull writes, "All these trials are not to be mentioned with England's great affliction"—the plague. He concludes with a plea: "the good Lord spare and teach our nation to draw near to him!" Within this system, God rewarded and punished human behavior individually and collectively. After a series of successes in raiding the French trading posts in Canada and narrowly averting armed conflict with the Pequots, the Bay colonists no doubt felt satisfaction, but "not to let wholly slip some chastisements of God unto the Commonwealth in general, and more particularly unto this town of Boston, one of the honored magistrates . . . was taken away by death." "Another such like providence befell us this year," Hull writes in recording the death of Major General Edward Gibons. Several years later Hull expresses, very simply and eloquently, the cosmology of providential thinking: "The spring was very wet; yet it pleased God to give a seed-time."[18]

In Puritan culture, commercial profits became visible evidence of God's blessings rather than of personal achievement.[19] When Boston received news of the safe arrival of all the ships "that sailed hence for England last year," Hull recognized "the Lord's gracious preservation of the estates of his poor, despised people." Again and again Hull repeated the phrase, "The Lord brought in," applying it in succession to a small ship "sent out by myself and others," "several vessels that I had adventures in," "the ketch *Adventure* whereof I was part owner," and "the ship *Providence*." In the fall of 1666, Hull "sent to England a considerable adventure in sundry ships. . . . And it pleased the Lord all that I sent arrived safe, and came to a good market." Later Hull returned to this entry and added a postscript, "The Lord make me thankful."[20]

When the world reflects God's judgments, history becomes a narrative of the working out of God's will on earth. Historians have focused intently on the New England Puritans' special sense of mission, their "errand into the wilderness."[21] Keith Thomas asserts that English Protestants claimed this spiritual mantle as well, declaring themselves "a people singled out by God for a special purpose, an elect nation called upon to play a particular part in the designs of providence." John Hull participated in this tradition by beginning the public portion of his diary with a brief history of the settlement of New England, when "God therefore moved the hearts of many to transport themselves far off beyond the seas, into this our New England." He chronicles how the newcomers "gathered into several churches" and formed a civil government peopled only by church members, "the churches and civil state thus mutually embracing and succoring each other."[22]

In Puritan providentialism the individual was expected to shape his or her behavior on Christian principles without any immediate expectation of rewards. They might come; they might not. God would decide. A person could only control his or her own behavior in hope of attracting God's blessings and ultimately God's grace. A believer was condemned to uncertainty. To combat doubt, Puritans engaged in a series of practices such as diary writing, frequent prayer, and a disciplined (but not necessarily ascetic) lifestyle. After Hull rose to the rank of ensign in the Boston militia, one of many prestigious positions and honors he achieved, he prayed for "a spirit of wisdom and humility, love, and faithfulness," to obey his superiors and be helpful "to my inferiors, and by him [God], be kept from temptation and corruption or pollution." Each time the town chose him as selectman, Hull responded with a private plea for "wisdom," "humility," and "grace," always seeking God's reassurance.[23]

Precise accounts, a crucial element in Puritan piety, constituted a critical element in a merchant's success as well. A set of sailing orders directed to John Harris exemplifies Hull's concerns. Hull instructed Harris and his mate to "daily so think thereof as to quicken your prudent, diligent, & frugal improvement of your time for the good of your Owners," and he stressed that Harris "daily forecast & write down what you have necessary to effect." Several years later Hull cautioned his cousin Edward Hull in London, "Cousin Let me tell you that if you be a factor and take Commission you must never neglect your accpts [accounts] and Especially your accpt of Sales."[24] Keeping careful track of moving goods helped to garner profits and to contain anxiety in an unpredictable business in an uncertain world.

Account books and letterbooks performed a function that paralleled sermon notes and diaries. Each helped to ward off anxiety about unforeseen and uncontrollable events. Each served to reassure through effort and the very presence in writing of God's blessings in goods and ships, and in life and spirit. John Hull began his diary so that he "may be the more mindful of, and thankful for, all God's dispensations towards me." His letterbook preserved copies of all his business correspondence so that he might be more mindful of the dispensations of his worldly goods. The parallel forms of writing ministered to shared concerns about the unknowable future.[25]

Capitalist goals and Puritan beliefs were not incompatible in an individual's life, but when applied to communities based on transatlantic trade, they worked in opposition to each other. While spiritual diaries and commercial accounts were part of a shared practice of coping with uncertainty, commerce introduced other elements which threatened to unsettle the delicate equilibrium of Puritan capitalism. Trade was absolutely essential for colonial settlements perched on the Atlantic fringe. The role merchants played in rescuing Massachusetts from its first depression in the 1640s, bringing goods and money into the colony, and transporting commodities overseas, made them powerful figures in early New England.[26] To the extent that they followed Puritan practices in their language and behavior, merchants contributed to the careful balance between piety and profits.

John Hull, for example, acquired his capital through a combination of artisanal skill, family connections, and public office. Born in Market Harborough in Leicestershire in 1624, Hull emigrated from England with his family at the age of ten. They settled in Boston, and after a short stint at school he began an apprenticeship as a goldsmith and "through God's help, obtained that ability in it, as I was able to get my living by it."[27] In colonial America, goldsmiths, poised at the peak of a recognized hierarchy of artisanal occupations, worked primarily in silver and carried on several other functions in port towns.[28] In addition to crafting valuable objects which denoted wealth, goldsmiths also acted as bankers because they were the most qualified persons to assess the value of foreign coins. They usually possessed a stock of specie and metal and often extended their services to taking monies and plate on deposit and making loans.[29]

Hull and his London-trained partner, Robert Sanderson, crafted the earliest pieces of colonial silver, in a late Renaissance or Mannerist style popular among merchants and gentry in northern Europe, the port towns of eastern England such as Norwich and Ipswich, and the metropolis of London.[30] The partners assembled and trained a group of talented apprentices who dominated the craft of gold and silversmithing in Boston for a hundred years.[31] In spite of his recognized skill as a gold and silversmith, Hull made only passing references to this work in his diary and letterbook, apparently preferring to feature his vocation as overseas trader.[32] In 1647, he married Judith Quincy, daughter of Edmund, the founder of an important Massachusetts family, in a ceremony performed by Governor John Winthrop.[33] Within ten years, Judith Hull gave birth to five children, only one of whom, daughter Hannah, lived to adulthood. While his wife was drawn into a narrowing circle of birth and loss, Hull widened his horizons and launched a career as a merchant.[34]

Situated at the edge of an Atlantic trading network, colonial merchants relied on local support and on a kinship network that often included commercial connections to London.[35] In 1652, Hull's business received a powerful jump start. The General Court, the legislative body of the Massachusetts Bay Colony, expressed concern over the amount of counterfeit coin circulating in the colony. Hull noted in his diary that "much loss [was] accruing in that respect (and that did occasion a stoppage of trade)."[36] The Court dealt with the problem by ordering a mint to be set up to coin Massachusetts shillings. The silver shillings were designed to weigh three-quarters of the English equivalent.[37] This coin became the famous "pine-tree shilling," and the court chose John Hull as mint master. For his work, the court authorized him to keep one coin out of every twenty he minted. This amounted to a 5 percent commission on the coinage of the colony and provided a windfall that Hull reinvested in trade.[38] Then, according to historian Bernard Bailyn, "young John Hull built up his many-sided business with the help of his uncle, Thomas Parris, a haberdasher, and his [cousin Edward] Hull at the 'Hat-in-Hand' within Aldegate, London."[39]

Dealing in transatlantic trade forced Bostonians and Salemites to breach their carefully constructed communities and reach beyond family or religious channels to deal with foreign merchants, with "strangers." Economic interests propelled Hull beyond the confines of Boston colleagues or Puritan overseas networks as he sought out trading partners unknown to him or his family. Yet, when Hull attempted to branch out and deal with others, the transactions did not always go well. On the advice of the wealthy Anglican merchant Samuel Shrimpton, Hull consigned a "small parcel" of loggwood and two hogsheads of tobacco to "Mountsier" James de la Ronde. A year later, he wrote sharply to remind de la Ronde, "Sir No colored silks are of any use here; onely black" and to complain of merchandise "not vendible" in Boston. In 1672, he requested another "stranger," Solomon Delyon, a Jewish merchant in Jamaica, to either pay interest or put up security on his debt of one-hundred pounds plus interest. Hoping for Delyon's "Ingenuity & Justice," in return for "being so Courteous & Civil" to a stranger, Hull promised to "subscribe myself your loving friend" if Delyon would repay the debt. Apparently that failed to persuade Delyon or to ease his circumstances because nine years later Hull wrote to Samuel Bradstreet, the governor's son and a physician in Jamaica, requesting assistance in collecting the debt from Delyon.[40] In spite of these difficulties Hull was reluctant to sue his debtors, preferring to use moral persuasion and familiar Puritan contacts.

Hull continued to develop his commercial empire through local networks and overseas contacts, always trying to keep a careful balance between community and commerce. His merchant ventures followed much the same patterns as those of other New England merchants— shipping furs to England, fish to Southern Europe, and food and timber to the West Indies. The key to success lay in the ability to command local commodities suitable for sale in distant ports. Like all Boston merchants trading overseas, Hull depended on the city's hinterland for supplies of commodities that would "sell dear" in English, European, and West Indian markets. In a colony that produced few manufactured goods other than homespun cloth and locally made leather items, this did not mean self-sufficiency. Early New England has been characterized as a region of small farms where each farm family aimed for a "competence" or economic independence.[41] However, Hull's business arrangements—partnerships, tenancy, barter of goods and services, wage labor, apprenticeships, and, later, moneylending and marine insurance—indicate that market relations penetrated the countryside in seventeenth-century New England, belying the myth of self-sufficiency.

In fact, the economy, led by prosperous merchants and landholders, exhibited increasingly complex relationships throughout the region. Hull, for example, owned farms in Medfield and on Hog Island in Boston harbor that were either leased to tenants for a portion of the produce or operated by managers employed by Hull. Leasing farms or employing managers and perhaps other wage laborers was a common practice among large landholders in Massachusetts Bay. This runs counter to earlier scholarship, but recent social histories have demonstrated the prevalence of this practice, based in part on English procedures.[42] In 1659, Hull and a surveyor went to Medfield, west of Boston, to lay out a three-hundred-acre farm on recently purchased land. Correspondence indicates that Hull leased the Hog Island farm to tenants for five years at five shillings per year. Hull, who held title to the island by order of the General Court, had problems collecting even that modest sum and in 1675 he empowered an agent to "sell the Island for money or any other verry Good pay." Like other overseas traders, Hull depended on commodities from the land, particularly grain and timber, and he experimented with various methods of acquiring them. In his diary and letter-book Hull detailed his business transactions, his difficulties with employees, his struggles to collect debts from distant strangers, and his efforts to find new commodities and reliable supplies. He always concluded his diary entries with providential interpretations, knowing for example that his supplies of grain would be ample when God gave a good seedtime.[43]

Hull, wealthy merchant, Massachusetts officeholder, and committed Puritan, exemplified how early Bay colonists negotiated the intersecting, and in many ways conflicting, claims of commerce and community.[44] Problems with debt collection tested the limits of Puritan morality.

Ministers reminded merchants of their obligations to others: "you aim at the getting of Silver and Gold, by your Occupation; but you should always act by the Golden Rule." In spite of ministerial injunctions some Puritan merchants used court proceedings to force debtors off the land, thus adhering too closely to diligence in their particular calling at the expense of their general calling, "which is, to Serve the Lord Jesus Christ." Hull rarely resorted to court proceedings and employed a Puritan language of providential causality to describe his commerce with strangers, by which he meant non-Puritans and/or non-Englishmen. He used the same Puritan discourse to transform his acquisitive search for profits into an anxious search for salvation, continually acknowledging that it was the Lord that brought his ships home and reminding himself that "the loss of my estate will be nothing, if the Lord please to join my soul nearer to himself."[45]

The complex negotiations between piety and profits with which early Bostonians mapped their imaginative universe mirrored the labyrinthine geography of the early town. Boston, whose shape has changed considerably since the 1600s, was then a peninsula connected to the rest of Massachusetts by the Neck, a thin strip of land. In the words of one recent arrival in 1687, the town was "almost an Island; it would only be necessary to cut through a Width of three hundred Paces, all Sand, which in less than twice twenty-four Hours would make Boston an Island washed on all Sides by the Sea."[46] On the small peninsula, streets curved around the North End, docks reached into the harbor, barricades supported decaying gun emplacements framing the waterside at North and South Batteries, while houses and shops clustered around the Town House, Dock Square, and Clark's Square, and thinned into a straggling row along the one road out of town.[47] A contemporary visitor remarked that "the houses are for the most part raised on the Sea-banks . . . many of them standing upon piles, close together on each side [of] the streets." Boston faced the water, and early representations of the town were drawn from the point of view of a visitor coming from the water. Portraying the contradictions built into Puritan Boston, the arms of docks stretched forward welcoming the visitor while an array of sharply pitched roofs behind the waterfront hinted at a more prickly, private society.[48]

The hub of this waterside community was Town House Square, just two blocks from the harbor. At this square, King Street, the widest and perhaps the straightest street in Boston, joined "the Street to Roxbury," the sole land route to the mainland. Bernard Bailyn, in his history of New England merchants, called Town House Square "the exact pivot

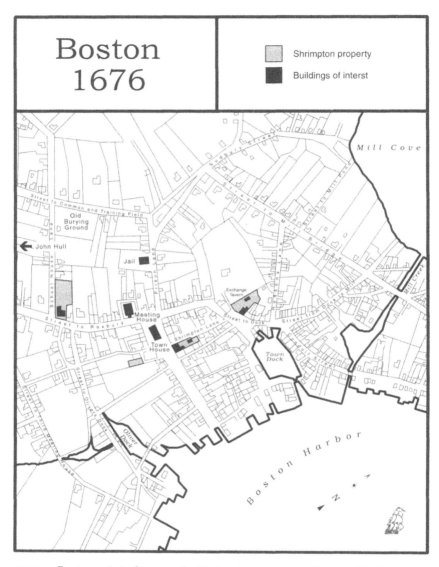

MAP 1. Boston, 1676, showing the Shrimpton property. Prepared by Tom Tricot for the author, based on maps by Samuel Clough at the Massachusetts Historical Society.

FIGURE 1. Boston's Town House, 1657–1711. Drawing by Charles Lawrence, 1930. Courtesy of the Bostonian Society/Old State House.

point of the primary orbit of Atlantic trade in New England." Here stood the First Meeting House, built in 1640, and the Town House, which echoed Tudor-Stuart market halls in provincial English cities like Aldersgate. The Town House, built in 1657 with a bequest from Robert Keayne, a successful and controversial merchant, was designed to provide shelter for "the country people that come with their provisions . . . to sit dry in and warm both in cold rain and dirty weather" and to furnish meeting rooms for courts, "the Elders," and other town groups on the upper floors. On the first floor, "the open roome between the pillars may serve for Merchants, Mr [Masters] of Shipps and Strangers . . . to meet in."[49] In his concern for a sheltered and orderly market site, Keayne initiated a continuing and contested effort on the part of wealthy merchants to shape and control the flow of goods and people in the town of Boston.

While goods flowed all along the crescent-shaped waterfront, the Town Dock, an enclosed harbor like the inner docks in Amsterdam, became an important commercial site for shops, warehouses, and taverns.[50] The streets linking Town House Square to Dock Square were lined with homes and commercial establishments of merchants and well-to-do artisans involved in overseas trade. The cross street closest to the water displayed this connection with the name "Merchants' Row." Facing the Town House, on the corner of one of these cross streets, later named Shrimpton's Lane, stood the house and shop of an enterprising brazier (brass smith) turned merchant, Henry Shrimpton. Like John Hull, Shrimpton was one of the leading merchants in Boston; in contrast to Hull, he never achieved important civic or social position. This contrast reveals much about the values of Puritan society.

Henry Shrimpton began without the Puritan connections that supported Hull. He was first admitted as an inhabitant of Boston and member of the church in 1639. On his arrival from England, he set up business as a brazier and entered into a few merchant ventures. His business grew dramatically; in 1687, only 1.4 percent of Boston's taxpayers reached assessments over £100 in taxable wealth, yet two decades earlier, Shrimpton's inventoried estate totaled £11,979. While assessments and estate values are not precisely comparable—inventories list personal possessions not usually included in tax assessments—clearly he must have ranked at or near the very top of Boston's wealth holders.[51] Even though he may have been the richest man in town, Shrimpton rarely figures in accounts of the social and political life of early Boston. He apparently did not have the requisite education and kinship connections to join the Puritan elite.[52]

By the midseventeenth century, New England material culture revealed the very beginnings of an international style transported and patronized by merchants and tied directly to the circulation of goods. The plan of Shrimpton's house and shop, like others in Anglo-American port towns, followed a building tradition full of accents of medieval England and urban France. Material culture historian Robert St. George describes the multiple origins of the town house courtyard design of Shrimpton's home. From 1600 to 1640 architects in England, inspired by French and Italian design books, developed classically influenced plans for town houses in London. Meanwhile, London and provincial merchants were copying French patterns of long, narrow houses with enclosed yards, which they observed on buying trips to Rouen and Saint-Malo. These appeared in London and the English ports of Exeter and Totnes as early as the 1550s.[53] Shrimpton's dwelling seemed to follow this layout while borrowing other characteristics from English Tudor houses. A large room on the first floor called the "hall," with its rough plaster walls and low, heavy-beamed ceilings, housed most family activity other than sleeping. Sunlight reached the house's dark interior from only a few Tudor-style diamond-paned casement windows. The Shrimptons' dwelling encompassed a hybrid heritage as did their stylish possessions.

The Shrimptons' goods were poised midway between an older Elizabethan character and the soon-to-come material and cultural domains of Georgian gentility.[54] Elizabethan gentry interiors featured multipurpose rooms and furniture that could be moved against the walls of the rooms to accommodate a variety of activities. Social occasions centered on grand ceremonial celebrations held in multipurpose halls, in contrast to repetitive daily rituals like tea drinking and separate rooms designed for specific functions that marked eighteenth-century gentility. In most early New England homes, rooms would be sparsely furnished with a table and benches and few carved wooden chests and cupboards pushed to the edges of the room. In comparison, Shrimpton's house was crowded with belongings that confirmed his business acumen.[55] As he accumulated riches, he invested in textiles for his home and clothing for his family. In Shrimpton's opulent environment, heavy wooden furniture cushioned with lengths of deep-colored silk, brocade, and velvet, stood on thickly patterned oriental carpet. Precious silver plate and other valuable objects were hidden away in chests.[56] The hall, furnished with window curtains, tables, stools, and ten leather chairs topped with high cushions (and one "great Quishin" for the master of the house), served as a dining and living room for the Shrimpton family.[57] A livery cupboard contained glass, earthenware, and pewter. The Shrimptons served dinner with uncommonly elegant equipment such as "two brass chafing dishes," thirty-three pounds worth of pewterware, and a case of knives. Even the kitchen was adorned with a cushion, a cupboard cloth, and curtains at the window.

Shrimpton demonstrated a close attention to changing tastes but that did little to endear him to Boston's Puritan elite. He owned many stylish goods that had only recently come into fashion in England. Across the entry from the hall, the "great chamber" displayed the most important pieces of furniture. A bedstead draped with red hangings dominated the room, creating a cocoon of privacy and warmth at night while making a bold assertion of wealth by day. Other items of great value were tucked away in Shrimpton's "great Chest with his wearing apparel" and one "trunk [marked] EL of woman's wearing apparel." Nineteen cushions in rose, Turkey work, and gilt adorned the chamber, which also contained a "Chest of drawers," a form of case furniture only recently introduced in England. Matching suites of bed hangings, table, chimney, and cupboard cloths, and window curtains, found in the great chamber and the "green room," indicated a sophisticated European influence. The fashion for matching fabrics within a room originated in 1619, when Madame Rambouillet remodeled the interior of her Parisian *hôtel*, including a *chambre bleue* for her literary salon.[58] In the 1640s, fueled by English fascination with French elegance, a fashion for textiles *en suite* was "commonplace in grand circles" in England, and by 1666 we find it in the Shrimptons' home in Puritan Boston.[59]

Like other early Boston and Salem merchants, Shrimpton drew on Old World family connections to expand his business. We know little of how Henry Shrimpton acquired his fortune of almost twelve thousand pounds from artisan beginnings; only scattered references remain. Shrimpton drew on his brother Edward, a London merchant, to begin his commercial ventures. His son Samuel, said to be the wealthiest merchant in Boston at century's end, expanded business further through trade with his in-laws, the Roberts family in London. We do know that Shrimpton's shop, a part of his courtyard complex, contained working tools for pewter and brass as well as finished products such as wine cups, three dozen "great Alchemy spoons," salts, chamber pots, porringers, barber bowls, smoothing irons, stewpans, and cowbells. These items represent just a small portion of stock on hand. The cellars stored raw material, stocks of metal wire and scrap, and food for the family. The garret and loft of the shop held more brass and pewter items while the yard also enclosed an outhouse, a wood yard, and at least one load of charcoal.[60] In addition, Shrimpton invested in several properties in town, including half ownership of a brewhouse, malthouse, bakehouse, warehouse, and wharf complex, and one-third of the Kings Arms, later known as Exchange Tavern.[61]

Henry Shrimpton and his family had assembled an impressive collection of properties and up-to-date goods in early Boston. Several items in Shrimpton's inventory offer important points of comparison with English practices and with eighteenth-century Boston inventories discussed in later chapters. The ever-present cushions—the Shrimptons owned forty-six—added comfort to high-backed chairs in a period before the advent of upholstered seating furniture; they also signaled an interest in consumer display of materials such as gilt and Turkey fabrics.[62] In the seventeenth century, window curtains stood out as a marker of wealth and cosmopolitan taste. One scholar of English consumption patterns found that only 13 percent of middle-class inventories in England and America between 1675 and 1725 recorded any window curtains. Among the wealthiest London group, 68 percent owned curtains in 1675.[63] Based on possessions, the Shrimptons would have been at home in a cosmopolitan environment.

In spite of financial success and dazzling possessions, Shrimpton did not appear as a leading figure in the civic records or personal accounts of Boston.[64] As an artisan and merchant he did not hold the traditional elements of gentry status in seventeenth-century Massachusetts—obvious Puritan piety, university education, kinship connections to elite families in England, and an established local reputation. Wealth alone did not bring him the companionship of the Winthrops, Dudleys, Bradstreets, Mathers, or any of the other leading Puritan families of Boston. Yet Shrimpton's separate kitchen, permanent bedsteads, "chest of drawers," many cushions, and fabrics *en suite* demonstrate an attention to an emerging aesthetic that would accompany the rise of an Anglo-American commercial elite, an elite that in the coming generations would supersede the Puritan elect.[65]

The expanding commercial world of mid-seventeenth-century Boston stood in sharp contrast to Puritan attempts to order, control, and hedge-in the disruptive effects of foreign trade and the multiplying sites of market exchange. The layout of houses, streets, public buildings, wharves, and warehouses took on much of the topsy-turvy character of English port towns, shaped, not by an ordered plan, but by gradual development over time. The streets and wharves expanded as a result of individual and group projects undertaken by prominent inhabitants and undergirded by growth in trade. Boston became a marketplace increasingly unconfined by traditional or Puritan strictures of the just price. Although Boston churchmen and magistrates censured merchant Robert Keayne for reaping excessive profits, twenty years later they accepted his bequest for a Town House that enthroned commerce at the center of Boston even as they placed trade at the heart of their plans for the town and colony.[66] But neither price nor trade could be fixed at a single location. Instead, hawkers traipsed through the streets of Boston and trade goods spilled out along the waterfront and the major thoroughfares. John Hull could claim to live "out of the crowd of trade," but his livelihood depended on trade and later his Cotton Hill neighborhood would become the site of Georgian mansions erected by eighteenth-century merchant princes of the principal trading town in New England.[67]

In a world increasingly shaped by mobility, migration, international trade, foreign goods, and alien merchants, many events seemed unpredictable. Puritans, inspired by their concern for salvation in the after life and for order and security in the present world, sought to bind and constrain individual behavior, material goods, and community mores; security was possible only within tight limits. Yet to arrive on the shores of North America and to support the fledgling land-rich and people-poor colony, Puritans had to rely on the "adventure" of overseas trade. Even more disconcerting to them, they had to depend upon the labor of other religious and cultural groups to sustain their city. While Puritanism and capitalism could combine successfully at the individual level—John Hull is a prominent example—when applied to the larger concerns of community order and well-being, piety and profits became competing impulses creating almost unbearable tensions for trading towns. In building Boston and the neighboring port of Salem, Puritan colonists embodied a contradiction between their need for open, expansive economic life and their desire for a closed, limited, and secure society. Continued pressures from other religious and ethnic groups drawn from throughout the Atlantic world to thriving Massachusetts ports would inevitably bring about a cultural transformation.

2

Much Commerce and Many Cultures

Order implies restriction ... disorder by implication is unlimited, no pattern has been realized in it but its potential for patterning is indefinite. ... Though we seek to create order, we do not simply condemn disorder. We recognize that it is destructive to existing patterns; also that it has potentiality. It symbolizes both danger and power.

MARY DOUGLAS, *Purity and Danger*, 1966

AS THE MARKETPLACE OF Essex County, Massachusetts, the town of Salem embodied a tension between the familiar and the foreign. Salem welcomed vessels and goods from throughout the Atlantic world. In the late 1600s, Salem merchants, like their Boston brothers, sent goods throughout a broad trading network that extended to and from the West Indies, Spain, Portugal, France, and England, as well as up and down the colonial coastline. Shipping merchants fashioned both a local community and a wider, transatlantic web of economic exchange, kinship, and friendship. In an era of limited currency, commerce depended on an exchange of labor, goods, and credit among neighbors, but transplanted English colonists also depended on an Atlantic lifeline that supplied necessary and exotic goods. Port cities, the "marts" of colonial America, embraced a contradiction. Trade, financed and directed by merchants, supported by artisans and laborers, and drawing on products from the surrounding countryside, made colonial settlement possible, yet it simultaneously undermined local norms. The marketplace, in the words of historians Peter Stallybrass and Allon White, "is the epitome of local identity ... and the unsettling of that identity by the trade and traffic of goods [and people] from elsewhere."[1] In Salem, Puritan efforts to fix an identity based on religion and English origins were continually challenged and unsettled by planters, artisans, mariners, merchants, and fishermen from other regions in England, and other countries in Europe. Drawn to Salem by economic opportunity, they complicated any single definition of community or of capitalism.

Much has been written about seventeenth-century Salem, prompted in part by fascination with the witchcraft crisis that erupted in 1692.[2] If we explore Salem by centering attention on the biography of the wealthy merchant and accused witch Philip English, this familiar material takes on a different coloration. Salem Town, which is often cast as a unified, Puritan, commercially oriented port—as in Richard Gildrie's history of Salem as a covenant community—emerges as a divided and conflicted place. Focusing on Philip English's career in Salem highlights the problem of drawing and maintaining community boundaries as diverse cultural groups arrived in New England. The material artifacts and spatial arrangements of English's world provide additional evidence of Salem as a space structured by a town center with a number of peripheral groups dispersed around the edges.[3] The urban layout and the town polity of seventeenth-century Salem were primarily determined by the powerful Puritan merchants who, after the 1630s, occupied the physical and metaphorical center of town. Late in the century, peripheral groups raised challenges to the town center in several ways: by achieving economic success from a marginal location, by shaping an oppositional tavern culture, by disrupting church services in witness to a God within, and by launching political efforts to gain control over common lands. As a result, an alternative portrait materializes of Salem as a conflicted town where a variety of ethnic and religious groups attracted by the magnet of economic prosperity challenged the Puritan goal of a unified community. In response, the dominant Puritan merchants sought to control, exclude, and/or marginalize other cultural groups in Salem throughout the seventeenth and early eighteenth centuries.

In order to understand Philip English's life in Salem we must examine the antecedents of the town's economic prosperity and the multiple peoples that came to participate in trade, fishing, shipbuilding, artisanal manufacturing, and agriculture. Founded four years before the Winthrop fleet arrived to establish the Massachusetts Bay Colony, the town began not as a refuge for Puritan dissenters but as an outgrowth of English investment plans.[4] The Dorchester Company, an English joint-stock company established by investors from Western England, aimed to reap financial benefits from a New England colony devoted to fishing and trade.[5] After a failed attempt at settlement on Cape Ann, a remnant of West Country Englishmen found their way to a peninsula, surrounded on three sides by sheltered bays, that was called Naumkeag by the native American inhabitants. Led there in 1626 by Roger Conant, the "Old

Planters," as they were later called, attempted to establish their commercial vision of an agricultural, trading, and fishing venture. They soon welcomed like-minded immigrants recruited from an English parish presided over by Conant's brother John. Two years later, John Endicott, representing the New England Company, arrived with a contingent of seventy colonists, many also from West Country gentry families. Salem's early inhabitants included an unusually large number from English gentry origins—more than one-quarter of the settlers received one hundred acres rather than the six to ten acres granted commoners in nearby towns—and most practiced a hybrid form of Protestantism "somewhere between Puritan and Anglican."[6]

Within its first decade, Salem became a pluralistic society as West Country planters received an influx of colonists from a different English region. Numerous families from East Anglia, an area northeast of London and just across the North Sea from the Low Countries, followed their minister, Roger Williams, across the Atlantic to Salem in 1631.[7] Seventeen families, all from the busy port of Great Yarmouth, Norfolk, formed a nucleus of familiarity and friendship in the new surroundings. Driven by the desire to practice a purified form of religion and influenced by the habit of practicing mixed agriculture in a natural environment much like that of New England, the East Anglians followed "strange" ways that led them into clashes with the West Countrymen.[8]

Accustomed to thriving ports, cloth-making towns, and compact villages surrounded by planting fields and grazing meadows shared by all, East Anglians, infused with dreams of both economic prosperity and Christian millennium in the new world, tried to impose their "imagined community" on the fledgling settlement.[9] The Old Planters had grown up in the very different environment of western England, a world of dispersed farms and manors, punctuated with occasional scraggly fishing villages and a few port towns dotted along an irregular coastline. Furthermore, Roger Williams, the newcomers' minister, espoused a radical Puritanism that called for separation from the Church of England and encouraged lay preaching by men and women. The divisions between Williams and his East Anglian supporters on one side and the West Country Salemites backed by the Boston church on the other, grew so troublesome that in 1635 the General Court banished Williams to Rhode Island, where he was joined by ten families from Salem.[10]

In the midst of this crisis, another shipload of newcomers arrived including men who were to assume leading positions in Salem's civic affairs for the next half-century. Coming from Wiltshire and Bedfordshire, they took up residence in the middle of Salem and forged a centrist position mediating between the ardent East Anglians and the Old Planters. Several more of Williams's supporters left town in 1638 in the wake of the antinomian crisis (a ministerial dispute over the role of good works in achieving salvation), following Boston's lay preacher Anne Hutchinson into banishment at Rhode Island, which further eased local tensions.[11]

These extreme antagonisms over religion, which had intensified cultural differences to the breaking point, led Salem's newly arrived minister, Hugh Peter, to attempt to clarify boundaries and redirect the townspeople's energies. To heal divisions and cope with exploding growth—between 1633 and 1635 the town population doubled—both groups agreed to adopt measures formulated by the leading Puritan divine. Peter's plan set the terms for Salem's continuing efforts to balance economic, social, and spiritual concerns. The minister suggested and the town leaders agreed upon two strategies. First, "it seemed to them that the way to prevent difficulty was to define Christian community more carefully."[12] Church members were required to sign a covenant or be excommunicated. Second, Peter advised the colony to take specific measures to foster a fishing industry. He moved beyond advice to action. The minister encouraged shipbuilding by putting together a group of investors and recruiting the shipbuilder Richard Hollingsworth to construct an unusually large three hundred–ton ship.[13] Peter's economic proposals thereby resurrected the corporate plans for a fishing and trading settlement first formulated by English sponsors in the 1620s. Unfortunately for Salem, his economic plans undermined his social aim of a unified commonweal bound together by a mutual covenant with God.[14]

The church covenant that Hugh Peter wrote for Salem expressed spiritual concern about a dissolving unity. "Having found by sad experience how dangerous it is to sit loose to the Covenant we make with our God: and how apt we are to wander into bypaths," Peter believed that precise directions for earthly and spiritual life would keep his flock headed in the same direction. It was essential to fix a single definition of church (and community) membership and to "oppose all contrary ways, canons, and constitutions of men in his [God's] worship." Peter asked Salemites for an explicit recognition of the right of the best men to lead and the others to follow. He called for "all lawful obedience to those that are over us, in Church or Commonwealth, . . . that they should have encouragement in their places, by our not grieving their spirits through our Irregularities" as Roger Williams and his followers had done. Peter and his supporters thought that obedience to a church covenant would provide a framework within which Salemites and other Massachusetts settlers could safely pursue economic opportunity based on ocean-going commerce and still keep the multitude of mariners and merchants soon to arrive on their shores either at the margins or within the covenant. Perry Miller explains that at "the core of each town was a church, composed of those who had given proof that they were visibly sanctified, joined together by a covenant into which they entered of their own will." Peter hoped to make all the inhabitants part of the covenant. Neither he nor the other Bay Colony leaders supporting his design could see that he was pursuing a contradictory strategy, seeking to impose religious and cultural conformity while at the same time promoting an economic base—the fishery and overseas trade—that would draw strangers from throughout the Atlantic world, many of whom would not be willing to follow the Puritan path.[15]

The plan worked for a time. By the 1640s, Salem's deep-water harbor and excellent network of waterways supported a developing fishery and the beginnings of overseas trade. As increasing numbers of settlers were drawn to Salem, the peninsula's narrow neck no longer accommodated large land grants to prosperous farmers. Instead, newcomers received property several miles inland in an area soon to be designated as "the Farms," later called Salem Village, and then, in the following century, recast as the independent town of Danvers.

The prominent men overseeing Salem's initial commercial growth—Edmund Batter, William Hathorne, Henry Bartholomew and Walter Price—did not concentrate their energies exclusively on importing and exporting goods. They continued to acquire large land grants, an important source of status and power, and to set up farms cultivated by members of their extended families or by tenants.[16] They also devoted considerable energy to town and colony affairs. Important town officials often worked their way to the top through a ladder of offices beginning at constable and culminating with selectman. Selectmen had immediate and continuing influence on many of daily life's small details and large issues. When Bartholomew, Hathorne, and Price won election to the group of selectmen (originally called "the seven men" in many towns), they took on the responsibility for managing activities ranging from doling out poor relief to licensing taverns, and for carrying out the will of the inhabitants as expressed in semiannual town meetings. In Salem, the selectmen had also acquired the de facto power to grant land and divide up the common area, decisions nominally reserved to proprietors who possessed "rights" in the commons that could be bought and sold like real estate.[17]

At the colony level, the General Court, chief governing body of Massachusetts Bay, consisted of one or two representatives from each town, called deputies, and a smaller Court of Assistants, or Magistrates. Deputies and magistrates were both elected annually, deputies at local town meetings and magistrates/assistants by the full body of the General Court. Magistrates functioned for the colony much like select-men did for their towns, carrying out day-to-day business and following up on decisions made by the full General Court. Magistrates often did double duty by acting as justices for the county court system in their home counties. Although the system of governance was based on elec-tion by most adult white male property holders—specific regulations al-lowing only freemen or church members to vote at town meetings were not always enforced—electoral outcomes reinforced existing ideas of deference. Magistrates were rarely ousted from their post, and the office of selectman rotated among acknowledged leaders, with sons often tak-ing their fathers' places. Deputies and magistrates represented the town to the colony and vice versa. Towns with several magistrates, like Salem and nearby Ipswich, had greater influence at the colonial level but often had greater expectations thrust upon them, especially in times of war.

To understand how a Puritan merchant group gathered much of the social and political power in town, it is useful to briefly review the ca-reers of some of Salem's prominent seventeenth-century leaders. Salem proved fertile ground for several men of respectable English back-ground who linked entrepreneurial efforts and political office with reli-gious conformity. Henry Bartholomew, William Hathorne, and Walter Price each forged a combination of the elements required—English ori-gins, Puritan piety, and commercial achievement—to gain a position among Salem's merchant elite. Bartholomew, an East Anglian merchant, began with a small half-acre house lot in Salem. He made the mistake (so some locals thought) of following Roger Williams to Rhode Island but returned after a few months, immediately rejoining the church. Two years later, the town enticed him to stay with a grant of 150 acres; a few years later, voters elected him to the most important office. Bartholomew was chosen as selectman or deputy to the General Court in Boston almost every year from 1643 to 1684.[18]

Joining Bartholomew and William Browne, another powerful Puritan merchant, on the magistrates' bench, William Hathorne, a peacemaker between East Anglians and West Countrymen, became one of Salem's leading representatives to the colony, and a magistrate for the Essex County Quarterly Court from 1650 until his death in 1681. These men and others such as Walter Price followed Hugh Peter's dictum, both fostering commerce and joining the church. Price, coming to Salem in 1644 as a single man from the bustling port of Bristol, quickly joined the church and married a daughter of a middling mariner / merchant, Benjamin Gerrish. Five years later, he began working his way up through the ranks of town offices, starting as constable. Within a decade of coming to Salem, while still a young man of thirty-four, Price began his long tenure as selectman. His rise to prominence was recognized by a gift from his fellow selectmen of one hundred acres. When he died in 1674, leaving an estate of £2,058, his son followed him into town leadership.[19]

As Hathorne, Bartholomew, Price, and others like them built docks and warehouses along the edge of the inner harbor, and occupied the front row seats in Salem's meeting house, the Old Planters moved to the outskirts of this activity, taking up dispersed farms across the outer harbor on "the Ryal Side" and "the Cape Ann Side." Farmers and West Country gentlemen found their role in town leadership diminishing, in part because several rural regions severed ties with Salem to form independent units. The town fathers and the General Court agreed to carve out separate towns from the most distant areas of Salem. Wenham Pond became Wenham in 1643 and the area around Jeffries Creek became the small coastal town of Manchester in 1645. Marblehead, home to fishermen and shoremen from a variety of ethnic groups, officially separated from Salem in 1648, but extensive economic ties between Salem merchants and Marblehead fishermen and shoremen kept Marblehead in the position of a client town well into the eighteenth century. The final secession in this redrawing of geographic and cultural boundaries occurred in 1668, when the West Country settlers of the Cape Ann Side, separated by water and culture from Puritan, commercial Salem, became the town of Beverly. Still concerned about the loss of these valuable agricultural regions, the town leaders would refuse to grant Salem Village's requests for separate status in the 1680s, further intensifying the conflict between townsmen and farmers.[20]

The early discord in Salem over regional origins and religious beliefs heightened awareness of difference but also gave townspeople confidence in the methods they had used successfully to contain or exclude difference. The prominent leaders of Salem during the middle decades of the century spoke with one voice in public affairs, the voice of a mercantile elite; they practiced similar business strategies—clientage arrangements in the fishing industry and shared investments in vessels and cargoes.[21] Members of Salem's emerging merchant elite worked together on town committees to erect a new meeting house, commanded the two Salem militia companies, and, as selectmen, authorized "settling of a highway" from Salem to Reading in the interior and widening bridges to Ipswich and Wenham. These same families shared ownership in vessels and commercial ventures, built stores and warehouses next to each other along the inner harbor, constructed large, gabled houses around the Town House and along Essex Street, and linked their children in marriage to each other, to Boston merchants, and to the grandchildren of the colony's founding families. The townspeople, at least the long-term residents, recognized and supported the growing dominance of mercantile families; from 1665 to 1700 voters chose six merchants to each farmer elected to the seven-man board of selectmen.[22]

Merchants built their budding empires, in part, on the fishing industry. Fishing expeditions, manned by English servants, launched from English ports, and financed by English capital, had come to Salem early, especially to the shores of Marblehead and Winter Island.[23] English crews spent summers on the shore drying and packing fish, but this was not the "resident fishing industry" Hugh Peter had called for in his master plan for Salem. Nor were fishermen—prone to rowdiness, hard drinking, and profanity—the "residents" Peter had in mind. Most householders who settled in New England preferred the life of the independent farmer to the difficult, dirty, and ill-paying job of catching and curing fish.[24] If town and colony wanted to support economic opportunity and commercial growth, they would have to accept strangers in their midst. The town and the General Court did not recognize the paradox built into Hugh Peter's prescription for Salem. The townspeople continued to struggle with this issue throughout the seventeenth century.

As Salem's commercial success grew, the groups of strangers within its borders multiplied. A small colony of fishermen had settled in the 1630s on Winter Island, attached by a causeway to the eastern end of Salem's central peninsula. The town encouraged them to stay by granting small half-acre lots on lifetime tenure and fencing off the causeway to prevent animals from destroying the fish spread out to dry in the sun. But during the early years, most fishermen came to Salem as transients, as members of a vast pool of British maritime laborers, many from the West Country, who "drifted into the fishery in the course of their travels."[25] With fish so readily available and so cheap that farmers used it to fertilize their fields, local merchants had little control and little incentive to organize and finance a local fishery. But Salem, and the broader commercial world upon which it depended, soon changed.

The onset of civil war in England (1642) altered circumstances for Salem, for the Massachusetts Bay Colony, and for the transatlantic world to which all Salemites were, at least indirectly, connected. The bustling growth of the Bay Colony came to an abrupt end. Without a constant flow of new immigrants to the colony, prices for farm products dropped to the cellar, and English goods, metalwares, cloth, glass, and tools disappeared from merchants' shops.[26] But the Civil War in England disrupted not only the flow of new settlers to Massachusetts but also the flow of fish from Newfoundland to England and Spain, creating an opportunity for Salem and Boston entrepreneurs.

The price of good "merchantable" cod escalated; the simultaneous growth of West Indian sugar plantations based on slave labor from Africa provided an outlet for broken, undersized, or damaged "refuse" fish that planters used to feed their slaves. Massachusetts merchants were able to fill the gap caused by events in England; the output of the New England fishery grew from six thousand quintals in 1641 to sixty thousand quintals annually in 1675. The fish trade spawned its share of "instant millionaires" in Salem and Boston, allowing men like George Curwen, Philip English, and Henry Shrimpton to enter the ranks of wealthy merchants.[27] Among them, only Curwen had the Puritan credentials and family connections to reach a prominent position in the social elite.

George Curwen arrived in Salem from Workington in the county of Cumberland, England in 1638 with his wife and two small children. He received a modest grant of twenty acres from the selectmen. He soon constructed a store and warehouse at the inner harbor, began to build his fortune, and proceeded to make himself useful to the town. Curwen, perceived as a "man of property and education," was chosen selectman within a decade of his arrival. His wife had joined the First Church in 1640 and his second son had been baptized that same year. Curwen probably attended church regularly, where he joined William Hathorne and William Browne on the "Magistrates' Bench," set aside for influential men. By the time Jersey merchant Philip English made his decision to marry and settle in Salem in the 1670s, George Curwen already held a very prominent position in town and often served as deputy to the General Court. Through his children's marriages, Curwen claimed connections to the Hathornes and Brownes in Salem and to the important Boston merchant families of the Sheafes and Gibbses. Curwen's oldest son John married Margaret Winthrop, granddaughter of John Winthrop, founder and longtime governor of Massachusetts Bay, and daughter of

Connecticut governor John Winthrop Jr. Curwen's estate, valued over six-thousand pounds in 1685, included five houses, four warehouses, and two wharves in Salem, a warehouse and wharf in Boston, three farms, and four ships.[28]

As George Curwen aged, his sons John and Jonathan stepped into their father's place, both serving as selectmen and deputies to the General Court. John, the elder son, took over as militia leader and handled the overseas trading. Jonathan supervised a lumber mill in Maine and climbed to the highest level of the Massachusetts judiciary system, while serving regularly first as deputy and then, after 1689, as magistrate / councillor to the General Court. Jonathan Curwen gained his greatest fame as judge on the Court of Oyer and Terminer during the Salem witchcraft trials in 1692. Captain John died in the summer of 1683 "cut off in the midst of usefulness and when his prospect was fair for unusual eminence." Within two years the elder Curwen was dead and Jonathan, a gifted jurist but not a skilled merchant, was left to carry on the family obligations, which included not only his own young children but also two teenage sisters, an eleven-year-old half-brother from his father's second marriage, and his dead brother's only son.[29]

The Curwens, mercantile winners in the early fish trade, began to experience grave difficulties in carrying on family and enterprise, just at the time when Philip English, leader of the Jersey French community, was developing his business, hiring captains for his ships, building a mansion, and eventually gaining provisional acceptance into the social and political elite of Salem. When Philip English came to Salem in the 1670s he had a crucial advantage over his established colleagues: he was already a part of the Anglo-European commercial network. English had matured in the midst of "foreign" traders, whereas most Salem shippers still struggled to move beyond dependence on London merchants by developing direct contacts with Spanish and French ports.

Curwen Sr. had built his prominence on several shrewd moves, taking advantage of the disruption in commerce and the fishery during the two decades (1640–60) of unrest in England. Although still dependent on London merchants, whose own crews and vessels had been impressed for service in the war, Salem merchants like George Curwen provided the financing to develop a resident fishing industry by offering credit to fishermen and their crews, leasing them vessels, outfitting ships for each voyage, and allowing families left at home to purchase supplies on credit. In return, crews promised their catch to their creditors / patrons, who then sold the fish abroad, parceled out the share of profits to the men, and started the cycle all over again. Merchant capitalists gradually increased the amount of funds invested in the New England fishery. During the 1660s Curwen carried over one thousand pounds in debit balances for eighty men involved in fishing "to the Eastward" off the coast of Maine. This investment ensured Curwen and other merchants an ample inventory of fish to supply their own creditors in London and their customers in the Caribbean.[30]

It might be well over a year from the time Curwen or his fellow merchants laid out funds for a fishing crew to the day a ship returning from Spain or England brought the "neet proceeds" back to Salem in the form of goods to be sold or credit to be applied to other obligations awaiting payment. Soon thereafter, or perhaps even before results were known, another cycle of credit and exchange would begin as fishing crews left their winter quarters in Salem and Marblehead to head for the Isles of Shoals, Monhegan, or Newfoundland. When fishermen headed out to sea, merchants could only hope that memories of debts owed, houses built, and families cherished would prove strong enough to inspire the smelly, heavy, and perilous work upon which the commercial success of Salem was coming to depend.[31]

The resident fishermen whose cottages and children spilled across Marblehead and Winter Island, and the seamen, ship's carpenters, and dock workers at the eastern end of Salem town, did not exactly fit the community norms articulated by Hugh Peter and reinforced by merchant officials. Few fishermen attempted to join the Salem church; of sixty-six fishing families settled in town before 1676 only four had accepted the church covenant. Most espoused a "combination of Anglican spirituality and English popular culture that . . . was an affront to Puritan tradition." From his pulpit, Cotton Mather often lamented their use of "the Pagan Language of a Good Fortune" to report their "Luck of Fish." Usually the poorest working inhabitants of any community, fishermen resorted to rough language and physical violence in direct contempt of community ideals and authority.[32]

Townspeople misinterpreted the work rhythm of the fishing industry, which differed from patterns in agriculture or trade. When out on a voyage, the crew of a fishing ketch spent "months of labor on an isolated stretch of shoreline in exclusively male company, punctuated only by visits from other fishermen or wine peddlers and by occasional trips home." Back in port between voyages or in the midst of a winter freeze, the men experienced enforced idleness. This seasonal labor pattern disturbed Bay Colony authorities. In 1674 the General Court complained that "when they are at home, & not imployed in their callings," fishermen come "to be spectators, or otherwise ideling gaming, or spending their time unprofitably." Fishermen and mariners, while economically essential, offered a bad example "where by such persons as attend their duty, & spend their time in that service, are discouraged." This pattern of bouts of intense labor at sea alternating with weeks of idleness at home developed in response to the physical environment and the demands of international trade. Because fishermen had to accommodate their lives to both natural rhythms and market cycles, they did not conform to the moral guidelines of the Puritan merchant leaders. As a result, most fishing families lived as a troublesome sub-culture at the margins of Salem Town.[33]

Another group of "outsiders," the Quakers, arrived in Salem during the 1650s and 1660s. Initially, they threatened the status quo far more than disorderly fishermen. Although many Quaker families settled in the Woods, a region at the outskirts of Salem near its border with Lynn, they refused to stay put, insisting instead on disrupting Sunday worship and marching down Essex Street naked. Selectmen were forced to imprison the offenders, who feared the fate of their coreligionists hanged in Boston. The initial Salem Friends Meeting began, just two years after the first "contagion" in New England, when thirty people, several of them members in good standing of First Church, gathered at Nicholas and Hannah Phelps's house to hear two traveling Quakers speak. Salem officials acted quickly. Two constables and merchant-selectman Edmund Batter broke up meetings and imprisoned local followers and visiting preachers. In one incident, Batter stopped a visiting Quaker from addressing the Salem Meeting by stuffing his mouth with a glove and dragging him out by his hair. The more harshly officials reacted, the more aggressive the Quakers became, until six Salem Quakers dared to disrupt the ordination of Salem's new minister John Higginson. The protestors, whose "dramatic forms of witness were fueled by hopes for the immediate end of the world," were sent immediately to jail in Boston, while Higginson proclaimed that the "inner light" was "the Devil's Sacrifice" and "a stinking Vapor from Hell."[34]

Gradually, as visits from traveling witnesses slowed and fewer new members joined the Salem meeting, town officials adopted an approach that relied more on fines than on physical violence and imprisonment.[35] Not surprisingly, the fines often equaled the assessment of rates for ministerial support, which the Quakers had refused to pay. A few Quakers managed to integrate themselves into the community—Thomas Maule, who arrived in 1668 after the most virulent hostilities had subsided, was able to purchase property in town and pursue a modest mercantile trade—but a sense of unease about the Society of Friends lingered. The

Quakers in Salem acquired a reputation for unscrupulousness, sharp dealing, and excessive litigation in business, the same charges that would be leveled at the Jersey "French." One angry mariner made the connections explicit. Railing in court about his Quaker creditor, ship captain John Vittum exclaimed, "the Quaker dog shall never have one of them [his missing cargo] again. . . . it is as good going a privateering as taking anything from him [the creditor] as from a French man for I doe account him noe better." Quakers, Frenchmen, dogs, what did they have in common in the minds of "English" colonists? It must have seemed that none could be adequately pinned down or penned out. Each spoke a different tongue—ranting or barking; each threatened to invade the very heart of Salem.[36]

As English, Welsh, and Irish fishermen spread across the waterfront of Salem and Marblehead harbors, the "French" from the Isle of Jersey formed a separate cultural circle with Philip English at its center. Driven from their island home by economic decline and waning opportunity, Jersey's youth had to look elsewhere. Word of Salem as an increasingly prosperous fishing center in North America, reached the island just as the inhabitants faced an imploding economy. A few Jerseyans tried Salem in the 1660s. Daniel Bacon, perhaps the first Channel Islander to become a permanent resident, set up a boatbuilding business at Knocker's Hole on the shores of a tidal creek at the southern edge of Salem's waterfront. In 1661 the boatbuilder William Stevens of Gloucester constructed a ship for three Jersey merchants; one of them, Jean LeBrun (John Brown), later settled in Salem. At least three Jersey fishermen worked as clients of Salem merchants. One of Salem's few prosperous fishermen, Job Hilliard, purchased a share in one of George Curwen's fishing ketches in 1663 and took up residence at the eastern end of town, which was to become an enclave of Jersey Islanders.[37]

Born into the Channel Island milieu of mixed English and French cultural practices marked by Anglican religion and loyalty to the English throne coupled with a French-patterned court system and French as the primary language, Philip English rose to ambiguous prominence in Salem's maritime world. His odyssey reveals much about how individuals and communities coped with the competing impulses of adventure and security in late seventeenth-century Anglo-America. Philip English, a Frenchman and Anglican, represented an anomaly in Salem. Throughout his life he experienced a series of events that served alternately to include him with and distance him from his fellow townsmen. For decades English ranked as one of the wealthiest merchants in a town run by affluent merchants and their ministerial kin, but both his French origins and his Anglican religion served to marginalize him in the merchant elite headed by the Browne and Curwen families.[38]

By the time Philippe L'Anglois's name entered the birth records of Trinity Parish, Jersey, in 1651, the people of the Channel Islands, northern France, and the West Country of England had developed a tightly woven fabric of commercial relationships that stretched across national borders and language barriers. It was a fabric that both sustained and limited L'Anglois / English in his search for economic and social mastery in colonial New England. The Channel Islands proved to be an ideal training ground for an ambitious mariner.[39] Jersey's topography resembles a great wedge tilted toward France, with high cliffs on the northern side, and on the west, the combination of prevailing westerly winds and the long, sweeping St. Ouen's Bay with its rocky coastline forming a death trap for sailors.[40] The low-lying south coast, facing France, shelters St. Helier, the best deep-water harbor on Jersey. Islanders on the eastern shore lived so close to France that "Churches and Houses may be easily discerned from either Coast." The "small and narrow current" that flowed between them posed a navigational danger in peacetime but provided an essential barrier during war.[41]

Navigation in and around the Channel Islands held many hazards, but the islands offered incentives for those willing to brave the winds and currents. The islands were perfectly located to carry on licit and illicit trade with France, to control shipping in and out of the English Channel, and to disrupt commerce (via the Seine) between French Atlantic ports and Paris.[42] Originally part of the Duchy of Normandy, the Channel Islands became part of the possessions of the English crown in 1066. In order to keep the islands loyal to the English king, in spite of their proximity to France, succeeding monarchs conferred special privileges that promoted island commerce. Imports from England entered the islands with no duties, and island-manufactured goods could come into English ports free of imposts. This made the islands a "place of common vent" for Anglo-French trade. Traders exchanged English cloth, lead, and tin for French canvas, linen, and wine. Merchant capitalists imported English wool into Jersey for its largest local industry, the knitting of woolen stockings (hence our word "jersey" for a type of knit fabric) which were sold primarily to France.[43]

Coming of age on the Isle of Jersey, Philippe L'Anglois no doubt learned the expert sailing and navigation techniques required to negotiate Channel waters and absorbed the atmosphere of an international trading community. In Saint Aubin every Monday, he could visit a market held "for merchants of foreign commodities," where Jersey traders exchanged wine, salt, iron, and wool from Spain and Portugal for fish, stockings, and surplus wheat sent to Iberia. Merchants from the Channel Islands like Simon Le Sebirell and James Lampriere, who fled to France when their home base supported the Royalist cause during the English Civil War, settled in the port of Saint Malo and formed close commercial partnerships with French merchants while still maintaining their Jersey connections. L'Anglois / English would parlay the international connections he formed growing up on Jersey into a substantial colonial fortune.[44]

After the restoration in 1660, just when Channel Islanders should have been enjoying the fruits of their loyalty to Charles I during the Civil War, they found their major industry—knitting woolen stockings—entering what proved to be a permanent decline. In their heyday, knitters on the Isle of Jersey had fashioned 240,000 pairs of colorful striped and patterned stockings annually for European markets. As the seventeenth century wore on, relations between England and France worsened. Imperial policies, like a French tariff on stockings (1654) and on other English goods (1678), began to affect the cozy commercial network among French ports, the Channel Islands, and West Country trading centers. Jerseyans faced economic troubles on other fronts as well. Having joined the French and English in the Newfoundland cod fishery in the late sixteenth century, islanders found it increasingly difficult, as did their English counterparts, to compete with larger French ships. At Trinity Bay on the Atlantic coast of Newfoundland, the typical Jersey fleet of twenty had declined by 1670 to only two or three vessels.[45]

Navigation in the vicinity of the Channel Islands was not easy nor relationships with France smooth, yet the inhabitants depended on both; by the second half of the century, island population had so exceeded the land available for its support that Jersey imported half of its grain every year. Under these conditions it was "not easie for a Man . . . to enlarge his Patrimony, in a Country so full of People," and since land value was reckoned in quarters of wheat, rising or falling "according to the Price that Corn [grain] bears each Year in the Market," estates were always "variable and uncertain." Like many Massachusetts towns a century later, the island's young people looked toward a future of diminishing prospects.[46]

As a young man whose homeland faced the beginning of what came to be a long era of declining fortunes, Philippe L'Anglois, scion of an upper-middling Jersey family and godson of the influential Sir Philip De Carteret, came to Salem. Initially Salem may have been simply another port-of-call, one made more appealing by L'Anglois's undoubted ability to speak English. Although French, colored with "a Barbarism or two" was "the common language" in Jersey, most "Gentlemen, Merchants, or Principal Inhabitants" also spoke English. Like many of the transient maritime traders of the Atlantic world, L'Anglois shuttled around England, France, Spain, and North America.[47] It was only when he wed that he, like other mariners, put down roots—or in this case took up his wife's roots. With his marriage, L'Anglois claimed the English identity immanent in his family name and began to shape himself into an English gentleman / merchant—a doubtful quest in an era of strict social divisions between English gentry and foreign nabobs, and in the Puritan stronghold of Salem, however commercial it might be.

Coming to Salem as a young man in the early 1670s, English boarded with the Hollingsworth family. The elder Hollingsworth carried on a coastal trade with a branch of his family established in Virginia. Shortly before Hollingsworth's death in 1675, Mary, his only surviving child, married Philip English. English did not simply continue his father-in-law's established coastal trade but, taking advantage of his Jersey and French contacts, reached for a wider role in burgeoning overseas commerce. The earliest accounts of English's trading ventures appear in letters written in French. In 1677, an agent in Saint Malo, acting for "sire Moise Coubel, gentleman of said Jersey," financed a voyage for L'Anglois in the amount of £208. The letter of indebtedness, signed before a notary, laid out the intended voyage: L'Anglois, master of the ketch *Speedwell*, would head from Jersey to Boston and then to "Bilbao, Biscay, Bordeaux or coast of England," and "afterwards return to said Jersey or the said harbor of Saint Malo."[48] English completed the voyage and repaid the funds in 1679.

Trade ventures financed by French merchants and financiers gradually appeared less frequently in English's accounts, and disappeared by the late 1680s. Instead, he developed commercial relationships with London merchants and local Salem traders. English owned several vessels, which he sent to St. Christopher's, Barbados, the "Bay of Indorows" [Honduras], and Surinam in the Caribbean; to Bilbao in Spain; and to Madeira and the Azores. By the 1680s, he began to employ others as masters and ship captains and stayed in Salem to manage his expanding ventures. When his sons Philip Jr. and William came of age, English operated ships in the colonial coastal trade from Nova Scotia to Virginia as well as overseas. From these voyages, his captains brought back "Barbados goods" such as rum, molasses, and sugar, and "English goods" such as "nailes, blew lining, Osnabrigs, Holland Duck, cordage," "felt hatts," and "pepper, nutmeg, cloves, and starch."[49] Exotic commodities were not the only foreign imports English would bring to Salem.

Philip English established himself in Salem by marrying Mary Hollingsworth and inheriting her father's coastal shipping business and family property at the eastern edge of Salem. Like many other Salem merchants, English maintained his own fishing fleet. Locating the fishing industry on Winter Island at the outskirts of Salem harbor isolated the men and their foul-smelling catch from the town center. The island provided generous space for yards and stages (wooden scaffolding on which fish were laid to dry in the sun). Wharves on the island served for loading hogsheads packed with dried and salted fish aboard ocean vessels and for unloading the essential supplies of salt, barrel staves, and hoops used to pack cod and mackerel for shipment to the Caribbean or southern Europe.

In his part of town, situated between the fishing colony and the town center, English began to gather a colony of like-minded French-speaking mariners, fishermen, and apprentices around him. Prompted by fears of increasing pauperism as Channel Island economies declined, officials there encouraged poor families to send their children to America as indentured servants. Service with Philip English, known by Jerseyans and sponsored by the island's highest nobility, must have seemed like a fortunate opportunity. In January and February 1675, English, only twenty-four years old himself, "being at present aboard his ship of which he is master," agreed to take on at least two Jersey boys, one as a joiner-carpenter and the other "to learn some vocation or trade according to what Mr. L'Anglois or said child may find suitable." English promised to nourish and clothe them "well and honestly" and provide two "well-made habits" for each young man.[50] Unlike most indenture arrangements in colonial New England, these documents made no reference to religion. English brought at least eight indentured servants to Salem via the Isle of Jersey, and probably many more[51] (see table 1). Often these young people worked, not directly for English, but in houses all over Salem and ships all over the Atlantic. Philip English Jr. and son-in-law John Touzel, also from Jersey, continued the tradition as they came of age and established themselves as innkeeper and ship's captain, respectively. Prosperous Jersey families like the Englishes continued to bring indentured labor to Salem and Marblehead at such a great rate that Marblehead schoolmaster Josiah Cotton claimed he spent more time "writing indentures for Jersey boys and girls" than teaching his pupils.[52]

Table 1. Indentured Servants Brought to Salem by Philip English and Family, 1675–1731

		Home	Years	Service
	Philip English			
1675	Phle. Gaudin	Jersey	4½	joiner / carpenter
1675	Jean Binet	Jersey	6	—
1676	Jacque Chevalier	Jersey	6	mariner
1677	Jane Masury	Jersey	6	domestic service
1677	Ellener Clarke	Jersey		domestic service
1677	Mary Pary	Jersey	6	domestic service
1683	John Lawrence	Stockholm	6	—
1684	Emanuel Francisco	Portugal	5	labor at sea or on shore
	Philip English, Jr.			
1718	Thomas Le Sebirel	Jersey	6	mariner
1723	Edward Garvey	Jersey	5	tavern servant
1731	David Le Sebirel	Jersey	4	mariner
	John Touzel			
1724	George Cook	Jersey	4	mariner

Sources: English Family Papers, Phillips Library, Peabody Essex Museum; George E. Dow, ed., *Records and Files of the Quarterly Courts of Essex County Massachusetts* (Salem: Essex County Massachusetts, 1911).

Not every Jersey family viewed Philip English as a welcome rescuer. Widow La Messurier (Masury), on learning that her father had agreed to bind her sister Jane to Philip English, testified, "I was troubled but seeing that she must be embarked, did Furnish her very well with all sorts of necessaries for her Apparel" and a "coffer" to keep them in. Unfortunately for Jane and her family, she did not survive the voyage to New England. Another young servant making the same passage, Mary Pary, cared for Jane as she lay dying. Mary attested that Jane "desired that those who tended her should have what was left in her chest of clothes." But English ignored her last wish. The merchant parceled out Jane's finery "among his other servant maidens." The clothes, worth fewer than twenty shillings, did not make up for the seven-pound cost of Jane's passage, which English tried unsuccessfully to recover based in part on her claim that her brother Benjamin, already in Salem, would pay the passage.[53]

For English these indentures served an economic and a cultural purpose. When the young people arrived in Salem, English would hire them out in Salem and Marblehead and receive their wages as annual income during their term of servitude. In 1682, he hired out twenty-three-year-old Thomas Nichols of Jersey as a seaman aboard the ketch *John* under

Edward Woodman of Salem for thirty shillings per month. The voyage took Nichols and Woodman from Boston to Barbados, to "Saltudus" (Tortuga), back to Barbados, and then to London, where the vessel was sold and Nichols left stranded and unpaid since his wages could only go directly to his master. As servants indentured to English, young people of Jersey, like Thomas Nichols, shuttled about the Atlantic maritime world. Often that experience was not pleasant, but if they survived, and most did, they might set up their own simple homes and raise families in modest circumstances—most likely in Philip English's neighborhood at the eastern end of Salem among other Jersey "French."[54]

By 1685, at least two dozen families formed a separate cultural community based in part on language.[55] It would have been no surprise to any Salemites to overhear conversation in French as they walked down English Lane or among the cottages of the Masurys, Hilliards, Whites, and Searles clustered along the lanes leading to the waterfront near the Marblehead ferry. Mrs. Baldin, "a French lady," offered her church confession in French, a Marblehead schoolmaster worked feverishly trans-

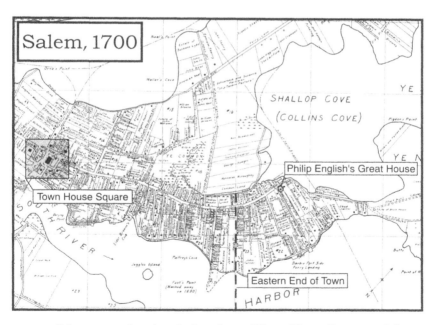

MAP 2. Salem, 1700, showing the locations of Town House Square and the eastern end of the town. Prepared by Tom Tricot for the author, based on a map by James Duncan Phillips at the Peabody Essex Museum.

lating indentures for Jersey youth, English corresponded with Channel Island and French traders in his native tongue, and the Essex County Quarterly Court accepted written testimony in French.

Most Jerseyans stayed apart from Salem's First Church, perhaps preferring private worship in accord with the customs of their homeland, where they used the *Book of Common Prayer*, translated into French, and recited the Anglican liturgy, again in French. In Jersey on "the Lord's Day," "public exercises" included "reading the Common Prayer." Worshipers received Communion four times a year, always including Easter and Christmas. The Jerseyans shared one practice in common with Puritans. They believed that "All Fathers and Masters of Families shall be exhorted and injoyned to cause their children and Domesticks to be instructed in the knowledge of their Salvation."[56] Perhaps this was such an ingrained article of faith for Channel Islanders that they saw no need to make such instructions explicit in an indenture agreement, or perhaps their less rigid Protestantism allowed them to omit the clause.

The Jersey French stood out and lived apart from other Salem townsmen, but as mariners and fishermen they also participated in a marginalized "alehouse culture" that developed beyond the realm of Puritan influence. In 1678, at least fifty mariners and fishermen resided in English's neighborhood in "the east part of Salem." Even though the fishing industry was in the midst of a shift from transient to resident labor, many strangers frequented Salem. The town drew crowds from all over Essex County on days when the Quarterly Court held its sessions. Young men from nearby villages came to the port to ship out on fishing crews or trading vessels. English merchant ships frequently disgorged their sailors for overdue shore leave.[57] All of these visitors needed refreshment; some found it at English's Blue Anchor Tavern.

Town officials distinguished between legal or licensed taverns and illegal drinking houses. While Boston claimed twenty-four authorized taverns, the General Court limited Salem to two wine taverns, four inns, and four retailers of wine and strong drink. Salem's ratio of one drinking place for every eighty people resembled the English homeland more closely than the rest of rural Essex County, which could offer only one tavern for 219 people.[58] Salem's minister directed a letter to the General Court in 1678 complaining about "too numerous" drinking houses, and people "too much given to drinking and not so well affected to Sobriety, Law & good order."[59] Reverend Higginson must have been pained to hear that a man having "a pot of beer and a cake" one Sunday morning "scorned to go hear old Higginson for he was an oppressor of the poor," or that another tavern goer, behind on his ministerial rates, threatened to have the constable hanged before he would have "any of it to pay Mr. Higginson." Jasper Danckaerts, a Dutch Pietist visitor to Boston, referred to "Sabbath revels," noting that "all their religion consists in observing Sunday, by not working or [by] going into the taverns on that day."[60]

Patrons also distinguished between licensed and illegal inns. Almost all disorderly tavern incidents brought to the court's attention occurred in Salem Town's eighteen and Salem Village's four illegal taverns. It was in these unlicensed, "easily established and often short-lived" drinking houses that an alehouse culture motivated by "festal sociability, entrepreneurial spirit, and indifference—or even hostility—to authority" developed. Women played an important role in running taverns where a "concourse of strangers" took food and drink.[61]

Philip English participated in tavern culture from an ambiguous perspective. As prospective inheritor and then owner of the Blue Anchor, a licensed tavern managed by his mother-in-law, Eleanor Hollingsworth, and an aspiring member of Salem's merchant elite, English had one foot in the door of gentlemanly sociability associated with upscale wine taverns near Town House Square at the heart of Salem. Yet the Blue Anchor Tavern, situated, like English's other properties, on the eastern waterfront, welcomed Jerseyans from the neighborhood, passengers from the Marblehead Ferry, and fishermen and mariners from Salem and abroad. It was in this tavern that English probably first met his future mother-in-law and possibly his future wife as well. It was no doubt his home port before his marriage to Mary Hollingsworth. Eventually it would pass to his son, Philip English, Jr.[62] As owner of a tavern patronized by many of the dissident elements in Salem, English placed himself in a paradoxical position, one that kept him closely connected to the French and fishing communities but also added to the income needed to join the merchant elite.

By operating local fishing vessels and drying, packing, and shipping facilities on Winter Island, by owning all or portions of several ocean-going ships trading with the Caribbean, southern Europe, and the Wine Islands, and by importing goods from London for barter or sale in Salem, English accumulated a substantial fortune. In 1689, less than twenty years after coming to Salem, English joined Major William Browne, Esq., Benjamin Browne, Esq., Major Redford, and William Hirst among the top five taxpayers in Salem.[63]

With financial success came an ambiguous social status for English. In 1683, English built a large Tudor-style gabled house in the eastern end of town. Known as "English's Great House," it contained a counting room and shop as well as expansive living space and a "great porch on the western end."[64] The house must have towered over its surroundings, for

FIGURE 2. Philip English's "Great House," built in 1685. Illustration by
George M. White, 1888, after drawings by E. V. Dalrymple and J. R. Penniman.
Courtesy of the Peabody Essex Museum.

he built in an area covered with small cottages occupied by fishermen,
mariners, and ship's carpenters. The other wealthy merchants lived in
the center of Salem, clustered near the town square and the inner docks.[65]
His mansion stood about a block inland on the corner of English Lane
and Main Street, which led from the center of town to the fishing stages
and wharves on Winter Island. Philip English commanded a substantial
domain, owning several houses, wharves, a tavern, a warehouse, and a
great mansion, but he held sway in a marginal location.

From his "Great House" beyond the center of town, English echoed
the ancient tradition of foreign merchants being forced to live and conduct business outside the city walls. In the sixteenth and seventeenth
centuries this custom of exclusion flourished in "the Liberties," an area
outside the walls of London that became a place of production and exchange beyond the control of guilds.[66] Recent English historians portray
the Liberties, site of insane asylums, hospitals, markets, and gallows,
and home to the poor, the infirm, the foreign, and the rebellious, as "a
domain of cultural ambivalence and excess."[67] As such, it served as a so-

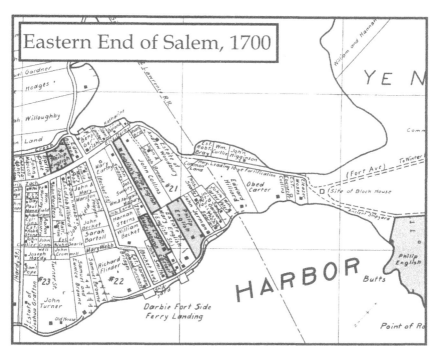

MAP 3. Philip English's neighborhood, the eastern end of Salem, 1700. Prepared by Tom Tricot for the author, based on a map by James Duncan Phillips at the Peabody Essex Museum.

cial and textual margin or commentary on the civic center. An area out-side Philadelphia named "the Northern Liberties," like its London pre-decessor, became a space where public rituals inverted the social hierar-chy. As described by Susan Davis, Philadelphia's Northern Liberties in the early nineteenth century consisted of "a poor working-class district clustered around boatyards and docks and pocked with small work-rooms."[68] If any area in Salem resembled London's or Philadelphia's Liberties it was Philip English's neighborhood. Given that the Liberties were often sites of subversive rituals and activities, English, the most visible and powerful representative of his site, must have threatened both the agrarian interests of Salem Village and the established mer-chants of Town House Square.

In 1683, the same year he built his "Great House," Philip English began his move up the ladder of town offices by becoming a constable for the eastern part of town. His duties included collecting taxes and keeping order in his neighborhood. In response to complaints from Salem, the Quarterly Court ordered constables and tithingmen "diligently to enquire and search tippling houses" to rein in "the increase of disorders amongst us." Salem's constables, in spite of their instructions, had very little success in penetrating alehouse culture especially in unlicensed taverns. In attempting to enforce official standards of behavior by halting fights and enforcing curfews, constables often met with verbal and physical abuse; sometimes they were attacked with chairs and andirons. Bystanders often refused to interfere and might even join an attack on authority.

Perhaps Philip English was chosen constable because the townsmen thought he could combine the authority of office with his local reputation to quell his countrymen and keep order in this unruly neighborhood. After all, the selectmen had often ordered constables to "take Spetiall care to watch the Eastward end of Towne."[69] Powerful as he may have been in his own neighborhood, English was unable or unwilling to collect taxes from mariners, who considered themselves transients and therefore exempt from town rates. English claimed that he should not be responsible for nonresidents; the selectmen did not agree. This dispute derailed English's integration into the Salem elite and his claims to the wider recognition and deference accorded every other leading merchant family.

Salem, whose name derived ultimately from the Hebrew word for "peace," thus represented a collection of sometimes bellicose communities. An inhabitant of Salem in the 1690s would be uneasily aware of several "sorts" of people within the town, distinguished, in part, by where they chose to live. The merchant elite built substantial Tudor-style gabled houses and simple but sturdy public buildings around Town House Square and along Essex Street at the center of town. South of Town House Square, along the inner harbor, merchants constructed wharves and warehouses; along Ruck's Creek several shipbuilders set up shop, giving this area its name of "Knockers Hole." The French-speaking immigrants from Jersey clustered together at the eastern edge of town. A mix of artisans, tavernkeepers, mariners, and laborers occupied smaller dwellings along the waterfront, around the periphery, and scattered along the roads out of town. Further to the east, beyond the Jerseyans, most fishermen were relegated to the Neck and Winter Island, where they lived in meager cottages among rough wooden platforms spread out across the fields for drying fish. In "the Woods," far to the southwest of town and nominally within the Farms, a number of Quakers made their homes. Each of these neighborhoods that made up

Salem Town defined themselves in part by their different ethnicities, religions, and economic positions. The Reverend Hugh Peter's dream of a covenant community had shattered under the impact of economic expansion into a kaleidoscope of shifting cultural groups.

1692 was a banner year for Philip English—at least it began that way. In spite of occasional problems with rotting fish, his trade with the Caribbean was flourishing.[70] He had several vessels, including the *Repair* and the *Susanna* (named after his daughter), shuttling between Salem and St. Christopher's loaded with cod, mackerel, shingles, pipe staves, and pine boards. The *Repair* made several trips across the Atlantic to the Azores & Madeira, returning with cargoes of wine, iron, raisins, and olives.[71] English had improved his fortune relative to the other leading merchants, rising to third highest position in Salem's tax rolls.[72] While no merchant was anxious to pay more taxes, English no doubt took pride in his growing fortune.

In March, English was elected selectman at the spring town meeting, finally achieving local power. This was his first elective office since his year as constable, which had ended with English embroiled in a lawsuit vs. the Board of Selectmen over uncollected taxes. With this new public recognition, he joined the ranks of the merchant elite, holding economic and political power over and for their townsmen. Of course, unlike English, these other families—the Brownes, Curwens, and Hathornes—shared English as a native language and the Magistrates' Pew in church. Their allegiances were clear, their backgrounds unambiguous, their names unchanged. These were the families that had dominated the Board of Selectmen; by joining their ranks, English had become truly "English"—or had he?

If 1692 began well for Philip English, it seemed to mark the end of a decade of sorrowful and disturbing events for the Bay Colony and for Salem. A series of increasingly distressing political conflicts with England produced a climate of fear and suspicion in Massachusetts. In 1683 England began the process of revoking the charter of Massachusetts Bay issued in 1629 and carried to New England with the Winthrop fleet. King Charles II and Parliament used a conflict over land claims in Maine as an excuse to move against a colony that, in their eyes, behaved too much like an independent nation.[73] In September 1684, Massachusetts Bay Colony governor Simon Bradstreet and the General Court learned that the Charter had been revoked. The cancellation had several important consequences for Bay colonists. For one, every property owner's claim to real estate was immediately called into question. Without the Charter in force, town meetings did not have the power to grant land. This meant that deeds granted to colonists over the last fifty years might be invalid. The following March the General Court, ignoring its own unauthorized status, confirmed all land titles and granted the county courts power to settle land disputes. These proved futile gestures.

The English Crown placed Massachusetts and New York under a royally appointed governor and abolished the General Court's elected assembly. The royal plan restructured the judicial system, replacing the county Quarterly Courts with Chancery Courts to handle land claims and a Court of Common Pleas for other complaints, all staffed by appointees from Boston. The new courts enforced strict legal procedures so that many Salem plaintiffs found their cases thrown out of court for minor details. Selectmen were constrained from suing in the name of the town; since most were reluctant to sue as individuals for town complaints, their power to regulate was considerably weakened.[74]

In just a few years, Bay colonists had lost their right to elect juries and to present cases before presiding justices from Essex County, often the same men they elected to represent them at the General Court. In Salem, figures like William Hathorne, William Browne, Sr., Bartholomew Gedney, and later Jonathan Curwen, while not always in favor with every resident, at least represented the choice of a group within Salem. Having to plead their cases before little-known outsiders forced on them by a distant, autocratic government angered Salemites. Massachusetts townsmen also lost control over legislation and taxation. Previously, the General Court had set the amount of colony tax to be paid by each town, but the towns themselves decided on individual assessments and, by assigning the task to constables for each neighborhood, handled collection of town, county, and colony rates. Without the charter in force, Salemites and other Massachusetts settlers were now in a position little better than subjects of an autocratic monarch. This growing impotency, coupled with anxiety over the right to own private property—the basis for much of the economic power of colonial North America and the only opportunity for most immigrants to claim a "competency"—threatened the very heart and purpose of society.[75]

Neither elimination of the General Court nor changes in the judicial system provoked as much written commentary or heightened feeling as the enforced toleration of Anglicans and Quakers. The Dominion government under Sir Edmund Andros granted religious toleration and revoked tax support for Puritan ministers.[76] A practicing adherent of the Church of England, Andros and some of the royal officials he brought with him to New England, joined by some Boston merchants, formed an Anglican church. At first they appropriated South Church for their services but in 1688 they built King's Chapel on a corner of the town burying ground. The site was commandeered by Andros in what one Bostonian later described as "a barefaced squat."[77] In 1690, three Massachusetts ministers, John Allin, Joshua Moody, and Samuel Willard, authored a pamphlet opposing toleration. They denounced their "Persecutors," implying that those who favored toleration also scorned godliness, "which their sore eyes feel an Ey-sore in."[78] Yet few pamphlets attacked Anglicans directly; perhaps at this moment they were too powerful.

The ministers reserved their most extreme antagonism for Quakers. The policy of religious toleration encouraged Quakers to renew the proselytizing efforts of the 1660s. George Keith, a Scottish itinerant preacher who aimed to rejuvenate original Quaker principles and passions, preached openly in the streets of Boston.[79] This "eye-sore" drove Puritans into a frenzy of vituperative language. Allin, Moody, and Willard asserted that "In Quakerism we see the Vomit cast forth in the by-past ages by whole kennels of those creatures . . . licked up again for a new Digestion, and once more exposed for the poisoning of mankind."[80] Casting Quakers as nothing more than beasts, they echoed the epithets voiced by defendants in the Essex County Courts. The new Charter attempted to enforce toleration and widen voting privileges by substituting property requirements for freeman status, which was often linked to church membership. In response, Puritan lamentations grew more strident still.

Throughout the colony in the years preceding the Salem witchcraft trials, feelings ran high. In 1689, after receiving news of the Glorious Revolution that installed William of Orange as King of England, Massachusetts colonists rebelled. Marching through the streets of Boston, a crowd of men and boys from all over Boston and Essex County, led by several magistrates who had been displaced by the Dominion government, captured and imprisoned Sir Edmund Andros and several of his supporters.[81] They reinstalled the aging Governor Simon Bradstreet, a long-time magistrate and Salem resident since his marriage to widow Anne Gardner in 1679.[82] But lacking a charter, burdened with a dismantled judicial system, and facing the specter of a harsh royal response to rebellion, Bradstreet's government remained ineffectual.[83] King William's War, beginning in 1689, raised another specter, the threat of Indian raids on rural towns. Many Essex County residents still remembered the horrific attacks by Native Americans on Andover in 1676. It was in this climate of anxiety and institutional weakness that witchcraft hysteria overtook Salem and spread throughout Essex County.

Philip English's election as selectman of Salem may have resulted from the change in voting regulations under the new Charter or a provisional recognition that he had more in common with the leading "English" merchants of Salem than the differences he displayed. With his election, English entered the coterie of the Salem elite, but he had only a few months to enjoy his newfound status. In February 1692, rumors of witchcraft rippled through Salem; by the end of the month three people had been formally accused.

Fears of witchcraft were very much a part of early modern culture. They represented one element of religious and magical thinking, one side of a literature of wonder, and one aspect of a belief in Satan.[84] However, executions for witchcraft were uncommon. Prior to Salem's outbreak, there had been ninety-three trials for witchcraft in New England; of these, sixteen resulted in executions. Many transplanted New Englanders had grown to maturity in East Anglia, particularly in the English county of Essex where the rate of witchcraft indictments and executions exceeded New England's. In northern European countries with significant Protestant populations, like Germany, Switzerland, and France, trials and executions of witches were more common than in England or its northern most colonies. The southern European, Catholic countries of Italy and Spain showed little concern over witchcraft, and only rarely did anxiety over witches reach the court system in the southern colonies. In any case, the practice of executing witches virtually disappeared by the end of the seventeenth century, and Salem was the scene of the last witchcraft panic in the Protestant world.

By exploring the Salem trials with a selective focus on Philip English and his wife—both accused by girls and women from Salem Village— we see the motivations underlying the hysteria as both more complex and more comprehensible. Betraying not only a deep-seated concern about emerging capitalism but also an anxiety about "the other" these fears were intensified by a period of confusing political transformation. It was not difference alone that elicited accusations; in each case, those singled out had crossed boundaries and placed themselves in an ambiguous relationship to the various groups uneasily occupying Salem.[85]

While whispers about witchcraft traditionally comprised a part of Protestant culture, this time, rumors and accusations swirled into hysteria. In April, a Court of Oyer and Terminer established to investigate the charges, accused twenty-two people and in May, another thirty-nine, among them Philip English and his wife. The process by which witches were accused and tried followed a similar sequence in England and New England. After a complaint by or on behalf of a victim, the magistrates of the local court gathered evidence, which consisted of depositions from witnesses including anybody claiming to have been harmed by the accused. Women suspected or accused were examined for a "witch's tit" (often a simple mole or blemish might be identified) where the demon was thought to suckle. With written evidence before it, a grand jury would either issue an indictment or throw out the case. At this point, the authorities often placed those indicted in jail for weeks or months to await trial. At the trial, the accused faced their accusers and a trial jury determined innocence or guilt. The sentence was passed by magistrates following the verdict. The records of Philip and Mary English's trial are missing, but a few depositions tell us that Ann Putnam, Marcy Lewis, Susannah Sheldon, Mary Wallcott, and Elizabeth Booth all complained against English while Mercy Lewis and Susannah Sheldon also implicated Mrs. English.[86]

Neither Philip English nor his wife fit the profile of a typical seventeenth-century witch. The most commonly accused were middle-aged women of English and Puritan background and low social status. These women, usually married with few or no children, had a reputation for abrasive, contentious personalities that they displayed in conflict with family members and in crimes of theft, slander, and assaultive speech.[87] While English may have been an aggressive litigator, as selectman and leading merchant he seemed an unlikely suspect.

Yet, in one respect, English's case fits a pattern of relations between accused and accusers highlighted by scholars of witchcraft in old and New England. In what Paul Boyer and Stephen Nissenbaum have characterized as a parody of the church covenant the presumed victim withholds something from the supposed witch, who retaliates with black magic. Philip English's encounter with William Beale of Marblehead, who testified against him, followed this pattern of request and rejection. In his statement, Beale, a man of about sixty, complained that in March of the previous year, "a very greate & wracking paine had seized uppon my body." As he lay in his bed early in the morning he saw a shadow of a man whose legs "weere of a very greate stature or bigness." He turned away and as he looked in that direction again, "I saw in the darkness aforesayed the plaine shape or else the person of Philip English of Salem." Beale wondered "what is this mans business heere now . . . or w'ch way came he hither so soone this morneinge by land or by water or hath hee been at marbllee Head all nighte & then laboring to correct my [?torn] not to thinke that hee was a wich;" Beale prayed to Jehovah and

"by secret ejaculations instantly the roome aforesayed became clear &
the shape shade or person vanished."[88]

Beale had had earlier dealings with English. He testified that in the
spring before New England expeditionary forces left for Canada, Philip
English came to a neighbor's house when Beale was present and "in a
fauneing & flattering manner" asked Beale to "give mee A good evidence in shewing me the bounds of my lande;" English tried to entice
Beale into giving supporting testimony in a land dispute with Mr.
Richard Reede of Marblehead by offering him "a piece of eight in my
pocket," but Beale answered: "doe not tell mee of your piece of eight for
if I bee called I must give evidence against you." English "seemed to be
moved & told mee that I lyed." That fall, English sued Reede and had
him arrested over the land dispute. Beale offered to testify for Reede and
even rode to Lynn to seek another witness who could support Reede's
claim. At the very moment Beale was "in discours about the titllee of the
lande aforesayed my nose gushed out bleedinge in A most extraordinary manner."[89] Beale's testimony ends leaving the court to draw the
conclusion that Philip English had practiced black magic on William
Beale.

Beale did not come to court with an unblemished record. He had appeared frequently in Essex County Court cases and had been convicted
of assault, lying, and swearing. Aware of his past, other Marblehead
men scoffed when Beale tried to assist the local constable in arresting an
angry drunk. Beale recounted that his neighbors "Called my [me] dog
rogue base fellow . . . and told me I deserved to have my braines beat out
for such absurd speeches." Beale had troubled relations not only with
his neighbors and the legal authorities, but also within his own family.
His wife was repeatedly unfaithful, giving him a reputation far and
wide as a cuckold. Worse yet, he was not only cast out of the marriage
bed but periodically driven from his house. One rainy night he appeared
at a neighbor's door, mattress in tow, complaining pitifully that his wife
"did upbraide him." Scorned by family and society, Beale fit the accepted profile of a witch at least as well as the man he accused. But Beale,
originally from East Anglia and "a man of some means," had the proper
pedigree of English origins and Puritan professions. He did not offer a
direct threat to the powerful elite of Salem Town who served as justices
in the witchcraft trials.[90]

Philip and by marriage Mary English did share one characteristic with
many other accused witches: they crossed boundaries. In Salem, as in
most other New England witchcraft episodes, a preoccupation with issues of mobility and boundaries underlay the accusations made against

individuals and acknowledged by the community. Witchcraft charges often seemed to be the escalation of personal quarrels expressed in the hysteria of adolescent girls, but they did not proceed to trials and executions without the support of a significant and powerful segment of the community. In the local conflict between factions in Salem Village, issues of birth, status, fixity, and mobility loomed large. From the perspective of the afflicted girls who launched the accusations, the areas beyond the Village bounds were "dangerous enemy territory." From the perspective of Salem's merchant elite who carried on the prosecutions, territories beyond the center of town were suspect. Members of the faction opposed to Village minister Samuel Parris were all logical targets. No accusations, however, were leveled at those "long-time Village residents who had been born to wealth and respectability;" they were *born* to respectability and their status was fixed. In contrast, those who were in motion socially and geographically like Rebecca Nurse and Philip English drew attention to themselves and were vulnerable because they were not fully a part of any group.[91]

Rebecca Nurse, "a respected older woman of Salem Village," married to a "once obscure artisan" in Salem Town, moved to the Village in 1678 when her husband purchased a "rich, 300–acre farm" near Ipswich road. Residents of the Ipswich road area, many targeted for accusation, while nominally of the Village, often seemed connected to town interests and to the travelers and traders who passed along this main artery to the north and stayed in taverns operated by Edward and Bridget Bishop, Joshua Rea, and Walter Phillips.[92] From the leading merchants' perspective, Ipswich Road was a marginal site. Rebecca Nurse had crossed both geographic and status boundaries and become associated with the fluidity of the Ipswich Road area; she was part of neither the isolated Village nor the mercantile center.

A concern with boundaries had become increasingly evident throughout Essex County in the decade preceding the trials. As longevity and population growth put pressure on availability of land, farmers began competing for less desirable land. During the 1680s, the Quarterly Courts handled a growing number of lawsuits over formerly negligible swampland. Farmers in towns laid out as open-field villages began to consolidate land and instituted lawsuits even in interior communities where no shortage of land existed. Absentee landowners were targeted for legal action because, as a Lynn farmer asserted about one such, he "cannot be contented to run lose in his own pasture but he must break over fences." Ministers and others expressed concerns in writing about problems of fences and boundaries. Minister William Hubbard of

Ipswich in his *History of New England*, printed in 1684, cautioned those who break through boundaries to "take heed . . . lest a serpent bite them while they are breaking the hedge that should secure others' liberties." Cotton Mather, a prominent Puritan divine, drew the association of transgressing boundaries directly to witchcraft. In his *Memorable Providences Relating to Witchcrafts and Possessions* he described metaphorically how "hellish Witches, are permitted to break through the Hedge which our Heavenly Father has made about them that seek Him."[93] Thus the connection between Jerseymen, Quakers, dogs, and witches becomes clearer; they all broke through boundaries constructed by the Puritan order.

English and his wife were the wealthiest and most influential of the Salem defendants, though by late summer the young women of Salem Village had widened their net to include several important Bostonians, culminating in their accusation of Lady Phipps, the wife of the newly appointed governor. English, unlike his fellow merchants the Brownes and the Curwens, proved vulnerable to accusation. One local historian, noting "that the storm burst mainly on the humble ones of the community," suggested that English's case was exceptional because he suffered from "the odium attaching to the English Church." I suggest that the odium of French origins played its part as well.[94]

Living apart, speaking, at times, a foreign language, participating in a fishing culture which transgressed Puritan norms, the Jersey French community also employed legal practices that further intensified their reputation as outsiders. The Channel Islands system of justice, based on French law and Norman practice, differed significantly from English common law, which formed the basis of the Bay Colony legal order.[95] The Catel Court, which handled cases of debt and bankruptcy on Jersey, operated by a set of procedures that encouraged creditors to sue quickly.[96] To satisfy merchants, the major creditors in Jersey, a "Saturday Court" met every week to make prompt litigation possible. Philip English continued this practice in New England and created a reservoir of resentment by acting quickly to sue debtors even if they had acknowledged his claim and made plans for repayment. In his own defense, English claimed that "it is every dayes waye in every trading towne, for marchants upon neglect of payment, for to arrest theire debtors."[97]

Throughout Essex County, the Jersey French carried a reputation not only of sharp legal practice and clannish conniving, but also of lying and theft. It was understood by most "English" townspeople that former Jersey residents would conspire together to cheat others. One Marblehead constable accused a Jersey fish seller, John Brock, of cheat-

ing as he weighed the catch. The constable voiced his anger and suspicion by calling Brock a "knave, cheater, and French dog." Several times,
men arrested for theft found it useful to direct suspicion toward a
"Frenchman" or "Jarseyman."[98] As a result of this climate of suspicion
and instantaneous litigation, local authorities were "more prone to resort to official action against these outsiders," and Jerseyans were quick
to object to local authority. One Jerseyan, Thomas Baker, called the venerable magistrate William Hathorne a "white hat [white-haired], limp-
ing rogue." He refused a warrant served him, asserting he "did not care
for all the laws in the country." The suspicion between the Jersey community and Salemites from the town center was mutual.

Suspicion of all things French was further fueled by a rumor that had
swept through Massachusetts in 1689. It was reported by two Salem men
recently released from a French prison in Canso, Nova Scotia, that Sir
Edmund Andros planned to deliver New England into the hands of ten
French men-of-war already sailing toward Boston. The fact that Andros
belonged to a prominent Channel Island family from Guernsey added
fuel to the fire of anti-French sentiment.[99]

Massachusetts colonists also drew on a broader Anglo-American feeling against the French. The revocation of the Edict of Nantes in 1685,
forcing many Huguenots to flee to England and British North America,
reminded England that France was a Catholic country. Fears that a
Catholic monarch, backed by French troops, would return to the English
throne prompted a series of Jacobite scares and fueled support for a succession of wars with France continuing for a century. Linda Colley in her
recent book, *Britons: Forging the Nation, 1707–1837*, suggests that this
anti-French prejudice had much to do with defining British nationhood
in the eighteenth century. According to Colley, "Britishness was super-
imposed over an array of internal differences in response to contact with
the Other, and above all in response to conflict with the Other" as embodied in Catholic France. The process which Colley describes is similar
but not identical to the moves carried out by the Puritan center in Salem.
British identity did not "come into being . . . because of an integration
and homogenization of disparate cultures," but rather emerged from
within when faced with the "other" of Catholic France and an overseas
empire; Salem Puritan merchants, on the other hand, wished to impose
homogeneity on other cultural groups or exclude them from the geographic and political center.[100] In each case, however, the French were
perceived as "other" and felt as a threat.

The negative feelings of many Salemites, particularly the leading merchants and those allied to them, did not result in wholesale accusations

of witchcraft against the Jersey French; instead, Philip and Mary English were singled out. It was not solely Philip English's "Frenchness" but also his ambiguity that caused concern. By rivaling other prominent Salem merchants in commercial success and joining them in the highest local offices, English moved from his marginal status, across powerfully imagined but experientially porous boundaries, to the metaphorical center of Salem, yet he continued to live among the Jersey French, espouse Anglicanism, own a waterfront tavern, and exceed local norms in aggressive court proceedings. This movement from margin to center and back, grounded first and foremost in English's origins in the ambiguous culture of the Channel Islands—like his very name, both English and French—condemned Philip English.

Accused, captured, and jailed in Boston to await trial, the Englishes managed to escape. They fled to New York and remained there until the following year. In their absence, a judge and a sheriff, both members of the Curwen family, seized the English family's trade goods, looted their mansion, and appropriated furniture and personal items. Philip English petitioned for years to receive restitution from the General Court of Massachusetts. One of his petitions listed commodities including Spanish iron and forty-three quintals (about four thousand three hundred pounds) of codfish from the "Ware hous att the Pint of Rocks [on Winter Island]"; 500 "butchells of Vorginiy Whet [Virginia wheat] and 203 bushels of "Engen Corn" from one warehouse; sugar, molasses, cordage, nails, and "1 Chist of Glass" from the warehouse in the Lane; and rum, twine, rope, and anchors in the warehouse on the wharf. On this wharf at the end of English Lane sat huge piles of fifty-eight thousand boards, ten thousand staves, and twenty-eight thousand shingles waiting to be loaded upon ships bound for the Caribbean. English listed several quantities of cloth taken from his "dwelling house" and "Luse in the Shop Chamber . . . besides a considerable quanitty of household goods & other things which I Cannot exactly give a pertickolar Acco[unt] off." His enumerated claims totaled £1,183. English avowed that this property was "What I had Seized tacking away Lost and Embezeld whilst I was a prisoner" and on "flight for my life." The estate "was so seisd and Tackin away Chiefly" by George Curwen, "Late Sheriff desesd [deceased]." After twenty-six years, a committee appointed by the General Court awarded English two hundred pounds "to be paid out of the publick Treasury in full satisfaction for what he may have sustained & suffered."[101]

The English family returned to Salem in 1693 to rebuild their lives. Mary English died soon after, supposedly of an illness contracted in the damp Boston jail.[102] With his goods expropriated and his home and warehouses ransacked, Philip English disappeared from the list of taxpayers in 1692–93. Few records exist to indicate how he managed to rebuild his fortune. We do know that he entered into occasional trade ventures with some of the leading merchant families of Salem. In 1695, for example, he consigned a shipment of wine worth almost seven hundred pounds to a partnership he formed with Samuel Browne, John Turner, and Edward Lyde (formerly a clerk of wealthy Boston merchant Samuel Shrimpton), and in 1700 he accepted a power of attorney from Benjamin Marston to facilitate trade arrangements.[103] Perhaps the "English" merchants of Salem sought a French connection to protect them from privateers on the seas during King William's War; more likely, English offered generous terms and important overseas contacts. Unfortunately, the few scattered pages remaining from his accounts of the 1690s offer only partial answers. What does stand out in the record is that English continued to ship fish to the West Indies and southern Europe and bring back wine from Madeira and Faial. He sometimes ventured shipments in partnership with other Salem traders. Economic interest apparently prevailed over cultural difference for members of the Salem establishment willing to share business arrangements with a French Anglican in their midst. In doing so, they assisted Philip English to recover from his losses sustained during the outbreak of community hysteria and xenophobia.

By 1699, having reestablished his overseas commerce, English again held the fifth highest tax assessment for the town, joining two of the Browne family, Deliverance Parkman and Benjamin Marston, as the wealthiest men in Salem.[104] Philip English's financial success may have influenced the property-holding inhabitants now able to vote for local officials. He won election to the Board of Selectman in 1700 for the first time since his brief service in 1692. Yet his ambiguous origins, part French, part English, continued to set him off from the other "English" merchants in Salem. And, once again, his tenure was cut short by social conflict.

How did Philip English and the Jersey French community challenge the Puritan communal ideal?[105] In Puritan doctrine, and for other Calvinist sects as well, merchants pursued trade as a calling, a particular employment ordained for each individual by God himself. Ministers exhorted the faithful to exercise diligence and care in the daily work of their calling. Yet wealth did not automatically result from diligence but came as a gift from God. New England Puritans added another conceptual layer to the matrix of obligations and rewards. They perceived themselves as God's people chosen to build a new city in the wilderness.

If riches are blessings from God, and New England Puritans are God's chosen people, then an Anglican Frenchman who achieves great wealth in the midst of Salem represents an anomaly—something out of order. Anthropologist Mary Douglas suggests that when the social system requires someone to hold ambiguous roles, "these persons [like English] are credited with uncontrolled, unconscious, dangerous, disapproved powers—such as witchcraft and evil eye."[106] An anomaly from his first entrance into Salem, Philip English refused to stay put. He built a "Great House" like other leading families—but on the wrong side of town. He became a selectman and then breached the rules of petitioning. He anglicized his name and gradually gave up French trading connections in favor of English partners, yet he refused to forsake his Anglican worship, rowing to Marblehead on Sundays to attend Anglican services.[107] English was neither French nor English, neither stranger nor brother. He remained indefinable, ambiguous, and threatening.

As with other Jersey French, English Quakers, and West Country fishermen, Philip English's personal and family history continued to be shaped by his marginality in Salem. Gathering more and more wealth through his successful trading ventures, English continued to represent a subversive element in the civic order of Salem. Shut out from the traditional avenues of power through public office, English attempted to preserve and extend his commercial empire. As his two eldest sons came of age, he quickly introduced them to commerce by employing them as ship captains and teaching them the trade. In spite of careful tutoring, Philip Jr. preferred dry land; after a few coastal voyages, he took over management of the Blue Anchor Tavern. After the untimely death of his son William, Philip Sr. looked also to his son-in-law John Touzel to carry on the family business.[108] In 1720, English, acknowledging "the Love and good will and natural affection which I have an do bear to my Son in Law John Touzel and Susannah his wife," granted them the deed to a seven-acre property on Point of Rocks, a promontory jutting into Salem harbor east of English's mansion, tavern, and wharf complex. Revealing a concern for family stability and lineage, he included "the children born after the said Susanna my Daughter unto my said son in law" in the deed.[109]

While firmly locating his descendants at the eastern end of Salem, English finally, in 1732, succeeded in planting his name in the center of Salem by donating land for the first Anglican church to be built near Town House Square. In that same year, a probate commission found that the estate of Philip English "is greatly wasted and daily wasting." The court judged English "not capable of manageing his estate" and appointed his "Particular friend & acquaintance" Thomas Manning and his son Philip joint guardians of the senior English. Later accounts referred to English's "cloudiness of mind," assumed to have been brought on by the unjust treatment he had received during the witchcraft episode forty years before. English, over eighty by this time, was sent to live with his daughter and son-in-law. During these same years, Touzel brought suit against his father-in-law for a debt of eighty-five pounds, which "tho often requested" English "hath not paid but detained the same from him."[110] Relations must have been difficult; one small list of charges squeezed into the middle of an account page submitted to the executors of English's estate concludes: "To my fathers Board & Lodgeing from 7 Oct 1735 when Mr Toozel turned Father out of doors to 10 March when he died." Marginalized once again, Philip English, in spite of his commercial success, never found full acceptance in Salem. English died as the ultimate foreigner, no longer launching transatlantic voyages, but condemned to passage on a ship of fools.[111]

A complex of issues crystallized around Philip English, who, with his financial success, threatened the Puritan definition of community and glaringly exposed the tension between a fixed social and religious order and a mobile and multicultural commercial economy built into Hugh Peter's prescription for Salem. Laid out so many years before, Peter's ideas pointed the community toward a cultural predicament which even the drastic remedy of executions for witchcraft could not solve.

Historians have interpreted the Salem witchcraft trials as a conflict between capitalism and a traditional, Puritan-tinged society, and this interpretation is partially correct.[112] But in Salem, a group of wealthy Puritan shipping merchants comprised the traditional order. The Browne family, like Philip English, sent ships to the Caribbean, southern Europe, and England. The Brownes headed the tax rolls and dominated local government.[113] Other wealthy merchants such as George Curwen and his sons, Benjamin Lynde, Benjamin Marston, and William Hirst participated in the shaping of civic society as selectmen and justices. Salem, then, could be described as a merchant oligarchy.[114] That oligarchy was threatened and almost overturned by the confrontation with rural Salem Village during the witchcraft crisis in 1692.[115] The challenge came not only from resistance to capitalism but also from those marginalized for reasons of nationality, religion, or cultural practices. Their "foreignness," their difference, threatened the social order built on both a capitalist and a Puritan foundation.

Philip English embodied the paradox built into Puritan town founding in Massachusetts. English, his sons, his Jersey French son-in-law

John Touzel, and the many young French-speaking apprentices and indentured servants he and Touzel gathered around them to assist at sea and on land, imperiled the closed world of Puritan community. For Salem merchants, the desire to increase profits through trade with "foreign," that is to say, non-English merchants conflicted with their search for an ordered and peaceful community of visible saints. Concerns about wealth and vice, which appear in the sermon literature, represented an anxiety resulting, in part, from the tension of overlapping communities and the tendency for profitable exchange to force and expand the limits of the local. Exclusion of the "other," not rejection of capitalism or wealth, marked the boundary of the Puritan community. The much lamented "decline" posited by Puritan ministers (and taken up by twentieth-century historians) was not solely a free fall into a market society— trade relations for profit were fully present in the first years of the Bay Colony.[116] It also reflected a fear of strangers' potential to unsettle the fragile culture of colonial towns wedged between oceans and forests peopled with the different and the disorderly. The threat came not from profits but from fortunes in the hands of outsiders, those of non-English origins and non-Puritan persuasions. Declension, long interpreted as a result of capitalist wealth and market forces, must also, be understood as the intrusion of the foreign. Philip English represented the foreign element in Salem. Wealth in and of itself did not offend the Puritan leaders, but riches owned and displayed by someone so different, did. English's success threatened the power of Puritan providentialism. How, they might ask, could God reward a "French Dog," an Anglican apostate?

3

Puritans, the Polite, and the Impolite

"Mr. Shrimpton, Capt. Lidget and others come in a Coach from Roxbury about 9 aclock or past, singing as they come, being inflamed with Drink: At Justice Morgan's they stop and drink healths, curse, swear, talk profanely and baudily to the great disturbance of the Town and grief of good people. Such high-handed wickedness has hardly been heard of before in Boston."

SAMUEL SEWALL, *Diary*, 1686

SEWALL'S SHOCKED OBSERVATION of behavior that "has hardly been heard of before in Boston" signaled the opening round of a prolonged and contested cultural transformation that would alter the physical and psychic landscapes of Boston and Salem. Riding in coaches and drinking healths would become respected social activities for Massachusetts gentry. A new culture, intimately linked with merchant capitalism, emerged first in London and in the ports of Britain and America. Possessions and manners replaced traditional values associated with landed property, family lineage, and religious affiliation as signs of status. Because much in the new culture could be purchased or learned, it opened up avenues of social mobility to wealthy merchants and rising professionals from various religious faiths, dubious family beginnings, or previously suspect European backgrounds. In a world of mobile people and property, the new manners and possessions of Georgian gentility allowed people to size up newcomers at a glance, a necessary skill in a social marketplace shaped by foreign trade and consumer goods.

Two paramount developments intensified this cultural change in Boston and Salem. First, expanding overseas trade created a need to come to terms with the exotic goods and foreign peoples arriving daily on the shores of ports throughout the Atlantic world. Secondly, the contradiction between economic expansion and community solidarity that was built into Puritan life, an opposition felt acutely in ports such as

Salem and Boston, produced extreme social stress. Tensions could be eased either by abandoning overseas trade, not a viable alternative in a colony dependent on shipbuilding and commerce for its livelihood, or by altering ideas and practices that constituted community, that is, by cultural transformation. I argue that the cultural contradictions inherent in the Puritan desire for a homogeneous community based on international trade prompted many urban New Englanders to embrace the new "polite and commercial culture" arising in eighteenth-century Britain. There, a genteel middle class of merchants, manufacturers, and professionals developed an urban culture based not on strict emulation of aristocratic style but on new ideas of self and others, ideas expressed in polite rituals and consumer goods. Social rituals and refined behavior, designed to incorporate foreign goods and peoples, in effect helped to smooth over religious and ethnic differences and energize consumer demand. The values and practices of this emergent transatlantic culture created a social marketplace where successful merchants and professionals of non-English origins and non-Puritan beliefs, like the Cabots, Faneuils, and Wendells, could purchase the goods and learn the manners that increasingly denoted character and defined value in Anglo-America.[1]

A changing relationship to material possessions lay at the heart of the broad transformations in Britain and America. Conflicts and negotiations over the meaning of goods and practices plagued many prominent families in Boston and Salem and affected middling and laboring people as well. A detailed consideration of the transition taking place in the early decades of the eighteenth century demonstrates how families and groups responded to a consumer culture and the social norms of gentility. Understanding at some level that new social practices have consequences in defining self and group membership, some embraced wholeheartedly, some rejected forcefully, and others reacted ambivalently to changes brought to Boston and Salem on the ships of the transatlantic trade. Examining varied responses—from Samuel Shrimpton's early embrace of polite and commercial culture to the staunch Puritan Samuel Sewall's fierce opposition or the Higginson family's journeys from Salem's pulpit to England, Barbados, and an East India Company factory in Madras—reveals the effects of large transformations in the experience of daily lives. Exploring how these transitional figures negotiated their connections to the fashionable goods and genteel sociability gradually gaining prominence in the towns yields a detailed map of cultural change at work in the provinces.

Intimations of a new cultural style shaped around a world of goods could be seen before the turn of the century in Boston. On 8 February 1698, Colonel Samuel Shrimpton, Boston's wealthiest merchant, died; six days later, he was buried in a monumental funeral ceremony.[2] The intervening period was filled with elaborate preparations that attest to the importance of goods in representing wealth and gentility. The tailor Peter Barbour fashioned four black morning suits and "westcoats" for Shrimpton's brothers-in-law Nicholas Roberts and Eliakim Hutchinson, and for Hutchinson's son William and the merchant Thomas Palmer at a total cost of forty pounds. The seamstress Anna Peacock sewed a black dress and hood for Madame Shrimpton. John Roulston made a coffin including "the frame for the coat of arms and fitting it up." Over four hundred pairs of kid gloves were purchased from the glover Roger Killcup to be delivered to the mourners. Extensive arrangements were underway at the grave site, supervised by a mariner, Thomas Walker, who brought in four hundred "hard bricks," three bushels of lime, and sand to build the tomb. Savill Simpson dug the grave; William Mumford assisted by laying steps and paving at the bottom. Samuel Sewall, who was among the mourners, noted the "very fair and large Paths [which] were shovel'd by great pains and cost." Benches were set up around the tomb, and a wooden cover was prepared to lay over it. At Shrimpton's home, yards and yards of black cloth draped the entry, the staircase, and the room where the coffin lay.[3]

The funeral day arrived, and the colonel's coach with horses "in Mourning: Scutcheon on their sides and Deaths heads on their foreheads" moved solemnly through the streets of Boston. The bearers included eminent figures such as Major General Winthrop and Lieutenant Colonel Hutchinson, while members of the family led the widow as they processed to the burying ground. Captain Clark gave the signal for the firing of "twelve great guns" as Colonel Shrimpton "was buried with Arms."[4] This ornate and solemn ceremony connected Shrimpton with a long tradition of elaborate funerals but also gestured forward in time to Georgian refinements. The observance carried Boston into a new era by honoring a man who had borne a novel standard of power and display.[5]

Shrimpton and his circle introduced cultural innovations to Puritan Boston by wearing scarlet, lace, and gold, sporting powdered wigs, traveling in coaches, and participating in a social style at odds with established Puritan standards of moderation. Sewall, son-in-law of the Puritan merchant John Hull, complained of Shrimpton and his rakish friends: they "drink Healths, curse, swear, talk profanely and baudily." Shrimpton, through his support of religious tolerance (he allied himself with Boston's Anglicans and also permitted Baptists to use his property on Noddles Island) and his connections with royal officials, signaled his participation in a group that would soon gain ascendancy in Boston. Men like Shrimpton (heir to his father Henry's substantial estate), his brother-in-law Charles Lidget, and other wealthy merchants joined with royal officials to form a nascent merchant elite that played an increasingly powerful and visible role in the town.[6]

Shrimpton's only son, Samuel Jr., carried the merchants' growing interest in self-presentation and fashion into something akin to dandyism. An account between Shrimpton and Boston tailor Peter Barbour covering the years 1694–97 shows entry after entry designated as "for your son." Young Samuel, twenty to twenty-five years of age during the period, had his silk waistcoats embroidered with silver thread and purchased six cloth coats, five waistcoats, nine pairs of breeches—some with silver buttons—and one "Surtout coat" or overcoat, all in an effort to keep up with the rapid fashion changes set in motion in urban areas of Anglo-America.[7]

To prepare for polite company and display his elegance, Shrimpton Jr. engaged in a dressing ritual in his bedchamber aided by an ensemble of a "blacke Japan Table, Looking glass, dressing boxes, two glass sconces, and two small [candle] stands." In "dressing his face," he employed an assemblage of entirely new objects not seen anywhere before the late seventeenth century. His dressing boxes contained small compartments to hold combs, brushes, powders, and ointments just coming into fashion to enhance the genteel face. With cultural values shifting to exterior visible signs, presenting the face in the best possible light was essential to impressing other gentlemen and ladies. One's character could be worn or seen on the body. This was "the age of public man," governed by an "elaborately coded conversation of dress, gesture, and speech that . . . city dwellers carried out in London's squares" and in Boston and Salem's streets. Jonathan Belcher, son of a prominent merchant and a contemporary of young Shrimpton, signaled his understanding of the new cultural imperatives during his years as governor of the province. Belcher planned his public appearances down to the last detail because for gentlemen in "publick Station, . . . every motion & Syllable, even the Gestures of their Bodies, must pass the Censure of the Staring Crowd." The symbolic aspect of public and private life, "the calculated gestures of civility and incivility," took on an inordinate significance in the theater of urban streets.[8]

In an era and in a business where coin was scarce—there was a constant shortage of specie in New England throughout the colonial era—and so much depended on credit, time and money spent on personal appearance not only furthered the social norms of gentility but also made good business sense. And that was the point. Capitalism influenced much of eighteenth-century life, from the desire for a fashionable appearance to the conception that authenticity resided in an accretion of details—in commercial accounts and in personal presentation.[9]

The Shrimptons were not the only family to change the social presentation of self. During the first half of the eighteenth century, well-to-do Bostonians participated in "the consumer revolution" which marked an "increasing interest in and availability of a wide variety of material goods designed to present the self, transform the environment into a comfortable and decorative stage, and, in the process, reshape leisure activities."[10] This new interest in self-presentation spurred commercial development. As the English merchant-economist Nicholas Barbon had proclaimed in 1690, fashion "keeps the heart of commerce pumping."[11] Fashion fused with capitalism to remake Boston and Salem into provincial Georgian ports, thereby shaping the lives not only of merchants trading overseas but of all who lived within the cities.

The Georgian gentility that became a marker for urban elites in Anglo-America included several elements: an emphasis on carefully controlled movement, an effort to disguise bodily functions, elaborate attention to self-presentation, skill in defined social rituals, and intense involvement in consumption of novel and imported goods. During the eighteenth century, a broader middle-class and genteel public adopted a self-conscious consideration or preoccupation with taste and appearance, a preoccupation that had been confined to courtiers in earlier centuries. In England, as court culture declined in the late seventeenth and eighteenth centuries, and in America where no entrenched aristocracy existed, an expanding commercial class with disposable income and leisure time turned its attention to niceties and refinement.[12]

Many of the behaviors that most middle-class Americans learn as children and now take for granted originated during this period as more casual behavior gave way to precise deportment. For example, in the fifteenth century, conduct manuals proclaimed it unseemly to blow your nose into the tablecloth or into the same hand with which you ate. Three centuries later, the handkerchief had come into widespread use and manuals cautioned readers to blow quietly into their handkerchief and not touch the nose too often. Genteel behavior imposed similar restraints on other bodily functions. Even the terms used to refer to digestive processes changed from "farting," "urinating," and "defecating"

(Erasmus, 1530) to "emit wind," "pass water," and "other natural functions" (La Salle, 1729), which apparently could not be named and should
be performed "where you cannot be seen."[13]

A growing emphasis on cleanliness accompanied the disguise of the
body and its workings. Essays in the *Spectator*, an early eighteenth-
century magazine, emphasized the significance of polite behavior. Joseph
Addison and Richard Steele's popular periodical quickly became an
arbiter of taste and refinement in England and America. One issue
included a letter on cleanliness aimed at polite and commercial people.
The writer asserted that the greater the fortune, the greater the duty
of cleanliness. "Not a speck" of snuff or powder should mar a man's apparel. Wearing a powdered wig and using snuff [finely ground tobacco
held between the fingers and sniffed] indicated an investment in self-
presentation that remained far beyond most Anglo-Americans. Only
those with considerable funds, available time, and powerful motivation
could uphold the dictates of refinement. Thus gentility became a con-
vincing sign for economic and social success. An immaculate body and
appearance, according to the *Spectator*, engendered not only politeness,
but also love, health, and "refined Sentiments and Passions." Cleanliness
and its attendant elegancies represented civilization. Professing the fundamental nature of refinement, the letter asserted that these "marks of
civilization" could distinguish not only individuals and groups but even
nations. Addison and his fellow authors understood that gentility created a kind of international, or at least transatlantic, imagined community.[14]

Writings in the *Spectator* and later periodicals such as the *Gentleman's
Magazine*, the *Ladies Repository*, *La Belle Assemblée*, and conduct manuals
like *The Instructor: Or, Young Man's Best Companion* and *The Ladies
Library . . . Consisting of general rules for Conduct in all the Circumstances of
the Life of Women*, portrayed a nascent psychology of politeness. In the
Spectator, an author explains that "the Love of Symmetry and Order . . .
is natural to the Mind of Man." Variety is also a natural trait and springs
from the "Additional Pleasure from the Novelty of . . . Objects." Because
the senses act as "Inlets to all the Images conveyed to the Mind," beautiful and elegant objects lead to "pure and unsullied Thoughts." Therefore,
the path to greatness leads through gentility, not, as previously assumed, through privileged birth. Essay 612 asserts that "we can have no
Merit, nor ought we to claim any Respect because our Fathers acted
well." A gentleman, does not brag about family lineage; he can "only
Boast of Wit, Beauty, Strength, or Wealth."[15]

Yet the new ethos sometimes exceeded the boundaries of refined behavior and vaulted into "eager competitions for Wealth or Power." Even

though membership in the polite and commercial culture required wealth and led to power, politeness necessitated a somewhat ambiguous attitude toward aggressive pursuit of money or rank. Perhaps this is why the well-to-do Boston merchant Nicholas Boylston chose to have himself painted in a leisurely pose, with his account books barely visible in the background. Obvious grasping offended polite society, but "Personal Excellencies"—"graceful Address in Horsemanship, in the Use of the Sword, and in Dancing"—inspired admiration. Elegant taste and "Complacences of Manners" marked a "Character of Distinction."[16]

Colonial America did not produce social arbiters like Addison and Steele or commercial pamphleteers like Daniel Defoe, but their maxims laid a foundation for the spread of Georgian gentility and the rise of a polite and commercial culture in New England. Bound volumes of the *Spectator* appeared in personal libraries and in the Social Library formed in Salem, Massachusetts. Knowledge of and participation in Georgian gentility appeared frequently enough in the early decades of the century for the short-lived *New England Courant* to satirize the excesses of refinement and stylish possessions. Using a format similar to the *Spectator's*, James and Benjamin Franklin and their collaborators inserted social satire into their newspaper as letters from fictitious authors. In one issue "Anthony Fallshort" comes under the spell of and marries "Sylvia the Fortune." Fallshort enumerates her expenses on fashionable silk clothing—£101; on glazing the House "with new fashion'd Square Glass"—£57; and on a "Tea Table with its Equipage, Sugar, Tea, etc." worth £157. All told, her expenses amount to over £1,800, while her dowry, "an Estate in rough uncultivated Lands, Rocks, Trees, Bushes, and Quag-Mires" brings only £350—a warning for men to beware "a *New-England* Fortune." Thirty years later, with the *New England Courant* long out of business and "square glass" the norm for "handsome" buildings, the "Equipage" and rituals of the tea table defined families of Massachusetts's merchant elite as members of the polite society of Anglo-America.[17]

Polite rituals and commercial ventures tied New England's colonial economy to a transatlantic network of production, exchange, and consumption. Boston and Salem shipped goods to distant shores, received vessels from across the Atlantic, and built numerous ships for local and English merchants. Table 2 indicates the number and destination or place of departure of vessels entering and leaving Boston in 1720. Based on entrances and clearances listed in the *Boston Gazette*, the data are not comprehensive enough for statistical analysis but do provide abundant evidence for the importance of trade to Boston and Salem. Almost 400 ships entering and leaving a town of no more than eight to ten thousand people, in the case of Boston, indicates an extensive involvement in long-distance trade. The table does not include the many lighters, fishing boats, and pleasure craft that darted in and around the larger commercial vessels. More than one hundred ships carrying lumber, meat, fish, grain, and horses made the long voyage to various destinations in the Caribbean. Trading with "foreign islands" under the control of Spain and France as well as with English islands like Barbados, vessels returned to Massachusetts with sugar, molasses, fruit, Dutch cloth, and French or Spanish wine.[18] More than thirty vessels entered from or departed for Spain and Portugal (including Faial and Madeira in the Wine Islands), where masters exchanged cod and fish oil for salt, iron, olive oil, and spirits. An active trade to London and the British ports of Cowes, Bristol, and Glasgow, with occasional forays to Ireland, Amsterdam, and Calais, confirms the close connections between Britain, continental Europe, and New England.

Charting the coming and going of ships, reading contemporary newspapers, examining merchant accounts, and delving into diaries of the period, one cannot escape the conclusion that many literate elite, middling, and laboring townspeople in Boston and Salem must have had an expansive mental horizon. All sources confirm the pervasive influence of the foreign in Boston and Salem. Ocean-going craft entered or departed Boston and Salem almost one thousand times, which meant carting, loading, and unloading thousands of tons of goods. Ships, cargoes, and seamen were constantly coming and going, to and from nearby New Hampshire and Connecticut, other coastal ports such as New York, Philadelphia, Charleston, and smaller entrepôts in Virginia, Maryland, and the Carolinas. Food, cattle, timber, fish, and fish oil poured into Boston to be crated and loaded onto vessels bound for the West Indies and even as far as Surinam, a Dutch colony of sugar plantations in South America. Local families sent their kinsmen to set up trading companies in various ports in the West Indies. Others established close relationships with English, French, or Dutch merchants resident in these ports. Ships returned to Massachusetts with sugar, molasses, rum, and visiting Caribbean planters. Other trade routes sent vessels across the Atlantic to Spain, Portugal, and the Wine and Canary Islands. Over twenty ships entered Boston in 1720 from England and the Netherlands, a sign of the continual flow of goods and people that traversed the Atlantic.[19]

While far fewer vessels entered or left port from Salem, the evidence for the predominance of Boston in transatlantic trade is not as clear-cut

Table 2. Entrances and Clearances from Boston and Salem, April–December 1720

	Coastal	Long-Distance						Combined Total
		Newfoundland / Nova Scotia	W. Indies / Surinam	So. Europe / Wine Is.	Britain	Other Transatlantic	Total	
Boston								
Entrances	245	32	95	15	21	20	183	428
Clearances	206	30	135	17	19	12	213	419
Salem								
Entrances	5	0	8	4	0	1	13	18
Clearances	21	0	16	22	0	3	41	62
Boston and Salem								
Combined	477	62	254	58	40	36	450	927

Source: Boston Gazette, 18–23 April 1720 to 28 December 1720–5 January 1721.

as might be assumed from looking at these figures alone. Ships owned by Salem merchants and piloted by captains resident in Salem often left via Boston. At least one leading merchant family in Salem, the Browns, had a warehouse near Long Wharf in Boston. Common destinations for Salem-owned vessels included North Carolina, the British islands of the West Indies, and the Iberian peninsula. In fact, in 1720, Salem sent more cargoes to southern Europe than Boston. That, coupled with the absence of trade with Newfoundland, suggests that Salem already dominated the fish trade to Spain and Portugal. Salem merchants often maintained their own fishing fleets and did not have to depend on supplies from Newfoundland and Nova Scotia as many Boston merchants did. This trade, referred to as "Fish for Gold" by one recent economic historian, supplied extraordinary gains for merchants. The commerce in cod also kept the local fishing fleet profitably employed helping Salem to avoid the most devastating effects of an increasing economic gap between elites and commoners that plagued eighteenth-century Boston.[20]

In both ports however, arrivals and departures of ships from all over the Atlantic world indicated a sense of connection to a broad geographic territory. Place names mostly unfamiliar today, like Vigo, Bilbao, Placentia, the Bay of Campeche, Cayenne, Ceuta, Cowes, Providence Island, all signified ports of call for New England ships and all denoted markets where money could be made or lost.[21] They also marked points on the Atlantic fringe that were part of an Anglo-American venture in domesticating the foreign. The anthropologist Benedict Anderson asserts that "the convergence of capitalism and print culture created the possibility of a new form of imagined community" and produced a fundamental change in "modes of apprehending the world." He goes on to suggest that two key forms of imagining in eighteenth-century Europe were the novel and the newspaper. Kathleen Wilson finds this same imagined community in studying colonial news in English papers, noting that "newspapers . . . functioned like imaginative literature in reproducing and refracting world events into socially meaningful categories and hierarchies," thereby producing an " 'imagined community' of producers, distributors, and consumers on both sides of the Atlantic." But part of this fundamental transformation also involved a geographic imagination that, fed by foreign news and global shipping traffic, stretched the community of Anglo-America to the shores of western Europe, Asia, and Africa.[22]

The place names became familiar yet the foreigners associated with them, "the strangers among us," were alternately (and sometimes simultaneously) welcomed and feared. Fleets from distant ports not only brought exotic and fashionable goods like tea, "China ware," chocolate, and silk, but also foreigners, with different cultural backgrounds and religious beliefs, to visit and settle in Boston and Salem. Foreign horizons and economic opportunities also called local residents to far-off destinations.

The broad reach of international trade shaped young men's aspirations and transformed families. The third generation of Salem's ministerial family, the Higginsons, influenced by the lure of distant lands and the possibilities inherent in commerce, took to the seas. Their grandfather Francis Higginson had been the first minister in Salem and his son John followed his father's calling and served for almost fifty years in the First Church's pulpit. His five sons chose different paths. John Jr. stayed in Salem and became a merchant "concerned in the fishing trade." Henry, also a merchant, migrated to Barbados, conducting trade for his brother and as a factor for other New England merchants. Francis, perhaps intending to continue the family's clerical tradition, studied at Cambridge University in England where he died of smallpox. Nathaniel, educated at Harvard, took a position in England as tutor and steward for Lord Wharton. A decade later Nathaniel traveled to Fort Saint George in Madras, where he rose to president of the East India Company's factory.[23]

The rise and fall of each son's fortunes dramatically portrays the possibilities of gain or loss that accompanied the long-distance reach for merchant capital. Henry, stricken with smallpox like his brother Francis, died after a short career in Barbados. Thomas, another son, apprenticed as a goldsmith in London, returned to Salem and embarked for Africa or Arabia "with privateers," never to be heard from again. John Jr. who had "obtained a comfortable estate," "met with losses by the French" in King William's War. Noting that the local fishing fleet had declined from sixty-odd ketches to six, he observed that "no town in this Province has suffered more by the war than Salem." John Jr. recouped his fortune after the war and became a justice of the peace and longtime member of the Governor's Council in Massachusetts. Nathaniel certainly had the most illustrious career of the five brothers. While in India he married an accomplished Englishwoman who spoke "Malabar, Genhow, and Portuguese languages very perfectly." After seventeen years he left India and the company, and with his family returned to London where he prospered as merchant until his death in 1708. Massachusetts was all agog at Nathaniel's presumed riches from the Indies. On hearing of the possibility of his return to Salem, a leading townsman, revealing the esteem increasingly attached to wealth, wrote, "Sir, it would be an honor and ornament to Salem to have so honorable and worthy a person well settled in it." The letter writer felt compelled to add that if "[Salem] should not suit with your inclinations or occasions, or grandeur, Boston may, which is much more populous, rich, and stately, than when you left it." Higginson's family in Massachusetts wrote frequently to request money because, as John Jr. avowed, "I hear that you have attained to a very considerable estate, some say £300,000, some say 2, some one." Even the third part would have well exceeded any fortune in New England, where ten thousand pounds sterling meant a very substantial estate.[24] The elder Higginson, recognizing early the necessity for melding spiritual and secular values, proclaimed in a 1686 sermon, that "you must do as those that have a rich Legacy bequeathed to them." He assured his listeners that God would comfort and protect those who disciplined their pursuit of wealth with self-conscious piety. But, like Hugh Peter before him, Higginson did not realize when he spoke that Salem's legacy as both a Puritan and a commercial port not only brought strangers to town but would also dispatch all but one of his sons to uncertain futures in foreign lands.[25]

In the 1720s, the *Boston Gazette*, a newspaper produced for the "trading part of the town," chronicled an extensive involvement in the Atlantic world and demonstrated a pervasive atmosphere of speculation, as if all the world were a market and everything in it for sale. Bulletins from foreign cities—London, Paris, The Hague, Hamburg, Vienna—recounted numerous get-rich-quick schemes. News ranged from lists of lottery prizes awarded in London and accounts of an English gentleman marrying a wealthy heiress worth thirty thousand pounds to a report that the Duke of Chandos had gained an equal amount in South Sea Stock. 1720 was the year of the so-called "South Sea Bubble," when shares in the British South Sea Company rose to astronomical levels and then collapsed.[26] Share prices were followed closely in the *Boston Gazette*, as were other enterprises like the Golden Wheat Scheme and the Mississippi Company, both financial ventures launched by John Law, a Scottish adviser to the French government, whose affairs, like those of a modern celebrity, were followed in great detail in the pages of provincial papers.[27]

But what goes up must come down. The local paper reprised a letter from Paris in June 1720 including "a long Account of the fall of the publick Credit there." The article wryly noted letters full of "the lamentable Circumstances of Families, who now lose by the fall of the Stocks, any more than it was formerly to hear of the raising and Riches of others by the first and sudden rising of the said Stocks." Other riches could disappear as quickly. That same year, the *Gazette* reported that London merchants received notice that one of five trading vessels "richly laden from Turkey" was lost in a storm; "the [East India] Company is in pain." Just a few weeks later came news of the destruction by storm of the

"Homeward bound London Fleet" from Jamaica. A few of the dozen ships were driven ashore on the western end of Cuba; 150 sailors survived while 200–300 perished along with an unestimated value of goods. Closer to home, the same issue of the *Gazette* informed readers that a Spanish privateer had captured a Boston ship loaded with lumber, fish, and oil. Later that summer, news arrived that pirates had destroyed most of the fishing vessels in Newfoundland, and a ship headed to Boston from London limped into port after being attacked by pirates who hoisted a banner of a white death's head on a black ground, the traditional pirate flag.[28]

Storms, disease, privateers, and pirates took a significant toll on commercial profits and continually reminded dwellers of busy seaports that trade was a risky business; riches quickly gained could just as easily be lost. The term "adventure," used to denote investment in a ship's cargo and passage, embodied the multiple meanings of a distant journey, an unpredictable outcome, and an orientation to the future. All of these culturally imprinted meanings melded in commercial investment. All depended on the mechanism of market exchange and the cultural values ascribed to money and goods.

By midcentury, the sense of wonder, speculative frenzy, and fascination with and fear of the foreign would be thoroughly domesticated by more predictable business practices, and genteel rituals—friends gathered for tea in the parlor, couples in dressing gowns from India sipping morning chocolate in the bedchamber, and elegantly gowned ladies and bewigged gentlemen joining in cards, concerts, and dancing in newly constructed assembly rooms. But in the early decades of the eighteenth century, speculation and spectacle contested with the seemingly more stable virtues of a godly calling and Puritan tribalism, each voice beckoning to the townspeople of Boston and Salem.

The interplay between commerce and culture transforming the social universe of urban New Englanders also brought extensive changes to the material landscape. Overseas traders invested capital in reshaping the economic and cultural infrastructure. Prominent merchants used part of their profits to build larger dwellings, often in brick, using symmetrical forms coming into style in England. They also invested their returns in constructing new roads, warehouses, and wharves to facilitate the flow of goods into and out of Boston. In addition, they donated funds and property to establish new religious and public buildings modeled after English examples. As trade expanded so did the ports of Boston and Salem, their look and feel changing from one of cramped winding and muddy streets with overhanging, multigabled dwellings and plain wooden meeting houses to a plan with some straight streets, long wharves extending into the harbor, well-proportioned buildings with sash windows arrayed in regular patterns, and brick churches with tall steeples stretching skyward, all expressing the Georgian refinements coming into vogue in British provincial centers.

The rebuilding of Boston, taking place in several phases, constituted an important aspect of the ongoing transformation to a polite and commercial culture.[29] Late in the seventeenth century, wealthy merchants like John Foster, Samuel Shrimpton, and his brother-in-law Peter Sergeant built large mansions in a transitional style.[30] They borrowed from a new type of architecture that had begun to appear in London, along major highways, and in English market towns. Called "artisan-mannerist," the new style favored by merchants and gentry stood in contrast to the Stuart court–sponsored architecture of Inigo Jones. The architectural historian John Summerson asserts that stylistic differences highlighted the "gulf between tastes of the Court and that of the City." Artisan-mannerist buildings featured brick construction, uniformly symmetrical facades with vertical windows that would later develop into the Georgian sash window, dormered hip roofs (thought to be Italian in origin), or gables with curved outlines borrowed from the Dutch.[31] The Sergeant House, later designated as the official residence for the royal governor of Massachusetts, may have been the first structure in Boston to sport this new style. It was built of brick with a symmetrical facade, high-pitched roof, and third-story dormers. During this period, the Anglicans built their first church in Boston, and Congregational merchants supported the formation of a new church on Brattle Street, both constructed of brick instead of the usual wood. Several of the design features of artisan-mannerist buildings, especially the square-paned windows, hip roof, and use of brick, became hallmarks of Georgian architecture. The style influenced many public and private buildings constructed by the Anglo-American commercial elite in the eighteenth century.

Merchants also joined together to rebuild the commercial infrastructure in Boston. In 1673–81, a group of forty merchants used their own money to construct a massive circular sea wall intended to fortify the inner wharves and provide military protection for the town if needed.[32] In return, the Colony Council granted the investors the right to build wharves and warehouses in the flats between the shoreline and the sea wall. The breakwater never served a military purpose, and ship captains preferred the inner docks. On the Bonner map of Boston, drawn in 1722, it appears as faint dotted lines, labeled "Old Wharf" (see map 4).

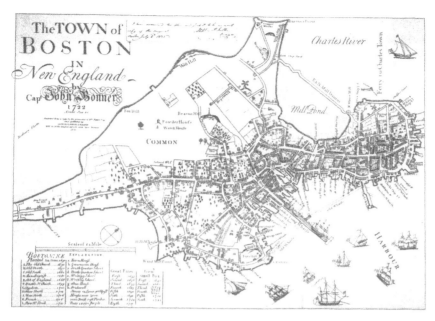

MAP 4. Captain John Bonner, *The Town of Boston in New England*, 1722.
Courtesy of the Massachusetts Historical Society.

In 1708, the selectmen surveyed the deteriorating "out wharfe" and required the owners, often heirs of the original builders, to repair their sections or forfeit them "to Others that will undertake and Maintaine the
Same." Those who gave up their interest were prohibited from extending their own wharves any further out to sea. This process created a realignment of merchant interests and opened the door for recent winners
to acquire more dock space, while families like the Shrimptons, whose
fortune was dwindling, escaped further obligation. This action by the
Council, whose membership included several leading merchants, coupled with an expressed interest in extending King Street beyond the low-
water mark, empowered merchants to build additional space for growing volumes of commodities and consumer goods entering and leaving
Boston.[33]

On the other side of town, Oliver Noyes, William Payne, Elisha
Cook, and David Jefferies, all overseas traders, joined forces to improve the road from the Neck, the main route for farm products into
Boston. At high tide the roadway often flooded, so the subscribers
agreed to "Secure and Keep off the Sea, from both Sides of the aforesaid

Highway." In return, the town of Boston granted the subscribers "all the upland, Beach, flatts, and Meadow ground on both Sides of the Highway down to Low water marke."[34] Thus merchants gained control over the only land route into Boston and, by improving the road, improved their own chances for profit.

A year later, several commercial gentlemen, including Noyes, Daniel Oliver, and Anthony Stoddard, proposed to the town to "Erect and build a wharfe . . . at the end of King Street." The group agreed to build, at "our own Cost and Charge," what came to be known as Long Wharf, and in return received title to the wharf and the right to "Possession and Peaceable Improvement of the Granted Premises." When construction was completed, the merchant group built an imposing row of brick warehouses along one side of the wharf. Their efforts created a route through which goods and people entered the area and simultaneously enhanced their real estate investments.[35]

In 1711, a huge fire swept through much of Boston, creating economic hardship for artisans and laborers. For a wealthy Anglo-American elite just coming into being, it offered a chance to reconstruct the town in early Georgian style. Most of the new buildings erected were of brick or stone, partly in reaction to fear of fire and partly in response to the Anglo-American fashion for brick. During this second rebuilding, Andrew Faneuil began his mansion house on the edge of town, while on Clark's Square, the center of the North End, the merchant William Clark commissioned a twenty-six-room manor house. The First Church and the old wooden, Tudor-style Town Hall, both of which had burned, were rebuilt as "handsome" brick structures. These new structures, coupled with the extension of Long Wharf and the brick warehouses and shops along the north side of the wharf, dramatically changed the appearance of Boston.

A third wave of construction began in the 1730s. Three new churches were built at the outskirts of the city. Sponsored by Governor Belcher, the Hollis Street meeting house may have been planned in part to increase the value of property owned by the Belchers and other merchants and land speculators. The Anglicans built their second church in the North End in 1723 and a third church, called Trinity, in the western part of the city in 1734, both modeled after English designs. The merchant Thomas Hancock constructed an important residence at the edge of town by the foot of Beacon Hill in 1737. He then used his distance from town as a reason for ordering from London a coach and four with Hancock and Henchman arms emblazoned on the doors. Most of the new buildings, churches, wharves, and dwellings were sponsored and financed by merchants, singly or in groups. This progression of construction projects in eighteenth-century Boston, illustrates how commerce and a changing set of values reshaped the urban landscape, and highlights the new elite's bid to reconfigure the town for its own economic and social purposes. They not only rebuilt roads and docks to facilitate the passage of goods; they also refashioned their homes and public buildings to announce their privileged status and modish tastes. The rebuilding of Boston demonstrates, in a most concrete way, the melding of mercantile aims and genteel designs.[36]

As Anglo-American cities began to remake their urban landscapes, they adopted an openness and regularity that expressed genteel refinement and the "love of symmetry and order." Houses designed or refaced with Georgian regularity smoothed out the jumbled appearance of the earlier Tudor aesthetic of gables and projections, of mixed materials and heavily patterned exteriors. Compare, for example, the jumbled shapes of Philip English's "Great House" of 1683 (figure 2, p. 54) with the single geometric block, highlighted by ranks of windows and an entrance flanked by classical pilasters, of Timothy Orne's "Mansion" (figure 4, p. 117) built in Salem about 1760.[37]

New vistas, walkways, gardens, squares, and buildings materialized to accommodate genteel leisure pursuits, appearing first in London and soon after in provincial ports and market centers in England and New England. As English historian Roy Porter observes, "Georgian public life increasingly revolved around the town itself, its streets, public spaces, and entertainments." The urban environment set the scene for "sauntering, shopping, sitting, strutting, and staring." In the fashionable village of Hampstead outside London, residents and visitors enjoyed the pleasures of a pump room, race course, bowling green, teashops, and concert hall. Greens for bowling, long an aristocratic sport in England, were situated near gardens and often included "houses" or rooms for entertainment. Lady Celia Fiennes described the playing area in Newcastle-upon-Tyne during her visit there in 1698, as "a very pleasant bowling-green . . . with a large gravel walk round it, with two rows of trees . . . making it very shady." On the fourth side of the green she noted "a fine entertaining house," and "a pretty garden by the side . . . where the gentlemen and ladies walk in the evening." Boston and Salem constructed similar public spaces. In 1714, the bowling green on Cambridge Street changed hands; the new owner, "Mr Daniel Stevens at the British Coffee House in Queen Street," announced in the *Boston News Letter* that the "Green will be open'd on Monday next" and promised that "all Gentlemen, Merchants, and others, that have a Mind to Recreate themselves, shall be well accommodated by the said Stevens."[38]

Dancing, a recreation favored by polite and commercial families in England and New England, became an important social performance. As one of the "personal excellencies" valued by writers in the *Spectator* and other social observers, dancing required controlled body movements and fashionable self-presentation, both important elements of gentility. Dances popular in the early eighteenth century, such as the minuet, included complicated figures where gentlemen and ladies circled and came together in a manner designed to showcase fashionable clothing and skilled body movements.[39] Dance, an art which required instruction and practice, necessitated dancing masters.[40] An itinerant teacher of genteel skills appeared in Boston as early as 1715, when Samuel Shrimpton Jr.'s widow Elizabeth was billed by George Brownell a total of £15 7s. od. for five and one-half months of "Dancing" lessons and five months of instruction in "playing on the Spinnet."[41]

Many of these pursuits provided not only entertainment but also an opportunity to see and be seen.[42] Clothing played an important role in defining self and group identity. Clothing had long been a marker of status in the traditional hierarchy, as evidenced by regulations about which status groups could wear what luxury items.[43] Changes in fashion and display constituted an element of the cultural shift from a domain of traditional values and landed property to a milieu of visible markers and mobile property. Luxury and refinement, previously signified by patina, by objects that bore evidence of longevity and witnessed to generations of family lineage, were now associated with novelty and foreign origins, an appropriate shift during the expansion of overseas trade and the rise of a mercantile elite in Anglo-America. In the realm of fashion, as with other aspects of the shift to gentility, some people embraced modern trends and others resisted. Interest in and knowledge of fabrics and styles increased gradually and fitfully in the decades before and after the turn of the century.

In 1684, Samuel Shrimpton's sister, a young woman of twenty-four, expended over thirty pounds on a "venetian Gowne lac'd," a "flowr'd petticoate," and various laces, ruffles, hoods, scarves, and knots.[44] In the seventeenth century, wealthy Bostonians gained much of their information about clothing styles through letters from their English relatives and friends. Samuel Shrimpton Jr., who evinced a strong interest in fine clothing, received tips from his maternal grandmother in London. With one letter in 1697, she sent him a "point cravat" and "lace to sew in your sleeves" explaining that "lace is much worn."[45] By the second decade of the eighteenth century, newspapers spread information of styles and fabrics through advertisements announcing English and European goods for sale in Boston.[46] In the *Boston Newsletter* of 22 March 1714, Stephen Labbe promoted goods "To be Sold at Publick Vendue or Outcry at the Crown Coffee House in King-Street, Boston" by claiming to offer the "Newest fashion Silk Satinets," as well as "European Goods" such as "Fans, Maps, and Pictures in gilt Frames" all at "very reasonable Rates."[47] As fashion information became more widely available, more people could recognize the markers of gentility and read the "face" of strangers. They could also move rapidly to acquire the appropriate possessions to claim their position among the elite.

Provincial newspapers offered ample evidence of fashionable objects and polite practices arriving in Massachusetts ports. Advertisements in the *Boston Gazette* in the 1720s touted Bohea Tea, sets of "fine China Ware," and Tea-Tables for sale in town.[48] Huguenot merchant Andrew Faneuil offered flowered Venetian silk "of the newest fashion . . . imported from London in the last ship" and James Stirling, a trader of Scotch origins, announced "a choice parcel of St. George's Wine just Imported" to be sold from his warehouse on Long Wharf.[49] Lost and found announcements featured precious objects like a "Triangle Steel Seal with coat of Arms," a silver toothpick case, and a silver spoon with engraved initials "SS," for which a twenty-shilling reward was offered. The Crown Coffee House on Long Wharf served as meeting place for merchants and public officials and a popular site for public auctions of real estate and genteel accoutrements like "a Collection of choice Pictures, fit for any Gentleman's Dinning-room or Stair-case."[50]

The privileged status of the mercantile elite was a distinctly white and European prerogative. Whites defined their privileged position by objectifying others. They gave alms to "objects of charity" and defined African American slaves and white indentured servants as possessions to be bought, sold, bequeathed, and displayed. Among the "objects" offered for sale in Boston and Salem were "a Lusty Negroe woman that can do all manner of Household work," "a Likely Negroe Girl of about seventeen Years of Age, to be disposed of," and a "young Negro Man that has been in the country two years." An African American house slave became an important part of maintaining a fashionable self-presentation for colonial gentry. Servants indentured for a period of time were also offered in the marketplace. An enterprising businessman could purchase five years' time of "a Jersey boy of about 16 years of Age." Perhaps even more desirable in a town quickly acquiring the trappings of gentility was four years' time of a "Likely servant Man" who could "shave and Buckle Wiggs very well."[51]

By the third decade of the eighteenth century, emphasis on change and style clearly overshadowed the importance of opulent materials.[52] Advertisements highlighted foreign manufactured goods and drew attention to their recent arrival, thereby implying quality and fashionableness. Merchant Jacob Wendell advertised goods "just arriv'd from England and Holland" on sale at his warehouse in Merchants Row. Along with Spanish and Swedish iron and German steel, Wendell sold "Silk Worsted London made Stuffs" and "sundry sorts of other European Goods." John Phillips, "Next Door to Mr Dolbear's the Braziers," sold "fine English textiles," "Fans, Masks," and "Silk Gloves."[53]

London artisans began to grasp the possibility of markets in provincial urban centers.[54] In 1733, the *Boston Gazette* carried the announcement of "Mrs. Elizabeth Hatton from London [who] makes Manteaus, Cloaks, Manteels, and all sorts of Women's Apparel after the newest Mode." Mrs. Hatton also "has new Patterns of Sleves by the last Ships, from the Queen's Manteau and Scarf Maker." Again the notice emphasized novelty and derived authority from a connection with London's highest social circle, the royal court. Mrs. Hatton signaled her knowledge of the importance of keeping up with the rapid changes in fashion by insisting that "she'l constantly be supply'd" by the queen's dressmaker "as the Fashion alters." Among the social elite, fashion became a code, a system of visible signs, which not only announced wealth but signaled social positioning, a knowledge of international fashion, and access to the latest designs and fabrics.[55]

Using references to the queen or phrases like "just arrived from London" or "on the latest ship from London," artisan and merchant advertisers transported the cachet of London and the court to products in the shops and warehouses of Boston and Salem. Coupling references to the queen and claims of rapidly changing styles, Mrs. Hatton's advertisement, and others like it, linked long-established cultural authority with the more recent emphasis on newness and constant change. The implication was that people discriminating enough to patronize that seamstress or purchase this fabric would, through the act of purchasing and then displaying at private teas and dinners or more public assemblies, dances, and promenades, put on the cultural authority of metropolitan connections, transatlantic horizons, and novel goods. In privileging novelty and change, the polite and commercial culture created a chain of recurrent desire essential to a modern consumer society.[56] For people surrounded by this ever-changing panoply of earthly delights, there was no longer time for pious contemplation of God's wonders.

It is no wonder, then, in this culture of the market or cultural marketplace, that notions about the meaning and value of possessions changed. The weight of inherited or internal values like family origin, religious affiliation, or English university education—attributes slowly acquired and not directly related to the marketplace—diminished, while the importance of accumulated possessions and polite behavior increased. In this bazaar of goods and skills, is it not surprising that objections to the new culture coalesced around religious tolerance, new forms of self-presentation, and novel kinds of sociability. Those wedded to Puritan practices, according to which public gatherings centered on lectures, sermons, and fast days, directed particular ire toward Anglican churches and genteel customs of wearing wigs, offering toasts, and performing dances. Not all townsmen welcomed the Georgian refinements or the enterprising foreigners who were changing the faces of Boston and Salem and transforming the meaning of things.

As first light broke over the horizon on 1 January 1701, four trumpeters, specially engaged by Samuel Sewall, "gave a Blast" to welcome "the Entrance of the eighteenth century." The performers marched from the Boston Common to the Town House where they "sounded" until sunrise, as strolling bellmen walked through various neighborhoods reading aloud from Sewall's poem *Verses upon a New Century*. The poem concluded:

> So Asia, and Africa,
> Europe, with America;
> All Four, in consort join'd shall Sing
> New Songs of Praise to CHRIST our KING.[57]

Had Sewall foreseen what the new century would bring to Massachusetts, he might not have hired trumpeters to herald its arrival. Sewall, a staunch Puritan, became a leading voice for maintaining the older ways. He sought to sustain a unified community of Puritan believers and was constantly concerned about the new manners and religious beliefs of "the strangers among us." Sewall unsuccessfully opposed many new developments that signaled change in Boston and Salem. As Anglicans, many of them merchants and royal officials, became more numerous and influential in Massachusetts, Sewall fought a rearguard action to confine and limit their religious influence. Small incidents tell the story: on one occasion he attempted to convince Harvard tutor Henry Flint to steer clear of the title "Saint" when speaking of Jesus' disciples. Sewall explained in a letter to Flint that this was a term "disused in New England." Sewall knew that he was in the minority in his refusal to gracefully accept the broadening of religious beliefs in New England as more and more "strangers" became townsmen. A few days later Sewall "was much surpris'd and grieved" to hear the [Book of] "Common Prayer" of the Anglicans read at the graveside of a member of the devotedly Puritan Stoughton family. He concluded, "there appears much Ingratitude and Baseness in it," and he reckoned it "an Indignity and affront" to Mr. Stoughton (a former lieutenant governor) and to an audience filled with descendants of the founding families—Hutchinsons, Byfields, and Winthrops. Sewall knew that he shared in what was rapidly becoming the perspective of a minority and that many resented his efforts to uphold an ideal that was in the process of being culturally displaced. When, a few weeks after his efforts with Flint, another minister referred to "Saint James" in his sermon, Sewall surmised that "he did it to confront me, and to assert his own liberty."[58]

In this same year of 1708, Sewall, as a member of the Provincial Council, was asked to approve building a Quaker meeting house in Boston. He opposed it, saying, "I would not have a hand in setting up their Devil Worship." Sewall continued to resist and denounce the establishment of other religious denominations in Massachusetts. A decade later, when reading London minister Daniel Neal's *History of New England*, Sewall noted, "it grieves me to see New-England's Nakedness laid open in the business of the Quakers, Anabaptists, Witchcraft."[59] Yet these indignities paled, in Sewall's view, when compared to the new customs of drinking healths and wearing wigs.

Objections to gentility coalesced around both goods and practices. The appearance of wigs early in the new century evoked negative attention from Puritan stalwarts like Sewall. Laboring to convince others to eschew wigs in favor of their own God-given hair, he spent one distressing day counseling and pleading with a young acquaintance who had shaved his head and donned a wig. Sewall explained to young Josiah Willard that "God seems to have ordained our Hair as a Test, to see whether we can bring our minds to be content at his finding; or whether we would be our own Carvers." Satisfied with his efforts, the diarist noted that Willard "seemed to say [he] would leave off his Wig when his hair was grown." A few years later, when attending the funeral of John Higginson, Salem's longtime preacher, Sewall observed with satisfaction that all six neighboring ministers "wear their own Hair." As he himself grew bald, he continued to withstand social pressure, and fashioned a unique black silk cap rather than adopt a wig that would have both warmed his head and covered the bald spot.[60]

While Sewall voiced strenuous objections to much of the new culture, others selectively resisted or welcomed change. Cotton Mather (1663–1728), one of the third generation of the leading Puritan ministerial family in America, moved further than Sewall toward a partial and selective acceptance of the polite and commercial culture gaining predominance in Massachusetts and other Anglo-American urban centers. Mather retained his Puritan antipathy toward Anglicans and frequently cautioned against preferring the pleasures of this life over the rewards of the next. Yet his interest and membership in the Royal Society, England's most august scientific organization, and his selective participation in genteel customs demonstrated a positive reception of the new styles and graces associated with politeness. His efforts to support inoculation for smallpox are the most famous example of popularizing the new science. Three years earlier, he responded to "the Agitation in the Minds of people throughout the Countrey" by quickly producing a scientific treatise on the aurora borealis designed to quell the town's fears of portents in the night sky.[61]

Almost simultaneously, Mather wrote logical explanations for natural phenomena and sought to make his son "a more finished Gentleman," while he continued to bewail the changing mores in Boston. He noted in his diary that the "very wicked" House of Representatives "have wickedly encouraged the People to cast contempt on the Order for the general Fast" (a public fast was a longtime Puritan practice for redeeming communal sin). Reading the proclamation of the fast from his pulpit in the Old North Church, Mather hoped to save his "Flock" from being "drawn into the Impiety." In despair at his declining influence, he cried "Lord, what shall I do, for a self-destroying People?" He called upon the "Hand of God" to deliver the Country from two or three "wicked Men." His powerful prayers were answered. "Within these few Hours, GOD has . . . smitten with an Apoplexy, one who has been . . . the greatest Hinderer of good, and Misleader and Enchanterer of the People." Dr. Oliver Noyes died the next day. Mather responded, "methinks, I see a wonderful Token for good in this Matter."[62] Apparently God's providence still ruled Mather's spiritual cosmology in contrast to his scientific understanding of the natural world.

Despite Mather's eagerness to participate in the new learning emerging as part of the Scientific Revolution, he maintained a troubled ambivalence toward a culture based on man's power to discern natural laws through reason, and on man's interest in accumulating value through earthly possessions. At times, he would pray "that all the enjoyments of this World might appear contemptible Things unto me" and "That I might be content with a poor; and hard, low, mean Condition in this World."[63] For Mather, Puritan piety seemed to be at odds with the polite and commercial world that was emerging in the expanding ports of Massachusetts and the trading towns of England.

Mather's colleague and sometime nemesis Benjamin Colman, who had trained for the pulpit at Harvard and gained social polish during two years of ministering to the English elite at the elegant resort town of Bath, took the lead in reinterpreting religious attitudes toward luxury and fashion. He ministered to a church of affluent merchants and, in sharp contrast to Sewall's condemnation of many genteel practices, Colman provided a blueprint for couching self-display in acceptable terms and in shaping an ideal of benevolence to coexist with vast wealth. In counseling a successful merchant's wife, Lydia George, who confessed to the "vanity of Vying with others" in fashionable dress, Colman reassured her: "You have been educated in the wearing of rich apparel; Mr. George chooses you should continue it," furthermore, "it is not offensive nor grievous to sober Christians."[64] Lydia's husband John became an important figure in Boston who invested in Long Wharf, supported King's Chapel, the first Anglican Church in Boston, and participated in founding Colman's own Brattle Street Church.[65] When George died suddenly at the age of forty-nine, Mather, again showing his attraction for "the enjoyments of this World," quickly began courting the elegant and wealthy widow George. She became his third wife eight months later on 5 July 1715, "the brightest Day in my Kalender."[66]

Cotton Mather exemplifies the partial and negotiated transitions taking place during this period in Boston and Salem. Despite his parochial antipathy to Anglicans, he shared the broad horizons characteristic of many residents in Salem and Boston. While not directly involved in merchant activity, he praised the benefits of commerce and depended on vessels traversing the Atlantic to carry correspondence in support of his own trade in influence and ideas. Mather envisioned himself as a key figure in an international intellectual community. An honorary degree from the University of Glasgow in 1710 and election as a Fellow of the Royal Society confirmed this. He corresponded with Bartholomew Ziegenblagh, a Danish missionary to the Hindus at Malabar (now part of Bombay) on the western coast of India, sent funds to distant missions, and offered prayers "Especially, a Smile of GOD upon what is doing for Him at Glaucha, and at Malabar." One of the letters to Ziegenblagh was expanded and published in 1721 as *India Christiana*.

Following his father's and grandfather's example, Mather maintained an extensive transatlantic correspondence with Dissenting clergy in England. He sought advice on marketing his works abroad from Anthony Wilhelm Boehm, a German chaplain at the English court, and expanded his circle of correspondents to include Boehm's teacher at Halle, the German Pietist August Hermann Francke. Mather envisioned a Protestant Union that would stretch across the Atlantic at the elite ministerial level; New England Congregationalists (Puritans), Scottish Presbyterians, English Dissenters, and German Pietists would combine to promote Dissenting beliefs and counter the Church of England.[67]

But when foreigners, even French and Irish Protestants, arrived close to home, he proffered a mixed reception. His congregation would provide funds for destitute Huguenots and Irish arriving in Boston, but his often repeated phrase "objects of charity" implied a certain distance between himself as benefactor and those less fortunate. Poor refugees, like the boatload of Huguenots arriving in 1687 by way of the West Indies, would have a relationship to Mather's international Protestant circle only as recipients of charity, not as full-fledged members. Furthermore, like the Puritan merchants of Salem, he deplored the seemingly undisciplined life and active tavern culture of seamen and fishermen. In his diary he bemoaned their impious life, saying, "and now, if I begin with the Sea-faring. Oh! What an horrible Spectacle have I before me! A wicked, stupid abominable Generation: every Year growing rather worse and worse, . . . Drowned in all Impiety and Perdition." His resentment of their continued resistance to his efforts to inculcate Puritan morality came through clearly when he wrote, "all the Prayers, and all the Pains I have employ'd in a distinguishing Manner for their Goods, they requite with making me above any Man living the Object of their Malignity."[68]

Again and again we see Mather's inconsistencies and ambivalence toward the polite and commercial culture taking shape in Massachusetts. He welcomed Scotch Presbyterian ministers to Boston, "more than two or three of them that are at this very time [1716] the pastors of our churches." But when they adopted too many attributes of Georgian sociability he complained that they were guilty of "drinking of healths, and pleading in defense of the games of lottery," and demonstrating "a vast indiscretion in their whole conduct, with attempts to sow discord among our people; among whom some of the more loose and profane sort (and scarce any but such) siding with them."[69]

Mather's biographer Kenneth Silverman maintains that Mather saw himself as a reconciler of two cultures. Rather than reconciling differences however, he seemed to waver from one position to another, accepting religious toleration for Baptists whom he had previously condemned but finding it impossible to extend that toleration to Anglicans. He continued to regard Anglicans as outsiders, "whose chapel is chiefly filled from strangers coming in among us." He welcomed many of the attributes of gentility: wearing wigs, marrying a fashionable woman who charmed him over the tea table, and desiring that his son acquire a gentlemanly polish. Other elements of polite sociability such as dancing, drinking toasts, and taking chances at cards or lotteries, all continued to earn his contempt. Perhaps Mather's concerns about many behaviors associated with the cultural transformations taking place in Massachusetts prompted his about-face as he approached one important social milestone. Near the end of his life, Mather sat for some preliminary drawings for a portrait by Peter Pelham, but before Pelham could complete the painting, Mather "repented of it"—ambivalent to the last.[70]

Varied responses to consumer goods and genteel society marked the transformation to a polite and commercial culture in England and America. Some members of the merchant elite, the Shrimptons and the East India Company's Sir Joshua Child for example, embraced gentility and used possessions and social rituals to identify themselves as Georgian gentlemen and ladies and to create further demand for imported goods; others, especially Puritan believers in New England, resisted some or all of the new customs and goods. Even in Britain, some objected to the growth of foreign imports and the increasing influence of fashionable consumption. Ambivalence about foreign goods prompted an unease even among devoted promoters of commerce such as Daniel Defoe, who lamented the craze for imported calico, saying, "it crept into our houses, our closets and bedchambers; curtains, cushion[s], chairs, and at last beds themselves were nothing but Callicoes or India stuffs."

The demand for calico, like other fashionable imports, showed the centrality of merchant capitalism in producing a culture of consumption. The introduction of Indian cottons into the English textile market, promoted in a calculated program by Sir Josiah Child, director of the East India Company, led to a craze for calico in late seventeenth-century England. Originally imported and sold to the middling and lower sort as an inexpensive substitute for "brocades and flowered silks favored by the aristocracy," Indian calicoes had soon become "the Ware of Ladyes of the greatest quality, which they wear on the outside of Gowns and

FIGURE 3. Cotton Mather. Mezzotint by Peter Pelham, 1728. The portrait Mather "repented of" was probably completed after his death in 1728. Courtesy of National Portrait Gallery, Smithsonian Institution.

Mantuoes and which they line with velvet and Cloth of Gold." Calicoes not only appealed to ladies but also spoke to the question of how to identify a gentleman. In 1699, a London pamphleteer exclaimed, "it was scarce thought about twenty years since that we should ever see Calicoes the ornaments of our greatest Gallants . . . but now few think themselves well dresst till they are made up in Calicoes, both men and women."[71]

Silk from the Bengal region in India also became a part of the quickly evolving consumer world of Anglo-America. English merchants both responded to and shaped an emerging "fashion pattern" that stressed change in color and decoration of material.[72] Directors of the East India Company recognized the importance of change and novelty in marketing a product of exotic origins. Writing, in 1681, to their factors in India, they stressed

> a constant and generall Rule, that in all flowered Silks you change the fashion and flower as much as you can every year, for English Ladies and they say the French and other Europeans will give twice as much for a new thing not seen in Europe before, though worse, then they will give for a better silk for [of?] the same fashion worn the former years.

The letter implied that the directors were simply responding to the inexplicable whims of the ladies. Their tone maintained an innocence of their efforts to naturalize demand in the name of fashion. Nicholas Barbon, an important contemporary writer on economic matters, recognized an explicit connection between commerce and gentility in his *Discourse of Trade*, written in at the height of the calico craze. Barbon observed that "Fashion or the alteration of Dress, is a great Promoter of Trade. . . . It is the Spirit and Life of Trade, It makes a Circulation, and gives a Value by Turns, to all sorts of Commodities; keeps the great Body of Trade in Motion." He accentuated the importance of fashionable consumption based on novelty to stimulate endlessly recurring demand and keep the heart of commerce pumping.[73]

By emphasizing the novel, Barbon and Child both responded to and further stimulated what a scholar of twentieth-century consumption calls "the organized creation of dissatisfaction." Almost upon purchase and certainly after one or two wearings, a fashionable dress no longer carried the message of novelty, and therefore immediately had to be replaced by one made in a newer style or with different fabric. The "fashion pattern," based on annual and even monthly changes in style, color, and fabric spread widely across England and its colonies during the eighteenth century. As Child, Barbon, and other entrepreneurs and theorists began to recognize, rapid changes in style stimulated the economy. The *Spectator*, too, explained the engine of consumer desire: "Novelty is a very powerful . . . most extensive Influence . . . the Source of Admiration, which lessens in proportion to our Familiarity with Objects, and upon thorough Acquaintance is utterly extinguished." But as the interest in fashion developed it produced a new attitude toward goods and their relationship to identity.[74]

In Tudor England, consumption among the English nobility had derived from "the cult of family status." Emphasizing the honor of long lineage, aristocratic families sought goods that possessed the "mysterious ability to grow more valuable as they grew more ancient and decrepit." For elite families during this earlier period, "new" meant "common," and even new goods required a simulacrum of patina. In his study of consumption Grant McCracken argues that it was in the late Elizabethan age, under the severe pressure of competition for the Queen's favor, that "certain goods began to communicate value not with patina but with novelty," and as one contemporary observed, with "the smell of beyond the seas." This initiated the shift from patina to fashion, but only at the exclusive level of leading aristocratic, courtier families, families increasingly cut off from their local seats of power and from the gentry and lower orders.[75]

As the calico craze, Barbon's instructions, and the East India Company's profits attest, the alteration from valuing longevity to seeking variety spread among the English gentry by the late seventeenth century and began to appear in Boston and Salem via wealthy merchant families like the Shrimptons. Invoking novelty and employing phrases like "à la mode" and "direct from London," merchants and artisans created the fear of becoming "a cultural laggard." This new language helped to shift ideas of value from permanence, age, and family lineage to possessions newly purchased and manners newly acquired. Foreign imports, "those not seen in Europe before," carried a particular cachet. Predating by two hundred years what is often considered a characteristic of twentieth-century mass consumption, Sir Josiah Child linked fashionable elegance with incessant novelty in promoting his company's wares.[76]

Not everyone could partake in the craze for foreign goods and incessant change. Investigating the arrival of a polite and commercial culture in Boston and Salem, has, so far, involved analyzing negotiations and differences among the gentry—not an opposition between two clearly identifiable groups but rather a selective appropriation of the new vocabulary of goods and a variable shedding of older values. Like Levi-Strauss's *bricoleur*, the Shrimptons or Mathers each chose different cultural elements to create singular myths or personal identities that had a similar dilemma at heart—how to stabilize a sense of self in a changing world?

But the account is incomplete without exploring the ramifications of burgeoning foreign trade and a contagious consumer culture for the lower sort, "the impolite." Not only elites could respond to consumer wares; another voice of ambivalence and resistance to the new culture came from those economically marginalized by unintended consequences of long-distance trade and the world of goods. English cloth workers pushed out of employment by competition from Asian fabrics, and Boston's struggling laborers and destitute widows facing scarcity amidst signs of plenty, had a different relationship to fashionable goods. They chose a vocabulary of crowd action to express their opinions about the effects of merchant capital and genteel presentation. Through controlled demonstrations, various groups of workers and unemployed exerted pressures on the emerging culture from a different position economically and socially.

As the obsession with calico swept through the Anglo-American gentry, it caused economic distress among those least able to afford fashionable goods at inflated prices. Workers in the silk-weaving workshops of Spitalfields in London rioted against the effects of foreign competition in 1697; as a result, Parliament prohibited the importation of Asian silks, which only temporarily cut back on imports and further fueled the demand for cotton calicoes. The silk weavers rioted again in 1719 "in a general assault on all wearers and sellers of the hated Calicoes," committing "several Disorders and Outrages on the Bodies of Persons wearing Calicoes, and printed Linnen."[77] The silk weavers' riots illustrated a form of forceful resistance to the changes prompted by long-distance trade and the growing influence of the polite and commercial culture. The demonstrations were covered extensively in the Boston papers. In early July, 1719, the *Boston Gazette* reported, under a Paris byline, that "the Journeymen in Spittle-Fields assembled themselves in a considerable Body, threatening the Wearers and Venders of Callicoes in Bishopsgate-street, [and] Aldersgate-street." Hundreds of silk weavers assembled at Parliament but "on the appearance of some Horse-Guards, they dispersed." A week later the *Gazette* reported that "a great Body of them . . . threatened the East-India House and several great Shops where Callicoes were sold." In response the House of Lords requested ideas for a scheme "for the Effectual Preventing [of] the wearing and using of Painted, Printed, and Stained Callicoes, which are so Detrimental to the Manufactures of this Kingdom."

The House of Lords had to satisfy demands from the demonstrators, assuage the powerful East India Company, and keep the beneficial Asian trade flowing. Two weeks later came word that "the Weavers who had been apprehended for the late Tumults, were discharged, with a strict Charge to avoid offending again in the like kind, least they should repent the abusing so much Clemency."[78] The following year, Parliament passed a prohibition against calicos imported from India that was honored mostly in the breach. The ban did not reduce consumer desire for printed cottons in England or America because, as one contemporary reported, "the Humour of the People [runs] so much upon wearing painted or printed Calicoes and Linnens." The ban did provide an early stimulus to the English textile industry. By midcentury, English workshops in Manchester and elsewhere in Lancashire began producing domestic calicos printed in London and available at a cheaper price than imported ones. The locally made cloth appealed to a wide body of customers who could appropriate the exotic allure of foreign-style fabrics at lower prices. After a generation of calico madness, a domestic product, through visible characteristics alone, could represent foreign origins and fuel consumer demand. The mechanisms of a consumer culture supported long-distance trade and over time produced the burgeoning demand that supported the Industrial Revolution. In the early decades of the eighteenth-century, merchants understood that demand for fashionable goods helped to keep them in business. Few, if any, grasped the long-term consequences of their business decisions and cultural preferences. Nor did Massachusetts merchants seem to acknowledge the short-term impact that their efforts to control commerce had on other groups in Boston and Salem.

Active resistance to the effects of merchant capitalism appeared in New England as well as England. While Samuel Sewall resisted cultural change by muttering into his diary, groups of concerned journeymen and laborers took more vigorous measures. As commercial leaders increased their power over the town's economy, conditions worsened for many, particularly in Boston.[79] Merchants and laborers occupied opposing positions in efforts to control the supply of foodstuffs in Boston. Residing on a peninsula with only a narrow neck of land connecting them to the surrounding countryside, townspeople depended on grain and produce from suburban farms. Because land was a scarce and valuable commodity, only a few residents could afford enough space for substantial gardens; those same residents, the wealthy merchants who had invested to improve roads, now controlled land access to the city. To meet overseas demand, they required a constant supply of grain and meat to feed crewmen on their vessels and slaves on the sugar plantations in the West Indies. As a result, they competed with local residents for foodstuffs. In some years there was plenty for all; in others, scarcity.

Some shortages resulted from natural disasters; others were created by merchants responding to international market demands.

Beginning in the late seventeenth century and accelerating in the early eighteenth, a series of local and international developments created an economic situation in which the majority of Bostonians and Salemites found it very difficult to maintain their basic living conditions. King William's War (1689–98) and Queen Anne's War (1702–14) required an extensive commitment of men and money from Massachusetts, including two thousand men recruited (or impressed) for an attack on Quebec in 1711. The attack failed and the troops sustained severe casualties. Governor Dudley estimated that the Quebec campaign alone cost the colony fifty thousand pounds.[80] The wars resulted in higher taxes, currency inflation, and rapidly growing numbers of widows and children in Boston. Threatened by French privateering, trade ebbed during times when England was at war with France and its ally Spain. The Salem merchant John Higginson, for example, claimed that his business was ruined and he had "met with great losses by the French" privateers.[81] In 1711, Massachusetts imposed an embargo on its own shipping to assure a plentiful supply of vessels for an attack on Port Royal in Nova Scotia. To add to the misery in Boston, a fire destroyed much of the city that same year. All of these difficulties combined to swell the ranks of the laboring poor and those dependent entirely on charity to survive. Cotton Mather, whose father had written of the wonders of God's providence, lamented earthly plights, noting that "the distressed Families of the Poor to which I dispense, or procure needful Relief, are now so many, and of such daily Occurrence."[82] Amidst this economic suffering, a number of merchants and land speculators accumulated sizable profits and displayed their riches openly. Andrew Faneuil and, following him, his nephew Peter, provided visible proof of their affluence and mastery over the complex and difficult transatlantic trade by acquiring expensive, opulent goods and constructing imposing buildings; it was in 1711 that Andrew Faneuil purchased a stone house with seven acres and began to fashion his Georgian-style mansion and gardens (see figure 7, p. 140). As the Faneuils and other merchants embraced gentility and began to display fashionable possessions and participate in polite sociability, they also took measures to increase their control over the local economy, thus concocting a formula for resentment and resistance.

A protracted effort on the part of leading merchants to regulate local procedures for buying and selling food products provides another example of popular resistance to the authority of the mercantile elite. The first legislative effort to confine markets to a particular site occurred in

1696 when the selectmen of Boston decided that a single marketplace should be established at the Town House.[83] Previous to the proposal of 1696, the town meeting annually chose clerks of the market to oversee the buying and selling that went on in the streets and squares of Boston.[84] Peddlers moved up and down the streets calling out their goods for sale and stopping from door to door while other men and women displayed and sold produce from outdoor stalls. Retail merchants and booksellers rented small enclosed shops under the Town House and artisans sold handcrafted goods from shops adjacent to their homes. Shipping merchants offered imported goods from their warehouses in Merchants Row and along the wharves and docks.

This haphazard method of marketing foodstuffs and other goods seems to be have been unique to Boston. Most larger towns and small villages in England and America had established defined sites and times for local markets and enacted laws to restrict peddling.[85] Officials in colonial Boston attempted to maintain order through licensing sellers, checking weights and measures, and appointing market officials annually. In 1691, the town offered twenty new licenses "To sell out of Dores;" twelve went to poor widows as a form of pension relief.[86]

In addition to the above regulations, clerks of the market were charged with the enforcement of the Assize of Bread. Adopting an established English custom, the selectmen of Boston and the General Court of Massachusetts passed laws regulating the price charged for bread in relation to the price of wheat. The Assize recognized three types of bread; white, wheaten, and household, each heavier (that is, made with coarser flour) than the next. As the price of wheat rose, the required weight of each loaf declined proportionately. The Assize regulated the baker's profit and aimed at controlling the price of bread for the poor.[87]

To tighten their command over the local economy, a group of merchants established, in 1696, a form of vertical integration that threatened to subvert the intentions of the Assize of Bread.[88] Andrew Belcher, one of New England's leading shipowners, controlled a large portion of the grain supply of Boston. Belcher allied himself with Elisha Cooke, leader of the "popular political faction" and Boston's largest mill owner.[89] Together they set up Nathaniel Oliver, Belcher's relation by marriage, as a baker, and he soon became one of Boston's largest provisioners of bread. The partners operated every element necessary to control the supply and cost of grain and bread in the town—except for distribution. With Belcher's and Cooke's support, Oliver gained a seat as selectman and apparently convinced his colleagues to draft legislation establishing a specific site for a public market. In this single location, Belcher, Cooke, and Oliver could dictate the price and supply of the most basic, most necessary food for the people of Boston. No records of planned collusion exist to confirm the three merchants' intentions, but his response to later crowd protests confirm that for Andrew Belcher profit took precedence over popular feeling.[90]

Plans to regulate the public market seem to have faded from view shortly after Nathaniel Oliver failed in his bid for reelection as selectman the following year. But issues over the supply of grain and bread continued to surface in Boston, especially during periods of warfare and / or economic difficulties. In 1711, when the city suffered from the effects of Queen Anne's War and a serious fire, Belcher seized his opportunity. As the largest grain merchant in New England, he garnered an appointment as commissary to the British forces fighting the French and Indians in Canada. To supply the British (and some of the Massachusetts men fighting with them), Belcher the merchant sold grain to himself as commissary, netting a substantial profit in the transaction. To keep the supply flowing, Belcher hoarded grain, severely depleting the supply of grain, flour, and bread in Boston. This rapidly pushed up the price of bread, creating a serious problem for those with marginal incomes— possibly over 60 percent of the townspeople.[91]

In a carefully restrained and precisely directed manner, the sufferers took action. One morning, the captain of a Belcher grain ship about to sail out of Boston harbor found the ship's rudder missing—cleanly sawn off. That evening a "mob" of men ran the ship aground to prevent the grain from leaving. An angry Belcher continued to let grain pile up in his warehouses and raised prices even further. The selectmen, unable to convince Belcher to lower prices or stop exporting wheat, bought what little they could find and resold it to the townspeople at pre-Belcher prices.[92]

In 1713, grain supplies again ran disastrously low, and when Belcher continued to export grain at a high profit to the West Indies, a crowd of two hundred broke into his warehouses and carried out their own distribution of grain. In each case, the mob took specific actions to alleviate a specific problem. They knew exactly whom to target—Andrew Belcher— and rather than attacking Belcher in person, they went after the grain, capturing a supply not just for themselves but for all the needy. This method of redress replicates eighteenth-century English food riots—another element of Georgian urbanity imported to Boston.[93]

In several instances, like the attacks on Andrew Belcher's ships and warehouses in 1711 and 1713, crowd actions followed the same pattern as protests in English provincial towns and market centers described by historian E. P. Thompson. Thompson explores the working out of what he denotes as a "moral economy" in food riots and crowd actions throughout England in the eighteenth century. The "mobs" or crowds followed a common pattern of behavior that avoided wanton destruction in an effort to focus on specific targets, such as granaries, flour mills, tax collectors, merchants, and markets. The crowd attempted to enforce what it perceived as a basic right of the working poor to a supply of food at a reasonable price. Often rioters paid merchants or millers for the grain or flour they took at a price reflecting the crowd's sense of fairness.[94] As Thompson and others portray it, the moral economy involved a process of changing "customs and usages" based on nonmonetary norms expressed "in resistance to the economy of the 'free market.' " The moral economy as understood by the common people of Boston, like Sewall and Mather's concerns for a "moral order," represented a form of negotiation over the authority of polite and commercial culture.[95]

In Puritan communities of seventeenth-century Massachusetts, a combination of plentiful food supplies, a system of "warning out" strangers who might become a financial burden to the town, and a strong sense of community among all who were subject to God's mysterious hand prevented market crises that might have motivated people to act on the ideas of a moral economy. In eighteenth-century Boston, as economic conditions deteriorated, a growing emphasis on visible wealth and new values reconfigured community alignments. Crowds took action as one response.[96] In times of scarcity, conflicting economic needs operated in what seemed a zero-sum game. The popular belief that every person had a right to food at a price he or she could afford opposed the profit-seeking goals of the merchants who controlled most of the economic resources. Like cloth workers in London, poorer Bostonians protested with a loud voice against the effects of new values that accompanied the growing ascendancy of a polite and commercial society. The streets fashioned by elite merchants had become contested terrain in the ongoing cultural negotiations.[97]

Public occasions, official and unofficial, polite and impolite, exhibited the arrival of a new outlook in New England, one that could be seen and heard. As the refined style of steeples and bell towers, first associated with Anglican churches, remodeled the skylines of Boston and Salem, church bells transformed public celebrations. Compare, for example, Boston's commemoration of the king's birthday in October 1686, when "many guns fired, and at night [there was] a Bonfire on Noddles Island" to the celebration in 1734 of a royal marriage when "at six o'clock in the morning all the bells in the town began to ring and continued ringing till night without intermission." The bells accompanied a parade and the evening ended with a Governor's Ball. Two years later, another royal marriage prompted another day-long ringing of "all the bells in the town," interrupted at midday when cannon fired a number of volleys equal to the ages of bride and groom and militia regiments paraded through the streets—streets that on other occasions might fill with impolite, rowdy protestors objecting to market controls. The festivities concluded with a ball and "genteel supper" for a "vast number of gentlemen and ladies."[98] Puritan diarist Samuel Sewall did not attend nor did he complain of the high living. He had put down his pen for the last time in October 1729.

Georgian gentility reshaped cultural values and social geography in Boston and Salem. The shift to outward presentation, based on purchased goods and learned manners, as the indicator of social and political status encouraged an acceptance of successful merchants from various European origins. If Philip English had arrived in Salem a generation later, as did his fellow Channel Islanders the Cabots, he might have found the acceptance and status he craved. The cultural changes in Salem permitted English, at the end of his life, to alter the social boundaries and move, literally and figuratively, to the center of town. In the 1730s, he donated land for the first Anglican church in Salem. Although the church planning committee met at English's "Great House" at the eastern end of town, the church itself rose at the very center of Salem, one block from Town House Square. Contributors to the building fund included other Jersey Frenchmen such as Philip Dumeresque and members of the German Crowninshield family. Merchants from Newport, Rhode Island, collected of forty-seven pounds; Gedney Clark, formerly of Salem, sent funds from Bermuda; and Lord Howe, the governor of Barbados, provided a substantial contribution.[99] The founding of St. Peter's Church represented a multi-ethnic, international community brought together by mercantile connections and sharing an acceptance of different religious affiliations and various family origins—an acceptance made possible by the new values of a polite and commercial culture. Cultural transformations enabled Philip English to finally take his place as a prominent merchant in the heart of Salem when, in 1736, he was buried in the churchyard of St. Peter's.

4

The Work of Gentility
in the Provinces

It is now the third Watch of the Night, the greatest Part of which I
have spent round a capacious bowl of China filled with the choicest
Products of both the Indies.

The Spectator, NO. 617, 1714

SURROUNDED BY A WELTER of fashionable possessions,
foreign news, and international commerce, residents of urban seaports
and trading towns in Britain and America gradually constructed new
identities to fit their altered circumstances. They drew from the goods
surrounding them to create, in the words of historian J. G. A. Pocock, a
"political society and social personality as founded upon commerce:
upon the exchange of forms of mobile property and upon modes of consciousness suited to a world of moving objects." In Georgian England,
the rising middle class, including wealthy merchants, incorporated unfamiliar objects and invented new forms of sociability—in effect, created
a new culture—to proclaim their growing influence, to identify themselves as genteel, and to integrate the products of foreign commerce into
everyday lives. The English bourgeoisie drew from the multitude of
goods available to shape a new refinement that borrowed some of its
cues from courtly fashions but moved far beyond simple emulation of
aristocratic tastes. English historian John Brewer describes the new middling sort or bourgeoisie as "men of moveable property" who distinguished themselves from "the patrician elite and the laboring poor."
Many financially successful merchants in England and the colonies invested some of their profits in acquiring and maintaining a fashionable,
and no doubt pleasurable, lifestyle. For leading merchants in American
ports, possessions and manners, though adopted from bourgeois forms,
signified a colonial aristocracy. Yet no matter how lofty their position in
the local hierarchy, when participating in Georgian social rituals in

London, they willingly joined the lesser gentry or middling sort rather than ape landed noblemen.[1]

Georgian gentility was well adapted for a world based on merchant capital and international trade. Employing portable and purchasable markers of status and character, it reinforced demand for consumer goods and affirmed a world of geographic and social mobility. Fashionable clothing and polite manners signaled almost at a glance the social and economic position of a newcomer and announced his or her ability and desire to be included among the genteel. Appearance and behavior communicated a shared set of values, even among strangers. As a culture that stressed the importance of material possessions, gentility had the additional benefit of supporting the growth of consumer demand and, ultimately, profits for merchants and manufacturers.

The need to create an appropriate identity was especially acute for European and British families who had moved to the colonies. Merchants like Anthony Stoddard, Peter Faneuil, and their colleagues took the lead in rebuilding their colonial communities into provincial Georgian cities, and in the process producing a rearrangement of personal and social space. They also refashioned their own identities based on a growing interest in possessions and polite manners. Joining with royal officials and professionals to form a powerful elite, they exercised, through control of trade and the urban landscape, an ability to remake society on the new principles of a world of goods.

While many artisans and yeoman farmers may have aspired to join genteel society, their limited efforts could easily be differentiated from the sociability of well-to-do merchants and professionals by both the type of materials from which their belongings were made and the scope and scale of their possessions and entertainments. Polite dinners, like those at the tables of Peter Faneuil, Timothy Orne, or Nicholas Boylston, required flatware, plates, and chairs for each guest, a requirement that could be met only by those able to invest in sets of eight, twelve, sixteen, or more silver utensils, porcelain plates, and leather-seated walnut chairs. A rural yeoman on the other hand might possess one or two inexpensive or chipped tea cups and a simply made ceramic teapot. In contrast, the elite of Boston and Salem would entertain with a silver tea service of myriad items and a dozen porcelain cups imported from China. Costly clothes, "tasteful" possessions, refined manners, and attending house servants defined a position at the top of the social and economic structure.[2]

In the early decades of the new century an uneven acceptance greeted gentility and the tenets of a polite and commercial culture in Boston and

Salem; by the 1740s Georgian gentility was a way of life for commercial families in both England and New England. Consumer goods had become an essential element in the shaping of identity. Economic tracts by Sir Joshua Child and Nicholas Barbon, both enterprising entrepreneurs, promulgated the importance of conspicuous consumption to the growth of the economy. But, the social consequences of a world of goods met resistance in both England and New England. When Bernard Mandeville, a Dutch physician living in London, first proclaimed frugality a vice and luxury a virtue, few could accept his views. Mandeville presaged the close connection of identity and presentation that developed during the century. He noted, "People . . . are generally honour'd according to their Clothes." At midcentury, Richard Campbell's *The London Tradesman*, attesting to the integration of fashion and identity, lauded the importance to genteel folk of a tailor or dressmaker who "not only makes their Dress, but . . . may be said to make themselves." By 1776, Adam Smith could proclaim in *The Wealth of Nations* that "consumption is the sole end and purpose of all production:. . . . The Maxim is . . . perfectly self-evident." And as consumption spread from London to the provinces, fashion and self-presentation became more central not only to political economy but also to a broader understanding of respectability and virtue.[3]

Practice of the genteel arts spread as quickly to colonial ports as to English provincial capitals. An English visitor to the port of Annapolis exclaimed that "the quick importation of fashions from the mother country is really astonishing." He marveled at the possibility "that a new fashion is adopted earlier by the polished and affluent American than by many opulent persons in the great metropolis [London]. . . . In short, very little difference is, in reality, observable in the manners of the wealthy colonist and the wealthy Briton." Sojourning in Boston in 1744, a Maryland gentleman, Dr. Alexander Hamilton, reported that "Assemblys of the gayer sort are frequent here: the gentlemen and ladys meeting almost every week att consorts of musick and balls." Hamilton, a connoisseur of gentility, insisted that he saw "as fine a ring of ladys, as good dancing, and heard musick as elegant as I had been witness to any where." After a midday dinner with a leading merchant, Hamilton enjoyed "a tune on the spinett from his daughter," who sang as she played. Other young women learned ladylike accomplishments that were practiced in Boston. One boarding school promised to teach "Flourishing, Embroidery, and all Sorts of Needle-Work, also Filigrew, and Painting upon Glas," as well as the more mundane skills of "Writing, Arithmetick, and singing Psalm Tunes."[4]

Polite sociability encompassed many new kinds of leisure pursuits.

Gatherings for concerts and assemblies represented the public (or semi-public) face of Georgian gentility. Assemblies, offering a mix of entertainment such as dancing, card playing, dinners, and concerts, took place in inns, market halls, town halls, and rooms built especially for these social functions in England and America.[5] Merchants often took the lead in financing and establishing assembly rooms and concert series. Some assemblies marked special occasions, but in many urban centers, entrepreneurs or civic groups provided entertainments on a regular schedule and sold tickets on a subscription basis. Church services now had to compete with social assemblies as key events in providing structure to the weekly calendar. In London's polite West End, the Hanover Square Rooms held concerts famous for performances of works by Bach and Haydn.[6] York, which in 1731–32 built some of the most magnificent rooms in all of England, held assemblies on a weekly basis in the winter and less frequently in the summer. Two hundred shareholders provided the initial financing of five thousand pounds for the rooms and elected directors managed the facilities. In York, as elsewhere, merchants played a leading role; a contemporary account from 1746 noted that "the design was first set on foot by a set of public spirited gentlemen" led by two merchants and an attorney. Resort towns such as Bath and Tunbridge Wells often had more than one set of assembly rooms built and managed by competing proprietors. Other towns took somewhat longer to establish gathering rooms; Bristol established its first rooms in 1755, and Newcastle-upon-Tyne in 1774–76.[7] In the winter of 1733, not long after York opened its famous building, Bostonians began a biweekly subscription assembly in "Mr. Pelham's great Room." Pelham published a notice in the papers announcing "to the Gentlemen and Ladies Subscribers and others, . . . [that his assembly series] will be Open'd on Wednesday the Tenth of January and continue Six Wednesdays during the Months of January, February and March."[8]

In the nearby port of Salem, the gentry also began a series of biweekly assemblies with music and dancing, similar to those established in Boston and English provincial towns. The gatherings took place at Jefferies' Tavern until 1766 when the Salem elite financed an assembly house on Cambridge Street, a short walk from the homes of leading merchants.[9] The new assembly building provided "an elegant room" forty by thirty feet with a very tall ceiling with "two handsome drawing rooms adjoining, . . . and a neat musick-gallery on the west side." Prominent local families participated in a constant round of visits, dances, assemblies, tea drinking, "turtles," and barbecues interleaved with births, weddings, and funerals. Thus Salem also created a local version of English cosmopolitan gentility.[10]

The polite culture in Salem and Boston depended on the commercial activities of merchants and their suppliers. One observer of the English scene in the 1730s marveled at the spread of gentility to the provinces and other locales. The writer described the large number of ship captains and seafaring men in theatre audiences, who "carry abroad a Taste of Politeness and Generosity, and give the World a Better Idea of *English* Manners." Because of their close transatlantic connections, merchants were often the first to see and acquire the new fashions and furnishings and to employ them to construct and define the polite and commercial elite in Boston and Salem.[11]

The interest in self-presentation associated with gentility required a substantial investment in and attention to acquiring the appropriate possessions. Nowhere did the material expression of polite and commercial culture exert its pull more than in the equipping and furnishing of private homes for the merchant elite. An inventory taken in May 1748 on the death of one of the builders of Long Wharf illustrates some of the changes taking place in Massachusetts. Anthony Stoddard, a merchant and judge, gained prominent connections through his marriage in 1705 to Martha Belcher, daughter of the leading grain trader and sister of a future governor.[12] After eight years at Harvard, Stoddard chose not to follow his famous uncle Solomon into the ministry but to join his father-in-law and grandfather in trade.[13] At the time of his death, Anthony Stoddard owned four warehouses and many thousands of acres of land in Massachusetts, Connecticut, and Maine.[14] Although his brick mansion on King Street contained both a shop and a warehouse, Stoddard exemplifies the occasional merchant who transformed himself from active trader into passive investor.[15] At the time of his death, all four of his warehouses were leased to others, and no evidence exists of his investment in ships.[16]

Extensive gardens surrounded Stoddard's mansion, reflecting the eighteenth-century interest in strolling through a manicured landscape as a leisure activity for men and women.[17] His home and its furnishings attested to prosperity. Inside the Stoddard mansion, a new emphasis on dining and partaking of hot beverages, and a much larger investment in furniture, distinguished Stoddard's personal belongings from Henry Shrimpton's collection of goods a century before. No longer were the most expensive items centered around the bedstead.[18] In fact, Stoddard's most valuable belonging was a "large clock with a fenered [veneered] case" worth £120. The clock with its tall angular case and silvered face personified a masculine patriarchal figure intent on counting and measuring time, and gaining a measure of control over nature—a primary goal for transatlantic shipping merchants. Most eighteenth-century tall case clocks provided information critical to anyone involved in oceangoing ventures, such as phases of the moon and tidal variations.[19] The wealthy trader Thomas Hancock ordered a London-made clock with "3 figures viz. Fame, Peace, & Plenty,.. Well proportioned & Guilt with burnish'd Gold" atop the case.[20] His decorations represented icons of merchant life: "fame," that is, in a widespread reputation for credit, skill, and solvency; "peace," so as to avoid wartime interruptions in trade; and "plenty" of goods to ship as well as "plenty" across the land to support strong demand, all of which equaled "plenty" of profit in the merchant's pocket. The heart of the tall case clock, the pendulum—a product of efforts to improve oceanic navigation—permitted the first measurement of seconds; from then on, clocks remained closely connected to merchant, and later industrial, capitalism.

Stoddard's front room, used for entertaining, contained the latest in fashionable items, including a large looking-glass and four glass sconces; a large round table and a small oval table displayed "China bowles" and tureens imported from the Far East. These possessions reinforced Stoddard's standing as a polite and commercial gentleman. In Stoddard's bedchamber, his bed hangings included a white calico quilt, again an Asian import, and an elegant high chest with twelve drawers.[21] The windows were dressed with four "diaper window Curtains" and two "valens," suggesting symmetrical sash windows. Pictures painted on glass of Queen Mary and Prince George, various mezzotints, and portraits of Admiral Shovell, King Charles II, and Admiral Russell adorned the walls. Stoddard's dressing ritual, like that of the dandified Samuel Shrimpton Jr., took place before a dressing table and looking-glass. The bedchamber closet held several "burnt Scollopt and pudding dishes" suggesting that the Stoddards ate informal meals in their bedchamber. During these relaxed hours, Stoddard would have forsaken his wig and worn his elegant and expensive "Damask Silk [dressing] gown" and cap.[22] Attention to furnishings and housewares set the stage for private socializing.

Stoddard's possessions gained importance by virtue of the attributes they conferred on the owner. Through advertising and personal display, merchants succeeded in coupling the idea of a particular and novel item—calico fabric, à la mode dress, japanned dressing tables—with a generalized concept of the fashionable. In terms of the values of a polite and commercial culture, "fashionable" implied a visibly refined and superior character. By these measures, Stoddard was refined indeed.[23]

The economic prowess of leading merchants allowed them to exert their civic and social influence while simultaneously refashioning the image of commercial men. Stoddard was one of a mercantile elite in Boston and Salem that defined itself in part by its attention to and interest in fashionable possessions. The commercial elite included royally appointed officials such as the customs officers Benjamin Hallowell Sr. and Jr., and rising professionals like the attorney William Pynchon or the merchant turned chief justice Jacob Wendell. Many of these men gathered at genteel social events, served together as public officials, founded charitable organizations, and established joint business ventures. Members of the Lincolnshire Land Company, who shared investments in large tracts of land in Maine, included Stoddard, Wendell, members of the Waldo merchant family, Stephen Minot, John Jeffries, and James Bowdoin. Many of these men or their families had earlier invested in the construction of Long Wharf and continued to associate in other financial ventures. As leading merchants, they occupied most of the important town offices in Boston and Salem. In 1740 prominent local officials came from many of the principal merchant families: Stoddard, Jeffries, Hancock, Wendell, Hutchinson, Belcher, Oliver, and Hallowell. Men from these families headed the list of elected offices such as selectman and overseer of the poor, and served as representatives from Boston to the the General Court. Jonathan Belcher, son of infamous grain dealer Andrew Belcher, served as royally appointed governor for a decade. The Council, the upper house of the General Court, counted many leading merchants as members including William Browne and John Turner from Salem, and James Otis Sr. from Barnstable; several merchants also accepted appointment as judges of county and provincial courts. They gathered in voluntary associations that combined civic and social purposes; the Wendell, Bromfield, Greene, and Hancock families joined the wealthy merchants Peter Faneuil and Charles Apthorp as supporters of the Boston Episcopal Charity Society, and many, including the customs official Benjamin Hallowell, belonged to the venerable Ancient and Honorable Artillery Company, an exclusive private military company and social club. These men and their families played a central role in bringing Georgian gentility to Massachusetts.[24]

A more public aspect of Georgian gentility appeared as local merchants and professionals adopted the urban architecture and suburban villas of merchants in London and the provinces. Earlier in the century, Boston and Salem merchants had transformed their cities by constructing an infrastructure of wharves, warehouses, and roads to support expanding trade. In midcentury, merchants, with the participation of professionals and royal officials, once again transformed the urban landscape. Borrowing from and adapting English models, they recast Boston and Salem into provincial Georgian towns.

In the metropolis a partnership of aristocratic landholders and commercially oriented speculative builders began to erect the famous Hanoverian squares of London's West End.[25] In 1724, Daniel Defoe, noting the wondrous changes, observed, "new squares and new streets rising up every day to such a prodigy of buildings, that nothing in the world does, or ever did equal it, except old Rome in Trajan's time."[26] One of the earliest real estate developments, dating from the late seventeenth century, grew out of the schemes of Nicholas Barbon, the economic writer and entrepreneur who promoted fashionable change as the foundation of commercial growth. Barbon, in partnership with an aristocratic landowner, the Earl of Southampton, leased and demolished a number of Tudor palaces along the Strand to build "affordable housing," creating a neighborhood of "noble streets and beautiful houses."[27] However, one critic lamented the changes as the area acquired "taverns, alehouses, cookshops, and vaulting schools." In another project, the aristocratic Sidney family, living primarily on their country estates in Kent, began the residential development of Soho from what had been their London garden and hunting preserve. Barbon, a part of this undertaking also, teamed with Lord Gerrard to develop Gerrard Street in Soho, home to artists and writers who gathered at the famous Turk's Head Coffeehouse.[28] Huguenot refugees from France also congregated in Soho; the area drew fashionable tenants such as Sir Isaac Newton, Sir Joshua Reynolds, and other artists, musicians, taverners, and master tradesmen and their workshops. Numerous affiliations between titled noblemen and builders on the make continued to expand and develop not only the genteel enclaves of the West End, known as the "polite" end of town, but also suburban villages like Marlybone, Kensington, and Islington. In the 1780s, a Prussian visitor, von Archenholz, noted of the West End, "the houses here are mostly new and elegant; the squares are superb, the streets straight and open—If all London were as well built, there would be nothing in the world to compare with it."[29]

Boston, too, had its West End. Wealthy Bostonian merchants such as the Faneuils and Hancocks chose to build their mansions on the outskirts of the city, away from their wharves and warehouses.[30] Many his-

torians of the eighteenth century, clinging to the concept of "the walking
city" where wealthy merchants lived over their warehouses next to the
docks, and poor and rich inhabited the same streets, have underestimated the rapidity with which provincial elites began to move out of the city
center in Anglo-America. Roy Porter asserts that "early in the century
provincial towns were still too small to support spatial elaboration. . . .
Class-segregated suburbs had not yet developed. . . . London was the
sole exception." But as we saw, seventeenth-century Salem already had
neighborhoods based on ethnic and occupational divisions that certainly
had class implications. A study of Newcastle-upon-Tyne finds the "principal residents," many of whom were merchants, leaving the lower town
and relocating in the more socially desirable uphill districts early in the
century. In his research on the "Urban Renaissance" Peter Borsay found
that "in post-Restoration Leeds the gentlemen merchants vacated the
main commercial street Briggate, for a district towards the south-eastern
edge of the town."[31]

In 1737, Thomas Hancock built his imposing Georgian house on the
Boston's Beacon Hill, while not a fully developed residential area like
London's West End, showed the hallmarks of an exclusive neighborhood. John Hull had built his home in the 1670s at the base of the hill facing the town but well away from the center of trade.[32] Later, in 1711, the
Faneuil mansion rose nearby, its gardens leading upward behind the
residence to a hilltop gazebo. Beyond the Faneuils, Beacon Street (hill
and street were named for the beacon at the summit kept lighted for sea-
farers) led past another fine three-story house built in 1722 by the merchant Edward Bromfield, who also designed a terraced garden capped
by a summerhouse "with a panoramic view of the harbor."[33]

In 1737, Thomas Hancock built his imposing Georgian house on the
south side of the hill, using his trading contacts to order the most fashionable tile, wallpaper, and custom-made furniture from London.[34] At
midcentury John Singleton Copley, would-be gentleman and favored
portraitist of New England's commercial nabobs, constructed a home
near the Hancocks. Attempting to replicate the styles of genteel England,
Copley added turned balusters, carved chimney breasts (fire surrounds),
a china closet, and classical arches all fashioned "in the best manner."
One architectural historian speculated on the impact of Hancock's residence, exclaiming that "nothing like it had been seen in the northern
colonies; it was of solid granite, with paneled walls and damask curtains, and brilliant carpets." While this author may have underestimated
the splendors already adopted by Boston's polite and commercial society, Hancock's edifice definitely made a powerful statement of economic and social mastery. A census of housing in America taken at the end of

the eighteenth century (1798) showed that only 15 percent of Americans lived in any kind of "two-story structure[s] fashioned out of permanent materials with differentiated rooms, a stairway, a brick chimney, and glazed windows." By contrast, these large two-and three-story, center-hall, twin-chimneyed Georgian brick or granite homes must have had a strong impact on those who viewed them.[35]

Salem experienced a similar transformation. Travelers described the town, with a population of about thirty-five hundred to forty-five hundred in the mideighteenth century, as a "pritty place" and "a large Town, well built." "One very long street, running nearly east and west" contained "many genteel large houses (which tho' of wood) are all plastered on the outside in Imitation of Hewn Stone," or "plan[e]d and Painted."[36] Each house "Covers a Great Deal of Ground, being at a Convenient Distance from Each Other, with fine Gardens back [of] their houses."[37]

Members of Salem's codfish aristocracy imported and modified Georgian architecture within a smaller urban landscape than Boston's. The successful trader Timothy Orne and other leading merchants built new and stylish mansions on Essex Street, just west of the civic and social center of town. Previously the most prestigious block in town lay on the east side of Town House Square, where the prominent Browne family lived and Governor Simon Bradstreet's gabled Tudor-style mansion stood until 1753; the site is now occupied by the Essex Institute. While William Browne's residence was still considered the finest house in town in 1760, the elite neighborhood was shifting slightly westward, first to Essex Street and later, in the nineteenth century, one block south and west to Chestnut Street, lined with federal-style mansions of merchants in the China trade.[38] Like other overseas traders, Orne located his home a few blocks from his warehouses and wharves on Town Cove. Along Essex Street, several of Orne's friends and fellow merchants occupied substantial homes including young Benjamin Pickman, Frances and Joseph Cabot, and Samuel Gardner. Supreme Court Justice Benjamin Lynde, the customs official John Higginson (grandson of the venerable minister), and the attorney William Pynchon also lived nearby. From their attractive homes, leading merchants could see Town House Square with the Court House and behind it First Church, and easily walk to the nearby Assembly House for social events.

A close physical resemblance between Boston's, Salem's and London's West Ends would not appear until the early nineteenth century when the well-traveled Boston architect Charles Bullfinch and his investment partners leveled off the peak of Beacon Hill and transformed the area

FIGURE 4. Timothy Orne's house, built in 1763 on Essex Street in Salem. Photograph courtesy of the Peabody Essex Museum.

from single-family mansions with individual gardens to symmetrically facaded terrace (row) houses surrounding park-like greens, such as Louisburg Square or Boston Common. Terraces, squares, and crescents like those in London and Bath began to appear all over the British Isles and British North America, especially, according to one architectural historian, "in the more rapidly expanding towns including the ports of Bristol and Hull"—and Philadelphia, Savannah, and the two main ports of Massachusetts.[39] Well-to-do New Englanders building commodious houses in the West End of eighteenth-century Boston or on Essex Street in Salem were participating in an Anglo-American urban renaissance, just as surely as the residents of London's Grosvenor Square.[40]

Many of the decorative and fashionable items owned by Anthony Stoddard and others of the Boston and Salem gentry originated not in England but in Europe or Asia. A la mode clothing designs featured French and Italian silks or Indian calicoes. Wallpaper began in France, and most designs retained elements of French scenes or patterned French toile. During the early decades of the eighteenth century, japanning—lacquering furniture with glossy ebony accented by dashes of vermilion and gold—signified the height of elegance; Stoddard, for example, completed his toilette at a "Japan Dressing Table" furnished with "one Japan dressing box with a nest of boxes and brushes."[41] Several of his rooms contained china bowls, teapots, and dishes. The daily ritual of teatime was based exclusively on foreign products—cups, saucers, and teapots from China, tea from East Asia, and sugar from the Caribbean. Demand for these products drove British imperial trade. Repeatedly, foreign goods were transformed into fashionable markers of genteel status, creating tremendous profits for merchants and embedding mercantile capitalism in the minutiae of social relations.[42] This is not to say that gentility and the fashion system were simply the product of a clever capitalist marketing scheme, but rather that through broad cultural transformations possessions displaced providence and took on a new importance in fashioning individual identity, defining economic and social relations, and shaping cultural expressions.[43]

Altered relationships to material artifacts and the changing urban landscape not only provided new sources of value, but also shaped new forms of self-identity and led to a redrawing of social boundaries. An increasing emphasis on visible wealth offered a pathway for successful merchants of non-English descent to enter the elite circles of colonial communities.[44] Merchants in the transatlantic trade played a key role in this cultural transformation by shipping Western and Asian commodities, bringing the latest English consumer goods to their warehouses and shops, building mansion houses and pleasure gardens, investing in modern wharves and streets, and financing public buildings and churches. These men and their families also played a critical role by acquiring and displaying high-style possessions as part of the circulation of goods.

In Salem, Boston, and other New England seaports, the penetration of capitalism and its emphasis on individual achievement created a social marketplace where wealth, possessions, and good manners could purchase a place in the highest circles. A transformation from Puritan ideals of a closed community to a world of goods fostered a greater acceptance of other Europeans and other believers, at least those who had the money to adopt the accoutrements of Georgian gentility. Puritans and their descendents were not the only groups to resent strangers. English dramas of the eighteenth-century sported stock characters such as "French fops, adventuring Irishmen, ridiculous Italians and bullying Spaniards."[45] Increasingly, European sojourners joined the English middle class and the Massachusetts merchant elite. Arriving in Salem in the early eighteenth century, "French" Jerseymen like Francis and Joseph Cabot joined in economic and social ventures with men bearing a long Anglo-American heritage. The Cabots were partners with Timothy Orne, grandson of a Puritan deacon, and other long-time Salemites in business ventures and in gentlemen's clubs. The Crowninshields, a family of German origin, who captained vessels for Orne and the Pickmans, also made their way into the Salem gentry. Not everyone accepted the changing boundaries of elite status. One of the Brownes, member of the former first family of Salem, caricatured Francis Cabot in a satirical verse as "a little Fretful man / Whose ease consists in scolding when he can." The same poet referred to the Crowninshields as "base Plebians" of "the Vulgar Race." His must have been a minority voice since the Crowninshields and Cabots were very much a part of the social rounds detailed in gentry diaries during the 1760s and 1770s.[46]

The story of the Faneuil family of Boston illustrates the extent of cultural change in colonial Massachusetts. Unlike Philip English, continuously pushed to the margins of seventeenth-century Salem because of his "French" origins and Anglican faith, the Faneuils, a Huguenot family arriving in New England a generation later, joined the Anglican Church and the eighteenth-century Boston elite by adopting the possessions and manners characteristic of English gentility. The cultural authority of visible wealth exerted such cachet that the Faneuils did not find it necessary to anglicize their name or obscure their origins. Instead they placed the family surname in the very center of eighteenth-century Boston—and in twentieth-century tourist guides as well.

The Faneuils came to America as part of the Huguenot emigration to Holland, England, and the Dutch and English colonies overseas.[47] In February 1692, the Massachusetts General Court drew up a list of "persons of the French nation admitted into the colony."[48] Among those named, three brothers from a merchant family in La Rochelle, Andrew, Benjamin, and John Faneuil, had arrived in Boston by way of Holland.[49] John soon returned to France. Benjamin settled in New Rochelle, New York. Andrew remained in Boston. Through marriage, the family allied itself to prominent Huguenot, Thomas Bureau, who established himself as a major London merchant and, with an investment of five hundred pounds, in 1694 became a founder of the Bank of England.[50] The Faneuil brothers quickly developed trading networks with their relatives in England, Holland, and France.[51] Andrew married a French woman, but the couple remained childless. In New York, Benjamin and Anne Faneuil gave birth to six children—two sons followed by four daughters.[52]

Upon the death of Benjamin Faneuil in New Rochelle, his sons Peter and Benjamin Jr. moved to Boston, where they trained as merchants under their uncle Andrew.[53] The elder Faneuil built up a substantial fortune during his years in Boston. Very few of Andrew Faneuil's business records remain to indicate precisely how he accomplished this. References in contemporary accounts continue to refer to Faneuil as a merchant, so presumably trade provided the bulk of his profits. He also began to purchase real estate in Boston. In 1703, he purchased a half-interest in a brick house on King Street (now State Street) and six months later purchased the other half of the house.[54] Nathaniel Oliver, a well-connected merchant, sold Faneuil an investment property of seven houses and land on a prime location at the corner of Cornhill and King Street near the Town House. In the 1730s, Faneuil bought and sold several wharves and warehouses including Oliver's Dock and a warehouse on Long Wharf. His main warehouse stood in one of the most advantageous commercial locations at the corner of Merchant's Row and King Street opposite the Bunch-of-Grapes Tavern, much frequented by merchants and ship captains. Unlike the City merchants of London, Faneuil and other colonial traders owned their own commercial property; Faneuil acquired a significant stake in downtown Boston.[55]

In 1711, Andrew Faneuil acquired a stone house and land on Tremont Street at the western edge of town, which he proceeded to fashion into a three-story mansion surrounded by seven acres of landscaped gardens.[56] Faneuil's house can be seen on contemporary maps and prints where it appears as a large, three-story, hip-roofed structure fronted with an arched gateway and fence (see map 4, p. 85). A member of the Quincy family of Boston remembered "the deep court-yard ornamented by flowers and shrubs, . . . surmounted by a richly wrought iron railing decorated with gilt balls." The mansion was "brick, painted white" and the entrance framed by "a semi-circular balcony." The memoirist described the hall and apartments as "elegantly furnished" and recalled "terraces, which rose from the paved court behind the house." From his elegant mansion, Faneuil simply crossed the street to attend services at King's Chapel, the first Anglican church in Boston. Although he provided generously in his will for the French Church, he regularly attended King's Chapel and supported the building of a second Anglican church in 1734.[57]

When Andrew Faneuil died in February 1738, the local press noted that "this Gentleman's Fortune was the greatest of any among us." A grand funeral, "as generous and expensive as any that has been known here," paid homage not only to his success in commerce but to the dramatic cultural changes evident in Boston. The *Boston News-Letter* of 23 February 1738 described "above 1,100 persons of all Ranks, besides the Mourners, following the Corpse; also a vast number of Spectators were gathered together on the Occasion." As in Samuel Shrimpton's rites in 1698, guns fired to honor the wealthy merchant. The family reportedly distributed three thousand pairs of mourning gloves and sent two hundred mourning rings to close friends and relations in New England, England, Holland, and France.[58]

No inventory of Andrew's possessions remains to tell us the precise extent of the fortune his nephew Peter inherited. But when Peter died just five years later at the age of forty-two, he left an estate valued at £44,453 in Massachusetts money or £7,557 sterling.[59] Peter Faneuil maintained or improved on his uncle's assets by aggressively pursuing commercial strategies, setting up fishing stations in Newfoundland, and maintaining broad overseas connections with merchants in Amsterdam and La Rochelle. During his brief reign as head of the family, he maintained its reputation for acquiring riches.[60]

Peter Faneuil lost no time after his uncle's death in enjoying his newly acquired riches. He and his sister Mary Ann, who lived with him in the family mansion, began to refurbish the interior and participate in a fashionable lifestyle. From his agents in London, he ordered a plentiful supply of china and glassware and one dozen each of silver-handled knives, forks, and spoons, "having the Crest of my Armes cutt on each of them." He enclosed "the Impression of the Armes that the goldsmith may take the Crest of" and also ordered a "Large handsome Lanthorn to hang in an Entry way."[61] A year after his uncle's death, Faneuil turned to the Boston upholsterer and dry goods merchant Samuel Grant, whose customers included other leading merchants like Thomas Hancock, Colonel Jacob Wendell, and the Orne family of Salem. Faneuil ordered several expensive and stylish pieces of upholstered furniture from Grant including "1 Elbow chair cov'd with Cha. [China silk]." He also requested six "Large chairs," twelve leather chairs, and two "Compass chairs [with rounded seats]." The following year, Faneuil ordered three dozen leather chairs and an "Easie Chair [wing chair] of morocco Leather and Callico Case [slip cover]." His expenditure of twenty pounds for the "Easie Chair" cost more than many less fortunate Bostonians could earn in a year. Faneuil did not confine his luxurious expenditures to interiors alone. A few months after receiving his inheritance, he ordered a "chariot" and two harnesses from London. At his death in 1743, he left "1 Chariot" valued at £400, one coach, a two-wheel chaise, a "4 Wheel

FIGURE 5. Peter Faneuil, by John Smibert, 1739. Courtesy of the
Massachusetts Historical Society.

FIGURE 6. Mary Ann Faneuil (Peter's sister), by John Smibert, 1739. Mary
Ann helped to entertain guests at the family mansion. Courtesy of the
Massachusetts Historical Society.

Chaise at £150," and fourteen harnesses valued at £770.[62] Frenchman Peter Faneuil rode through the streets in style—English style.

The inventory of Peter Faneuil's estate reveals an extensive collection of opulent furnishings. In the parlor, guests, called to tea by the chimes of an eight-day walnut case clock, sat on "Carved Fineerd [veneered] Chairs and [a] Couch" gathered around a marble table, and all arrayed on a Turkey carpet from Anatolia. Faneuil and his sister, dressed in English fashions and assisted by a black slave from Africa, served tea from East India, sweetened with sugar from the Caribbean, in "Cupps, Saucers, Tea Pott, Stand, Bowl, and Sugar Dish," from China.[63] These foreign goods transported by merchants were then transfigured, by the ritual of teatime, into the defining symbols of English gentility. Through an assemblage of goods and learned performances Peter Faneuil transformed himself from Huguenot descendant into Georgian gentleman.

Faneuil and other elite merchants exercised power and influence through displays of wealth and by rebuilding the local townscape. But their influence penetrated urban society in less visible ways as well. Connected with all levels of society through economic relations, traders wove a web of mutual obligation. Using surplus profits, some of the most successful merchants not only offered credit to those who worked for them and to local consumers, but also extended loans of large and small amounts to townsmen and sometimes throughout the region.

One figure, Salem's foremost merchant Timothy Orne, extended his financial network throughout eastern Massachusetts. As his various businesses grew, his reputation for good commercial practices—that is, his credit in both senses of the word—spread well beyond Salem. Orne exercised his influence and reinvested his capital in the regional economy through an extensive private banking enterprise, and in so doing, Orne made a major contribution to the development of capital markets in the inland economy of Massachusetts. One of the most significant private bankers in pre-Revolutionary Massachusetts, he loaned money at the legal maximum of 6 percent per year as set by British law. He extended loans from as little as six pounds to amounts over two hundred pounds to numerous individuals in towns throughout Essex and neighboring counties. He used the greater security and smaller rate of return to offset the risk of overseas trade.[64] The emergence of capital markets, often considered a mark of modern capitalism, occurred even as book credit remained the primary means of accounting for debts and credits. The wide reach of Orne's loans paralleled the midcentury availability of all capital funds in Worcester county, as calculated by historian Winifred Rothenberg, and exceeded the indicators for rural Massachusetts until after the Revolution, an impressive achievement for a single individual. Mapping Orne's banking activities highlights the economic power of leading merchants.[65]

The extent of Orne's economic relationships underlay the power of his cultural influence. In 1765, for example, Orne loaned at interest a total of £2,020 to thirty-three different people in Salem.[66] In Salem Village, established as the town of Danvers in 1760, thirty-two inhabitants owed Orne a total of £2,124. Another thirty-five of Orne's borrowers, owing principal amounts from £15 to £150, lived in the farm communities of Topsfield, Boxford, and Middleton. His customers for loans included twenty-nine borrowers from the inland towns of Andover and Wenham and the ports of Beverly, Ipswich, Lynn, Marblehead, Gloucester, and Newbury. Orne's regional orbit of capital flow reached to towns northwest of Boston like Reading and Medford and stretched as far west as Shrewsbury (near Worcester) and Lebanon, Connecticut, and as far north as Wells, Maine. Orne invested almost £9,000 in the people of Massachusetts. To what extent this increased the productive power of the local and regional economy is impossible to determine, but it certainly established Orne as a power center and perhaps increased the demand for overseas products within his sphere of economic influence. These financial relations, and the profits they reaped, supported Orne's ability to transform economic capital into cultural capital.

Employing local fishermen and artisans and purchasing supplies from nearby farms and sawmills also helped to extend Orne's personal influence and economic clout through Salem and surrounding communities. John Brewer uses the phrase "client economy" to describe the web of credit relationships between artisans and their patrician customers in England.[67] Craftsmen and women depended for their livelihood on the wealthy as consumers. In turn, aristocratic patrons expected long-term credit from artisan-producers. Without a broader base of consumers and an alternative source of credit, economic transactions remained tied to social relationships. Brewer's analysis of English practice applies to the colonies too. In a recent book exploring the radical nature of social change during the American revolutionary era, Gordon Wood characterizes the social structure of eighteenth-century America as a world of patronage. "Personal relationships of dependence, usually taking the form of those between patrons and clients, constituted the ligaments that held this society together and made it work."[68] Consequently, deference was tied closely to economic well-being. Orne's ledger reveals these re-

lationships at work. Covering the 1740s, the account book details economic exchanges with over 272 individuals, ranging from correspondent merchant Gedney Clarke Esq. who sold whole cargoes in Barbados,
to "simster" (seamstress) Rachel Pippen (who purchased small quantities of rum), or shipwright Samuel Bacon who took sugar and a set of
oars in payment for his labor.[69] Most of the accounts involved an exchange of products running over several years, with the balance sometimes in favor of the purchaser, who may have just delivered a large load
of fish or farm products, and sometimes in favor of Orne. The most frequently purchased items included sugar, rum, and salt (in that order),
and the most common forms of payment included barrels of fish or labor
for Orne. Those who supplied Orne's requirements for overseas voyages—providing fish to sell in the West Indies and Spain or building and
repairing his many vessels—carried the largest balances. Philip Sanders,
a baker, purchased sugar, rum, cloth, and flour, and paid with bread to
provision Orne's ships. George Deland, a local dock worker, purchased
rum, cloth, and small sums of money from Orne and repaid his debts
with fish. Beverly cooper Isaac Dodge paid for his salt, rum, sugar, and
cloth with kegs for shipping liquids.

Fish supplanted scarce paper money and specie in Salem. A few customers paid Orne in money; many more paid in fish, helping to supply
the substantial quantities needed to support his trade with Spain and the
West Indies. Orne owned his own fishing boats and also purchased fish
from shoremen Charles King of Salem and Christian Bubier and David
Furniss of Marblehead. All of these men maintained accounts reckoned
in hundreds of pounds (£515 to £834), substantial amounts when a simple laborer might earn only twenty pounds a year.

As part owner of over fifty vessels during his career, Orne, like other
leading merchants, kept a number of blacksmiths, shipwrights, rope-
makers, and coopers busy building and repairing his vessels. He seemed
to rely most heavily or expensively on blacksmith Jon Mansfield of
Lynn, ordering over one thousand pounds of nails in the course of a few
years. Boston ropemaker Edward Gray traded his cable for Orne's
hemp, while Samuel Field, a boatbuilder from Salem, built small boats in
return for salt, sugar, rum, and foodstuffs. Local instrument maker
Daniel King and goldsmith Joseph Gardner fashioned astronomical
equipment, buckles, and metal fittings for many vessels, for which Orne
paid them in rum—the other local currency—as well as sugar farm
products and cash. Connected by exchange relationships that often continued for many years, Orne stood poised at the center of an extensive

agricultural and industrial complex through which capital and commodities flowed.

Patronage alone does not capture the complexity of social and commercial relationships in Timothy Orne's range of businesses. His retail
trade, which combined extensive barter with occasional cash payments,
represented face-to-face transactions shaped by ideas of creditworthi-
ness as well as client-patron obligations. A merchant or his clerks had to
record a price for each item credited or debited, thereby establishing a
precise unitary value to represent barrels of cod or scoops of sugar. The
process of agreeing on a value for goods purchased and sold included a
complex negotiation between overseas prices and local consensus.

In Orne's insurance business, and in his role as a local banker, we see
what might be characterized as a rational approach to investment, one
less exclusively dependent on patron-client relationships than the trades
most historians have focused on. Regardless of how well Orne knew a
borrower or ship captain, he lent only relatively small amounts and carried only a portion of the insurance risk.[70] The symmetrical columns list-
ing his insurance contracts for 1761 reveal a shift in emphasis from personal to impersonal relationships under the influence of the market in
risk. Each entry indicates a claim, a possession, a monetary interest related to but separate from social ties. Relations of patronage and friendship that bound Orne to his favored ship captain Jacob Crowninshield
are, in the insurance records, reduced to a simple entry: "—60—
Crowninshield—11P—6.12—," which means that Orne insured £60
worth of a voyage of Crowninshield's at the rate of 11 percent for a pre-
mium of £6 12s. The name, bracketed by numbers, diagrams a social relationship bracketed, that is set aside, by market relations and the possibility of profit. But few of the names on the insurance rosters of 1761 are
among Orne's merchant and ship captain partners or among the leading
mercantile families of Salem. Absent are the familiar names of Lee,
Gardner, Lynde, Lovett, and Pickman. Nor do they appear as customers
or employees in Orne's ledger of the 1740s and 1750s. The names in the
account books signify not personal or patronage relationships but rather
monetary transactions, arbitrary units in the market of risk transactions.
Here capital, rather than the personal influence wielded between patron
and client, gave Orne his power. Yet much of his capital was contingent
on personal relations with Salem's and Boston's leading merchants and
ship captains, and his on patronage of local artisans and fishermen. So
Orne, like other Massachusetts merchants, depended on both personal
and business relationships to support his economic and social credit.[71]

He inhabited a world that defined social identity by wealth, accumulation, and display at the expense of traditional relationships among kin and among a body of Christian believers. In Orne's universe, economic and social relationships were interwoven in a complicated mix that served to reinforce the eighteenth-century world of goods and accentuated exterior, rational, material sources of authority and value.

Other forms of patron-client relationships altered during this period. The Puritan ideal of community had required Massachusetts towns to take care of their less fortunate Christian brethren. However, under the pressure of growing population, economic difficulties, and cultural transformation, charity evolved into genteel benevolence toward a more impersonal category of "the poor." The phrase "objects of charity,"[72] used repeatedly in eighteenth-century Boston, expressed a world of meaning. Placing another person in the position of object implies a power relationship in which the person giving charity exerts control over the recipient. The refugees and the growing ranks of impoverished widows, laborers, and artisans in eighteenth-century Boston, like the Jersey French in early Salem, lived "outside the walls," but for different reasons and within a different social matrix.

Having appropriated the authority to change the spatial environment by building port facilities and designing elegant buildings for social gatherings, the merchant elite of Boston and Salem also took on a measure of obligation to care for the "deserving" poor. In the process, they reinforced their status and distanced themselves from the supplicants. No longer were rich and poor subject equally to God's benevolence or judgment. Now, successful merchants and their ministers worked as God's appointed agents in dispensing charity and overseeing poor relief.[73] Operating from a very different understanding than that shown in early Puritan calls for Christian charity, wealthy donors and their recipients no longer shared a full belief in subjection to God's providence. Instead, they often stood on opposite sides of a gulf shaped as much by men as by God. Commercial success, no longer conceived as a blessing from God, instead provided a source of gifts to God.[74]

Ministering to many of Boston's leading merchants at his Brattle Street Church, Benjamin Colman expressed this eighteenth-century "enlightened" view quite clearly.[75] In a sermon of 1736 titled *The Merchandise of a People; Holiness to the Lord*, he asked rhetorically, "Shall not your Merchandize and your Hire be Holiness to the Lord?"[76] In a paean to the benefits of trade and commerce (seventeenth-century Puritans would have referred to God's blessings), Colman asserted that "the Knowledge of Christ has been propagated by Trade far and near." Echoing Dudley

North's praise of fashion, he proclaimed that "commerce . . . enlarges Peoples Hearts to do generous Things, for the Support of Divine Worship and Relief of the Poor."[77] Here, it is not God but commerce that enlarges men's hearts. Contrast this with John Hull's expressions of wonder at God's gifts, or with Cotton Mather's sermon on "Durable Riches" delivered in 1695, and the magnitude of change becomes clear. Mather, a transitional figure to be sure, remarked "that when Riches do without any Interruption flow in upon us, we grow but the more Hungry and Craving after them; . . . Tis well therefore that our God, Orders now and then a Loss for us."[78] For Mather and his followers, riches and losses "flow" from God to humans, not from humans to God or the needy. One generation later, Colman and his congregation found agency and power not in the supernatural but in the skillful practices and careful accounting of shrewd traders.[79]

Merchants responded to ministerial calls for philanthropy, sensing the dual role charitable gifts fulfilled, both marking the donors as men of importance, affluence, and generosity, and ameliorating growing social problems.[80] In Boston, successful merchants consistently served as overseers of the poor.[81] Overseers and visitors in the early decades included members of the Hutchinson, Clark, Brattle, Cushing, Pitts, Palmer, Stoddard, Walley, and Bromfield families, all involved in significant trading ventures and drawing funds and social prominence from commerce. By selecting them, the townspeople may have hoped to put their most affluent citizens under obligation to contribute to town relief.[82] The office also provided a platform for merchants to act out their benevolence in very visible ways: visiting the poor, constructing and supervising almshouses and workhouses, and dispensing "outdoor" relief to destitute widows and families.[83] Every three months, a small group of overseers, accompanied by a constable, walked through each ward of Boston "to Inspect, Prevent, and Suppress Disorders" in poor neighborhoods and give alms.[84] Historian Christine Heyrman characterizes this street procession as a "theater of legitimation" where the merchant elite "could begin to exhibit their authority, to exact deference, and to establish monuments to their cultural hegemony."[85]

Initially, the justices, selectmen, and overseers of the poor joined to visit various quarters of Boston "in Order to prevent & redress disorders." These inspections included all "the Familyes of this Town," but by the 1760s the leading men concentrated their visits on poor families and charity schools. During one midcentury observation, the merchant and overseer John Rowe noted that "the Selectmen paid a visit to one Mary Phillips who was born Deaf and Dumb and has remained so ever since and is now upwards of 80 years of age." He does not mention that Mary received funds, but commonly these visits were the primary method of dispensing outdoor relief to the indigent. The overwhelming majority of overseers of the poor chosen by the town of Boston continued to come from the ranks of elite mercantile families. In the 1760s Rowe was joined by mercantile colleagues such as Ezekial Goldthwait, Colonel Brattle, and Nicholas Boylston. When they undertook their annual visitation of the schools in Boston, the assemblage of gentlemen expanded with the addition of "a Number of the Ministers of the Town and Country" and "a Number of other Gentlemen."[86]

The parade of gentlemen who bestowed alms and evaluated young scholars had a deeper symbolic meaning for the eighteenth-century denizens of urban centers. The contrast in appearance between gentlemen schooled in polite manners and garbed in elaborate wigs, velvet coats, and embroidered vests, and the destitute and handicapped men, women, and children on the charity rolls reinforced the cultural values of a polite and commercial people. Not only could the elite congratulate themselves on their success, thrown into relief by lower class surroundings, but they could also feel the warmth of giving their time, attention, and money to those less fortunate than themselves.[87]

Viewed as a social drama, visitations of the poor provided a moment in which difference, although seemingly overcome through an act of giving, also produced a form of class consciousness. The very term 'overseer of the poor' implied an upper class looking down on, and taking charge of, a lower sort. To reinforce their position as a privileged elite, the Boston "visitors" would retire to a "Genteel Entertainment" at Faneuil Hall where Rowe recalled that "we all dined together . . . and everything went on with Pleasure &c" for the seventy gentlemen joining the dinner in 1768. Symbolic forms and rituals like visiting the poor molded interpretations of economic and social divisions.[88]

Benevolence sometimes took precedence over personal gain. In distributing funds collected from England and the colonies for the relief of those suffering from Boston's great fire of 1760, the overseers of the poor and selectmen gave money first to the "Widows, 2nd to the Tradesmen, and 3rd to the Middling People." The officials in charge of apportioning charity met more than one hundred times during an eighteen-month period to choose recipients and disperse monies. Leading merchants accounted for the largest portion of the one hundred thousand pounds lost in the fire as it destroyed "Houses, Stores, Merchandizes, and Furniture." The merchant and judge Jacob Wendell sustained damages of four thousand, eight hundred pounds in buildings, wharves, and ships, and thirteen others claimed damages of more that one thousand pounds. But a benevolent awareness of need and a consciousness of status obligations meant that "the Rich had none from the collection." Once again, generosity reinforced the privileged position of prosperous gentry.

A debate in the Boston newspapers in 1728 sheds more light on economic divisions. As the record of fire relief to "the Middling People" attests, there was a middle class in Boston; it was comprised, in part, of small merchants in local trade and a large number of artisans who manufactured goods both for the populace and for shipment to the Caribbean. Building, repairing, and outfitting trading vessels supported many craftspeople. Three different budgets designed for "Families of a Middling Figure" were published, each purporting to calculate the annual expenses for a family of nine. The median budget came to £244 17s. 1d., but this figure omitted costs for housing and fuel as well as excluding expenses for "the Tea table, the Coffee-cup, the Chocolate bowl, . . . and several sorts of Fruits foreign and domestick." These desirables, "tho' expensive," are the "Comforts of humane Life." By comparison, a maid's annual wages (probably including room and board) were computed at £11 per year and a journeyman might expect an annual income of about £45 per year.[89] However, the declining economy and increasing inequality of wealth put pressure on those in the middling ranks. The records from the great fire substantiate a pronounced inequality of wealth and limited ownership of property in 1760s Boston. Two merchants, Francis Borland and John Rowe, together paid 20 percent (£221 and £160 respectively) of Boston's annual tax bill in 1760. In 1771, leading merchants such as John Hancock, who was assessed for £18,000, formed a substantial portion of the top 10 percent of taxpayers, who owned over 60 percent of the taxable wealth in the town. The mercantile elite of Salem held a similar position at the top of the economic and social hierarchy—Samuel Gardener's assessment of his estate and income in 1759 reached £14,747, and in the following year, Timothy Orne calculated his worth at £20,000 and it grew by £2,000 per year until his early death in 1767. Due in part to the continued strength of the fishing industry, Salem did not experience as intensely as Boston the growing divergence in wealth between the commercial elite and the middling and laboring groups. However, as a result of economic and cultural differences, only two voices could be heard in the controversies that plagued Massachusetts in the eighteenth century: the voice of the elite who gained increasing control of economic resources, and the voice of an opposition whose composition varied depending on the issues at stake.[90]

Informal associations also provided for the poor, while enhancing gentility. Affluent merchants, among them Faneuil and Wendell, influenced members of the Episcopal Charitable Society of the 1740s; a later Charitable Society active in the 1760s included principal merchants John Rowe and Joseph Greene. Like so many civic associations, the Charitable Society took on the characteristics of a gentleman's club. Several of its evening meetings began with "a Genteel dinner" or "a fine Salmon for Dinner" at the British Coffee House or the Bunch of Grapes Tavern. Churches also took responsibility for helping the poor. As vestry members, prominent traders took part in doling out the annual portion of "the Poor's Money" on New Years Day. In municipal and voluntary giving, the mercantile elite occupied primary positions, thus reinforcing their economic power, benevolent image, and membership in polite society.[91]

In eighteenth-century Boston and Salem, refashioned social boundaries now delineated greater divisions between haves and have-nots than among religious and ethnic groups. Merchants of French and Dutch origin no longer seemed threatening to the Anglo-American gentry when they displayed high-style goods and partook of English gentility by riding through town in coaches, drinking tea in elegant parlors, and walking through gardens dressed in the latest fashions from London. Gentility smoothed over ethnic and sectarian differences among the elite, creating a community defined by wealth, power, and refinement. Fortunate people of the middling sort improved their circumstances through retail trade and artisanal production and began to acquire modest assortments of genteel goods. The lower sort—unemployed and poor artisans, mariners, dock workers, day laborers, destitute widows, orphaned children, and the disabled and infirm—unable to accumulate goods or attend to the minute distinctions required by genteel manners remained on the other side of what must have seemed like a deep divide.[92]

In both Boston and Salem, elites and the lower sort participated in different kinds of public gatherings. Civic rituals like court days, and celebrations of royal birthdays and weddings, became occasions for the leading merchants, professionals, and appointed and elected officials to parade, dine, and dance in fashionable dress and with genteel bearing. To celebrate the marriage of "the Princess Royal of Great Britain" to the prince of Orange in 1734, Bostonians turned out in style. The governor put on "several noble entertainments . . . to many of the first rank here." The day began with a gentlemen's breakfast and then a procession to "his Majesty's Ship" with "drums beating & trumpets sounding before

the procession as they passed along." Guns on navy ships saluted several times during the day. After "a most splendid dinner" at Castle
William, the officers of the British garrison in Boston Harbor, with the
gentlemen and their ladies, attended a ball at Mr. Lutwyche's Long
Room in King Street. Several gentlemen "being invited By Colonel
Wendell to his seat in School-Street," processed again and "made a most
gallant appearance, having 6 drums and 2 trumpets before them." We do
not know if the streets were lined with crowds to watch the parading gentry, but on this occasion and many like it, most commoners were excluded
from participating—they could only stand and watch. Massachusetts governors and high officials often entertained the local gentry. On one such
occasion, Governor Barnard's son gave "an elegant ball, at the Assembly
Room" in Salem, "to a very considerable number of ladies and gentlemen
of this town." Walking and riding in carriages to and from the ball, the
Salem elite made "a brilliant appearance."[93]

"The People" had their days to celebrate in public as well. On Pope's
Day (November 5), an anti-Catholic demonstration called Guy Fawkes
Day in England, commoners took to the streets. Groups of young men
from the North and South Ends would each fashion an effigy of a pope
or the Devil, hang it from a tree, and then try to capture the other side's
"pope." As the winning side marched through the streets, "several
thousand people follow[ed] them, hallowing &c." The revels often cli-
maxed with the burning of both "popes." In Salem, Pope's Day also
drew large crowds. Like most gentry, John Adams, in town for a session
of the Essex County Court, would only observe the festivities of "Popes
and Bonfires this Evening" and "a Swarm of tumultuous People attending them." Gentry spectators commented privately on the "foolish custom of Carrying about the Pope and the Devil &c" and evaluated the
"decorum" or "tumult" of the crowds; one November 5, John Rowe
confirmed that "The People have behaved Well, being Pope Day." In
England, Guy Fawkes Day commemorated the exposure of a Catholic
plot to blow up Parliament. In Massachusetts, Pope's Day became both
an anti-Catholic/anti-French protest and a commentary on aristocratic
pretensions. The pageantry of patrician and plebeian street theater defined differences between genteel and common. Social position dictated
whether spectators viewed a public gathering as legitimate ceremony or
extravagant display, as customary ritual or mob excess.[94]

Elites and commoners continued to negotiate in the streets for the
power to define and control their changing world. As well-to-do merchants and provincial officials transformed the landscape with Georgian
mansions, orderly streets, and extensive commercial structures, mid-

dling and poor artisan and laboring families continued to assert their own visions of street life. Mercantile buildings and marketplaces embodied the ordered ethic of a polite and commercial people and thus drew the hostility of others seeking to establish their own place in a changing world. The volatile combination of profound social changes and immediate economic necessity focused extraordinary interest and concern on the issue of central marketplaces in Boston.

Boston's merchant elite, many of whom had used their purchasing power to fix their own social identity in a modern cultural marketplace and continuously fixed the value of commodities in account books, also attempted to fix the time and place of commodity markets in Boston. The desire to circumscribe markets was part of a long tradition of ambivalence over foreign trade and its middlemen practitioners. During the Middle Ages, marketplaces first emerged at crossroads outside the jurisdiction of cities. As trade increased, markets moved into town centers, often in open squares overlooked by the church. This shift enabled urban officials to enforce orderly procedures and exact fees. In Elizabethan England, town corporations made up of "the trading element of the town, its merchants, artificers, innkeepers, shopkeepers, and stall-holders—perhaps the upper third of its population" regulated the marketplace. Market towns, developing all over England after 1570, supplanted regional fairs, like the famous Sturbridge fair, that had been the predominant means of exchanging trade goods. By 1640, over eight hundred towns in England held at least one market day per week, often near or under a small pavilion with a covered area and raised platform called a market cross, where local officials might read announcements of importance. The construction of market crosses in the town squares of English villages and cities invoked traces of their original location within sight of church.[95]

In London and Paris, extensive market areas like Leadenhall and Les Halles developed to accommodate the explosive growth in trade. Leadenhall, built after the great fire of 1666 and a focus of civic pride for Londoners, consisted of four large buildings surrounding an expansive open square which held hundreds of stalls—over 100 butchers' stalls for beef alone, and 140 more for other meats. Other English towns began to build more substantial structures for their markets, often combining the function of a marketplace under arches on the first floor with a large room for meetings of local officials on the second floor. Called variously the Town Hall, Market House, or Guild Hall, these buildings were frequently built and rebuilt as architectural styles and economic purposes changed.[96]

Borrowing from this English (and European) tradition, Boston built a town hall in 1657 with funds bequeathed by controversial merchant Robert Keayne (see figure 1, p. 27). Twenty years earlier, Keayne had been censured for "taking above six-pence in the shilling profit; in some above eight-pence; and in some small things, above two for one" or nearly fifty percent profit on English goods. His lingering chagrin over these charges prompted him to leave a lengthy "Apologia" in his will and a substantial sum for the construction of a market house/town hall.[97] Boston's first town hall resembled heavily built Tudor enclosures of early market houses in England. After a major fire in 1711, the Town Hall was rebuilt in Georgian style—a symmetrical facade with rows of larger windows. Sometimes towering at the edge of the town square or overlooking a separate open area set aside for markets, such buildings symbolized the growing influence of towns and markets.

But trade escaped the bounds designed for it in both London and Boston. Within two decades of the building of the massive Leadenhall project, stalls and vendors were spilling out of designated areas and clogging the streets of London.[98] In a similar fashion, shopkeepers filled the shops and stalls sheltered by Boston's Town Hall, and peddlers and hawkers thronged the streets in noisy, disorderly fashion, bringing the placeless market to every doorstep. While this disorder spelled liberty to some, to others, the leading merchants included, it appeared as a dangerous lack of control.

The controversy over markets in Boston came to a head in the 1730s and 1740s. It was part of the struggle over resources between emerging capitalists and increasingly marginalized laborers and "objects of charity." The first legislative effort to confine the market to a particular site occurred in the late seventeenth century. On 23 June 1696, the selectmen of Boston, meeting with the justices, "agreed that the market Appointed by Law should be kept at one place at Present viz in and about the Town house."[99] But in spite of the edict, peddlers continued to move up and down the streets calling out their goods for sale, men and women displayed produce at outdoor stalls, artisans sold handcrafted goods from shops adjacent to their homes, and shipping merchants offered imported goods from their warehouses in Merchants Row and along the wharves.

Early in the 1720s, several pamphlets appeared proposing and opposing a specific location for selling produce. One, written in favor of central markets by Benjamin Colman, brother to one merchant and minister to many at his Brattle Street Church, laid out the benefits in terms of "moral values of social harmony."[100] Colman insisted that with strictly regulated market sites, "housewives and tradesmen would be more courteous, servants would not idle their hours away while on market errands," and the end result would be "thrift, frugality, and diligence." Here the theme of social order and the values of gentility served as a main impetus for regulation. In 1733, with the election of five new selectmen (out of a total of seven), including members of the leading merchant families of the Bromfields, Lees, Jefferies, and Winslows, proposals for a town market surfaced again. At the town meeting in March "It was voted . . . That a Market under proper Regulation, would be of great Service and Benefit to the Town." The voters chose four members of Boston's merchant elite, Honorable Thomas Fitch Esq., Edward Hutchinson Esq., Thomas Palmer Esq., Jacob Wendell Esq., and Mr. Nathaniel Cunningham, as a committee to designate "Three suitable Places for Erecting Markets."[101]

Wendell, who figured prominently in the central market plans throughout the 1730s, arrived in Boston early in the century as a "poor Dutch boy." As a religious and ethnic outsider, he made an unlikely candidate for a leading role in Boston's Puritan elite.[102] But with the changing cultural values in eighteenth-century Massachusetts, Wendell was able to apprentice to a merchant and marry into the prominent Oliver family. He became a wealthy trader and an important provincial official.[103] Records of Wendell's trading activities are scarce, but we know that like Peter Faneuil, he developed a network of overseas contacts that reached beyond England to include Dutch merchants in New York and Amsterdam.[104] His marriage to an Oliver and his rise to social and political prominence, including a judgeship and a place on the Council, demonstrated the shift in social values that effaced ethnic and religious differences and accentuated economic power and genteel manners.[105]

While Wendell took advantage of the new ethos to construct a social and economic position at the center of the town's elite, he and others on the market committee were unsuccessful in gaining control over the daily buying and selling of local produce. The issue of central markets revealed Boston merchants' inability to fully command the physical and social landscape they had worked to create.

On March 26, the town agreed on three places and voted seven hundred pounds to construct "fit and commodious" buildings.[106] The proposed market scheme exempted all provisions coming into Boston by sea, which left the shipping merchants free to regulate their own businesses. The controls applied primarily to farm goods brought into Boston by land, including "flesh, fowles, butter, eggs." Again, the rules excluded grain and flour vital to overseas merchants. Fish from ocean waters continued to be sold at the wharves but freshwater fish fell under the new rules. The market began at "the Rising of the Sun," every day except "the Lord's Day" and continued until 1 P.M. No "huckster" or retailer could purchase provisions for resale until after one o'clock.[107]

In the midst of anxiety over economic depression and divisions among the townspeople, an anonymous pamphleteer came out against the plan. In *Some Considerations Against the setting up of a Market in this Town*, the author argued that centralized markets threatened to deprive townspeople of "a Liberty we have always had of buying at our own Doors," which represents a "Privilege that Nature seems to allow us."[108] Employing both established custom and recent concepts of natural law, the tract ignored Puritan providential language; God was never mentioned—another indication of cultural change occurring in Boston and in the larger Anglo-American world.

A town meeting held to reconsider the market proposals drew such a large crowd that the meeting adjourned to the old Brick Meeting House. After debate, the scheme passed by only 25 votes, 364 to 339. In the afternoon, the townsmen read, debated, voted and passed each of the twelve articles.[109] One month later, "the great Affair of setting up of Markets here came again into consideration." Over eight hundred voters attended to hear a report of costs involved and decided to postpone any further decision. This episode has often been interpreted as a city versus country issue or as an expression of the conflict between political factions in the General Court.[110] However, the marketplace issue also represents another example of different classes vying for their own economic interest and legitimate status in the new world of cosmopolitan Boston.

The following March, the town voted again in favor of the markets, and allocated seven hundred pounds to complete the project.[111] Perhaps the plan passed easily this time because just a few days earlier the town had appropriated money to establish a granary and for "Purchasing Grain, for Use of the Town, the Year ensuing" to assist the poorest townspeople.[112] This assured adequate provisions of bread for those in need and defused one of the more threatening aspects of central markets.

At sunrise on 4 June 1734, bells rang for the opening of the first public markets in Boston. "The Concourse of People, (Sellers, Buyers, and Spectators) at the Market Places" on the road to Roxbury, at the Town Dock, and at the Old North Meeting House, "was very considerable." The markets drew an "abundance of Provisions," and those that "exceed in Goodness & Cheapness, went off quick" while those "poor or dear" sold more slowly. Newspaper accounts claimed that markets would be "very beneficial" to the "great Town in general" and to "our Country Friends in particular." However, not all townsmen perceived country sellers as friends. Ten days after the markets opened, a town butcher "had a fancy to impose on" a country butcher by taking a quarter of a lamb "in a Clandestine manner, very much like unto Stealing."[113] The thief was caught and fined treble costs.

Not only did amity between sellers at the markets dissolve quickly, but attendance of buyers diminished as well. Apparently the author of *Some Considerations Against the setting up of a Market in this Town* perceived correctly that Bostonians preferred the liberty of "buying at our own Doors." In less than two years, the town meeting discontinued employing clerks and ringing bells at the start of business. There were few transactions to oversee and little reason to announce an opening. In the spring of 1737, "Sundry Inhabitants" petitioned the selectmen to appropriate the markets to some other use. A group of young men disguised as clergymen had already demolished the "Market on the Dock." The town recommended the sale of the South Market and the dismantling of the North Market House.[114] Daily transactions again spread throughout the neighborhoods and streets of Boston, escaping the scrutiny and control of preeminent officials and merchants. Like the cloth workers in England and the grain protesters in Boston a few decades earlier, those at odds with the polite and commercial elite exercised a visible though limited power in Boston.

In the wake of extended concern and debate about central markets, Peter Faneuil's offer, three years later, to build a substantial brick market house for the town at his "Own proper Cost and Charge" raised a furor. In July of 1740, Boston held a town meeting to consider Faneuil's offer. Again, so many citizens assembled that the meeting had to be moved from the Town House to Brattle Street Meeting House. Although Faneuil promised "to erect and build a noble and complete structure or edifice," debate ran long and fierce over whether to accept the proposed building. Influential townsmen insisted that the assessors stand by with their "Lists of Valuation of Estates and Facultys" to make certain that only legally qualified men voted. 367 men cast their votes in favor of accepting Faneuil's gift, and 360 were against. Few of the poorest townsmen would have passed the assessors' scrutiny but numerous Bostonians of the middling sort apparently resisted the merchants' efforts to reshape the landscape and control local markets. Perhaps they also resented the commercial elite's powerful influence in most areas of town management.[115]

Although Faneuil received "the thanks of the town" and never drew the obvious ire of Boston crowds, he played an important role in bringing about and profiting from a realignment of religious and social values based on consumer goods and polite manners. Faneuil reaped profits from transatlantic commerce by selling fish to supply the need for cheap protein in southern Europe and the West Indies, and by transporting sugar, tea, rum, and other exotic goods to satisfy consumer desires in England and North America. He then invested his returns in an assemblage of fashionable belongings essential to the new definition of English gentility. Using commercial contacts from his French background, he fashioned himself into an exemplar of the Anglo-American gentleman. The Georgian brick market hall by which he announced his transformation remains to this day one of the distinguishing buildings of Boston.

Faneuil Hall marked the climax of the final phase of eighteenth-century rebuilding in Boston.[116] In 1743, a Boston mapmaker and engraver, William Price, in a commercial venture designed to capitalize on the controversy over and interest in Faneuil Hall following its benefactor's death, paid homage to Faneuil's role by dedicating *A SouthEast View of the Great Town of Boston in New England in America* to "Peter Faneuil Esq." (see figures 7 and 8).[117] Price limned a view in which Faneuil's public and private buildings frame the center of the townscape. If a visitor entered Boston via Long Wharf, as most did, and looked up King Street toward the civic center of the town, a glance to the right would reveal Boston's latest "handsome" public building, Faneuil Hall, topped by a grasshopper weathervane, a replica of one atop the Royal Exchange in London.[118] If the visitor looked to the left, another cupola with a grasshopper vane appeared, crowning the summer house of the Faneuil estate. The "Frenchman" Peter Faneuil had helped to fashion a Boston skyline of cosmopolitan forms and commercial icons, making visible the new values at the center of the merchant's world.

Peter Faneuil's conception of a town meeting hall and a town market under one roof continued to provide a focus for the growing division of Boston society marked by those who could provide charity and those who became the objects of it. Faneuil never lived to see his grand design completed. At the first town meeting held in the new hall, the schoolmaster and orator John Lovell addressed the crowd which had "assembled in the deepest Sorrow for his Decease . . . on Occasion of the Death of Peter Faneuil, Esq." Lovell praised the merchant, "whose *Largeness of Heart* equal'd . . . his *Power to do Good.*" Rather than wasting his riches in luxury, "tho' Plenty always crown'd his Board," Faneuil gave to the needy and felt "that divine Satisfaction" from giving happiness to others. His largess to the "hungry, naked, fatherless, and widows in their afflictions" was so great that "none but they who were the Objects of it" could know the amount. The concept that "riches enlarged the heart to do good" had replaced earlier Puritan jeremiads against luxury; wealthy

FIGURE 7. Boston in 1743, showing Faneuil Hall with its grasshopper
weathervane to the right and the Faneuil house and summerhouse topped
with a grasshopper weathervane to the left. The hall and the house frame the
center of Boston. Rendered by Tom Tricot for the author and based on
William Price's engraving of Boston at the American Antiquarian Society.

FIGURE 8. The cartouche dedicating William Price's View of Boston to Peter
Faneuil. Courtesy of the American Antiquarian Society.

merchants like Faneuil had become benevolent middlemen dispensing God's blessings. Lovell suggested that God, in giving riches to "this Man, seems to have scattered Blessings all abroad among the People."[119]

In spite of the praise heaped on Faneuil, the townspeople remained reluctant to support a central marketplace; no sellers rented space in the first floor of the hall until nine months later when Anthony Hodgson paid twenty shillings to sell butter, cheese and flour from stall number eight. The market never prospered and was closed for a time in 1747 and again in 1752, while market issues continued to provoke contentious debates.[120] Today, Faneuil is remembered not for generosity or gentility, but for a gesture that inscribed the commercial and cultural authority of the merchant elite into the landscape of Boston.

French families like the Faneuils in Boston and the Cabots in Salem, who arrived with money and established transatlantic trading connections, flourished both financially and socially in the eighteenth-century cosmopolitan culture emerging in port towns. A Huguenot refugee chronicler, writing from Boston in 1687, astutely presaged this world of goods by warning that "whoever brings Nothing here, finds Nothing. . . . Those who bring much, do well in Proportion."[121]

Merchants' influence reached beyond parades, patronage, or charity. Using their financial capital to "purchase" cultural capital, the mercantile elite brought print culture, especially newspapers and libraries, to Massachusetts. As the most significant promoters of print culture in Boston and Salem they shaped the institutions of what is called the "public sphere." In *The Structural Transformation of the Public Sphere*, German sociologist Jürgen Habermas offers an explanation for the importance of social gatherings and print culture in the eighteenth century. Habermas argues that with new kinds of sociability—coffeehouses, salons, table societies—people educated by an expanding print culture came together on a hypothetically equal footing. In these settings they could discuss institutions and politics in reasoned debates that were free of the constraining influence of the church or the state. Habermas alludes to the influence of capitalism on the development of the public sphere in eighteenth-century Europe but never clearly spells it out. However, when we look at the development of the new sociability in Boston and Salem, the integral connection between commerce and culture becomes clear. In starting gentleman's clubs and patronizing coffeehouses, in establishing and supporting newspapers, in founding local libraries, and in transporting the wares of booksellers, leading merchants played an essential part in creating a public sphere in Massachusetts.[122]

Gentlemen's clubs, a feature of eighteenth-century England, often formalized the connection between commerce and culture.[123] Meeting in coffeehouses and taverns, "Our modern celebrated clubs," the noted English periodical the *Spectator* affirmed, "are founded upon eating and drinking." But clubs also provided a group setting that reinforced shared values, promoted civility, and fostered informal business arrangements among friends. In February 1745, Timothy Orne, his Essex Street neighbors and merchant partners the Cabot brothers and David Britton, and the young attorney William Pynchon, a descendant of the patriarch of Springfield, formed a club which they named "The Civil Society." The men agreed "to meet together at Mrs. Pratt's," a nearby inn, on Tuesday and Friday evenings "for the Preservation of Friendship & Conversation." The group set out written rules: fines for cursing and quarreling enforced refined behavior, introducing new members to the group required unanimous consent. In its first rule the group agreed that "Every Member shall pay his Club," invoking the dual meaning of the word club. As John Brewer observes, "in the eighteenth century the term 'club' was understood as a verb, rather than as a noun: '*to club together*' to pool one's financial resources for almost any collective activity, automatically created *a club*." "Club" also meant a bill for food and drink, so that a club connoted a pooling of friendship, civility, and business interests, and a continuation of face-to-face contact which promoted social and commercial investments. The Civil Society of Salem aimed for a free exchange of ideas and participated in what Joseph Addison in the *Spectator* styled as bringing philosophy and political economy "out of the Closets and Libraries, Schools and Colleges, to dwell in Clubs and Assemblies, at Tea-Tables and in Coffee-Houses." Market relations influenced not only the flow of goods and capital but the equally crucial flow of information and ideas.[124]

The Civil Society enlarged its membership and a few months later ten members raised fifty pounds for the relief of "the poor people in Salem whose Husbands or Sons went for the good of there Country in the land Service against Cape Britton." The French had attacked Massachusetts fishing boats off Newfoundland and captured Canso, a fishing port in northern Nova Scotia. In return Massachusetts, led by Council members like Benjamin Pickman of Salem, sponsored an attack on Louisburg on Cape Breton Island under William Pepperell, a leading merchant from Maine. The French port was captured and Pepperell knighted by the king of England for his services, even though Louisburg was returned to the French three years later in the treaty of Aix-La-Chapelle which ended the war in 1748.

The Civil Society subscription for the relief of widows and families of war veterans demonstrated the pooling of funds for charitable purposes, which developed outside of religious circles. As with the careful sharing of risk among shipowners and insurers of cargo, the Civil Society members each contributed a share of five pounds to create a substantial bank of funds rather than dispense separate sums. For Salem gentry, as for gentlemen in Boston, charity had become evidence of gentility and the wielding of economic power. Dr. Alexander Hamilton, leading member of the Ancient and Honorable Tuesday Club of Annapolis, reported attending several clubs during his visit to Boston in 1744. The leading merchant and clubgoer John Rowe often attended meetings several nights a week, belonging to the Merchants's Club, the Wednesday Night Club, the Possee, the Charitable Society, and the first Masonic lodge in Boston.[125]

Just as provincial social life recast itself in terms of regular repetitive rituals enacted in public sites such as promenades and assemblies, commercial interchange centered on daily visits to the docks, the exchange, and the coffeehouse.[126] The proliferation of coffeehouses in late seventeenth- and early eighteenth-century Anglo-America was closely linked with the rise of newspapers and the growth of capitalism. Lloyd's Coffeehouse in London produced the insurance firm of the same name and Jonathan's Coffee House in Exchange Alley became the home of stock jobbers.[127] An advertisement from the *Salisbury* (England) *Journal* for John Child's coffeehouse gives the flavor of these establishments and indicates their importance as a center for the exchange of information and a site of pleasurable experience. At Child's coffeehouse could be found

> the Votes, King's Speech and Addresses, the *Gazette, Daily Advertiser, General Evening-Post, Evening Advertiser* and London Chronicle, *Salisbury Journal,* Monthly Magazines, Sessions Papers and Dying Speeches; the best Coffee, Tea, Chocolate and Capillari, will be constantly provided, with all due and proper Attendance. . . . The Room is conveniently fitted up large, light, and warm, and subject to no annoyance whatever.[128]

An observer of the London scene in 1726 confirmed that "what attracts enormously in these coffee-houses are the gazettes and other public papers," for "all Englishmen are newsmongers."[129]

Like their London counterparts who gathered at the Royal Exchange, Boston merchants met daily at the covered walkway underneath the Town House or across the square at the Royal Exchange Tavern owned at one time by the Shrimpton family. They gathered at the London

Coffeehouse or the Bunch of Grapes Tavern across King Street at the beginning of Merchant's Row.[130] John Rowe met frequently at the British
Coffee House with other merchants and professionals to conduct town
business, to discuss commercial affairs, and to exchange pleasantries. The
coffee house often seemed to be his office or at least his conference room.

Few historians have fully acknowledged the constitutive role that merchants played in bringing print culture to a wider public. Just as many
coffeehouses became sites of commercial negotiation as well as social and
political conversation, many newspapers originated to serve the needs of
overseas merchants. In some cases, merchants actively sponsored publi-
cations, corralling subscribers and even hiring a printer/publisher.
Timothy Orne and Admiralty Judge Samuel Curwen, also from a leading
commercial family, organized a subscription to fund the publication of a
local newspaper for Salem. A letter from the printer-bookseller John
Mein of Boston notes receiving "the additional subscribers from Mr.
Orne." The somewhat differing commercial interests of publisher and
subscribers required some negotiation. Mein agreed to honor the subscribers' wishes, even if "advertisements be ever so numerous, to keep
always Six pages of our Paper for News & Essays." The first issue of the
Essex Gazette appeared on 2 August 1768.[131]

Continuing his leadership in bringing print culture to Salem, Orne
joined the prominent merchant Colonel Benjamin Pickman and Judge
Curwen to found the Social Library in Salem. Organized in 1760, the
Social Library paralleled private subscription and proprietary libraries
being established in England's provincial cities. Numerous polite and
commercial people such as members of the Cabot family, attorney
William Pynchon, Dr. E. A. Holyoke, and several of Orne's business
partners including Richard Derby, John Crowninshield, and Samuel
Gardner participated in funding and using the library.[132]

The books Orne owned and borrowed indicate a familiarity with
Enlightenment arguments for a rational approach to life—a value he
practiced so carefully in his economic ventures. Orne donated several
books to the library to offset his membership fee, including three volumes of Locke's works. He borrowed studies in political economy such
as Cato's letters, Mandeville's *Fable of the Bees*, and a response called
Answer to Fable of the Bees. He chose volumes on husbandry and religious
tracts like Hoadly on the Sacrament and *Sermons at Boyles Lectures*, and
indulged in an occasional novel such as Fielding's *Tom Jones*. Other novels taken out under Orne's name, such as *Fortunate Countrymaid* and
Betsy Thoughtless, probably reflected the taste of his daughters Rebecca
and Sarah, who were nineteen and fifteen at the time. Orne digested

French works in English translation like Rollin's *Belles Lettres*, which attempts to reconcile classical learning and Christian morality. In reading Voltaire's "Letters"—probably a translation of Voltaire's *Lettres anglaises*, Orne encountered praise for Locke and Newton, criticism of the French monarchy, and acclaim for British freedoms. A wide-ranging reader, Orne borrowed an eclectic list of forty-five titles during the three years documented.[133]

Prominent overseas traders dominated the Salem library association in a pattern similar to that of the establishment of many English libraries. The Library Society of Leeds, begun in 1768, included all the major merchant families on the organizing committee. In his study of the newly rich in eighteenth-century Britain, James Raven suggests "the cultural development of Leeds went hand-in-hand with local mercantile self-esteem." The commercial elite "permitted the theater to open, they enabled the operation of the newspapers, they imported artists and architects, they effectively ran the local library committee." Eighteenth-century Leeds, like Boston and Salem, absorbed émigré merchants into the local hierarchy, and like Boston and Salem it became a town constructed both physically and culturally by the "polite and commercial" people.[134]

In the career of Salem's Timothy Orne we see three major transformations of eighteenth-century Anglo-America coming together. Like others in Boston's and Salem's polite and commercial elites, Orne played a significant role in expanding capitalism and reshaping the urban landscape of Salem. He became a central figure in the emergence of a merchant elite which defined itself through the display of visible wealth, accentuating the difference between rich and poor, between Essex Street and English Lane. Orne also took a leading role in bringing print culture to Salem and fostering the growth of a public sphere separate from religion and from state control. For Orne, exchange of commodities, currency, opinions, and ideas flowed together in the life of an eighteenth-century colonial gentleman. By bringing together commerce and literature, Orne formed his identity as both a gentleman and a merchant, combining what had, in previous centuries, been two separate categories.

Orne's good friend and mentor, Colonel Benjamin Pickman, an acclaimed leader of the town's "codfish aristocracy" and member of the Massachusetts Provincial Council, fashioned the commercial icon for which Salem is often remembered. When he built his Georgian-style, gambrel-roofed house on Essex Street in 1749, Pickman commissioned a carved and gilded image of a codfish to decorate each stair riser in his new mansion, acknowledging that the foundation of his gentility rested

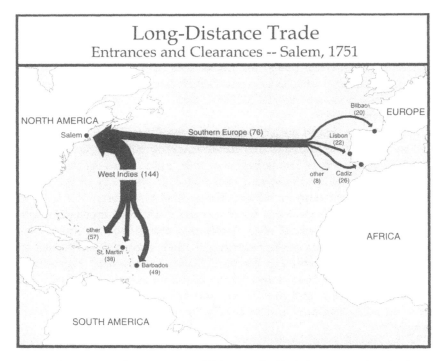

MAP 5. Overseas trading patterns of Salem's "Codfish Aristocracy" including Timothy Orne. Prepared by the author and Tom Tricot, based on Salem Customs House Records at the Peabody Essex Museum.

on profits from the humble cod. A generation later, in 1784, John Rowe's last recorded public action was to propose "to hang up the representation of a Cod Fish" in the House of Representatives hall "as a memorial of the importance of the Cod-Fishery to the welfare of the Commonwealth." The codfish can still be seen in the Massachusetts State House.[135] However, by the time of Rowe's proposal, the polite and commercial ideals of eighteenth-century Boston and Salem had been eclipsed by the republican values of revolutionary Massachusetts. Georgian gentlemen had either fled to Britain or adopted a new American identity.

5

A Return to Homespun

Last night 3 Cargoes of Bohea Tea were emptied into the Sea. . . .
this destruction of the Tea is so bold, so daring, so firm, intrepid
and inflexible, and it must have so important consequences, and
so lasting, that I cant but consider it as an Epocha in History. . . .
this however is but an Attack upon Property.

JOHN ADAMS, *Diary*, 1773

AFTER THE CONCLUSION of the French and Indian or
Seven Years War, Americans coped with a postwar depression just as
British ministers attempted to wring more revenue from the colonies.
The political developments during the early part of the revolutionary era
(1764–1776) have been thoroughly studied, but the various cultural expressions that accompanied ideological change have only been noted in
a piecemeal fashion. If we look closely at the responses of townspeople
in Boston and Salem to the rapidly developing changes, we can see a cultural transformation that recasts societal divisions. The class differences
constituted by economic resources and consumer display that characterized polite and commercial culture were, if not alleviated, at least cast
into the shadows by the flaring political divisions articulated in oratory
and print, in crowd actions—and in new uses and meanings for consumer goods. The economic and cultural influence of Georgian gentility
was undermined by a diminishing audience and a declining ability to
contain or mask political differences. A culture of homespun emerged to
challenge the meaning attributed to goods by the polite and commercial
elite in Salem and Boston. With a return to homespun and all it connoted, the Patriots created new uses and meanings for material possessions
and thereby severed the connection between fashionable British goods
and esteemed character. Political action and popular protest redefined
the connotations of material objects usually associated with the polite
and commercial culture—imported fabric, silver punch bowls, and East

India tea. From its early appearance during the boycotts of the late 1760s the reinterpretation of imported products became a crucial ingredient in forging a new American identity.

We can see the potential for change in the experiences of the young lawyer John Adams in January of 1766. On Wednesday, 15 January, Adams "spent the evening with the Sons of Liberty" in the group's Boston meeting place, the counting room of a distillery on Hanover Square—"a very small room"—where Adams and nine Sons of Liberty enjoyed "punch, wine, pipes and tobacco, bisquit and cheeze." Comprised of "mechanics"—a brazier (maker of brass objects), painter, jeweler, two distillers, and a ship's master—the gathering, Adams observed with approval, engaged in gentlemanly conversation: "no Plotts, no Machinations." For the cautious country lawyer just beginning to test the political waters, it was a first contact with the Boston radicals. The next night, Adams accepted an invitation to join a small company of ladies and gentlemen for a fashionable dinner party at Boston merchant "Mr. Nick Boylston's." Clearly less at ease than the previous night, Adams seemed surprised by the lavish table and the high spirits of his male dinner companions—several of them high Tories and "Hotspurs all."[1]

As a man in transit—from modest village origins to a career as a national statesman, from rusticity to refinement, and from unfocused identity to disciplined selfhood, John Adams's response to material circumstances and social gradations during these two back-to-back January evenings in 1776 reflected an established polite and commercial culture at its most sophisticated and, in contrast, a nascent material and political culture still in the process of formation.[2] While instinctively more comfortable with the Sons of Liberty, he responded uncharacteristically to Boylston's newly refurbished mansion. Reared in the rural environs of Braintree, Adams had gained a slight veneer of cosmopolitan manners during his years at Harvard and riding the circuit court at Salem. Later, he would decry the pomp and circumstance he saw as ambassador to the courts of European royalty and would lead the fight for American independence not only from the laws of imperial Britain but also from the potentially debilitating luxury adopted by well-to-do Anglo-Americans. But that night he was entranced. He pronounced it "an elegant Dinner indeed!" The company took a tour of the house to see what one thousand pounds sterling would buy. Adams gushed: "the Turkey Carpets, the painted Hangings, the Marble Tables, the rich Beds with crimson Damask Curtains and Counterpanes, the beautiful Chimney Clock, the

Spacious Garden, are the most magnificent of any Thing I have ever seen."[3]

Nicholas Boylston and his brother Thomas were among the social leaders of Boston's merchant elite. Nicholas and his partner Joseph Green owned seagoing vessels and imported English goods to their warehouse in Boston.[4] Thomas Boylston made a portion of his fortune importing Dutch goods illegally, as did several other notable merchants in Boston including Thomas Hancock, John Rowe, and the soon-to-be famous Patriot William Mollineux.[5] The Boylston brothers inherited their father's import business and elegant "Mansion House," and they continued to advance the business and refurbish the house.[6] As part of their stylish self-presentation, the Boylstons—mother, brothers, and sisters Rebecca, Lucy, and Mary—hired John Singleton Copley to paint their portraits in 1767.[7] The family commission represented one of Copley's major orders and generated continued opportunities as Copley was asked to paint a second view of Nicholas in 1769 and a full-length, posthumous likeness for Harvard College in 1773.[8]

Far from showing any semblance of a Yankee trader, Boylston's pose of indolence, draped in silk and velvet, leaning languidly on closed ledgers, summoned images of a Middle Eastern pasha. He donned a silk gown called a "banyan," from a Hindi word that means "merchant" or "trader."[9] In his elegant garment, he embodied the economic and cultural power of Massachusetts's merchant elite to transform commercial ventures and foreign imports into signs of Anglo-American gentility. Boylston's body, draped over its chair and swathed in fragile, luxuriant materials, obscures any hint of barrels of cod, casks of rum, quickly copied letters, scribbled account books, or the shrewd bargaining required to transform quantities of goods into surplus funds. The exotic gown and indolent pose suggest that only an artful alchemy, a decorous touch of the wand, could have produced such treasure; but we know it was the work of cultural transformation that allowed India goods and leisured poses to highlight the social position of New England's leading merchants.[10]

Nicholas Boylston, member of the Charitable Society and Fire Club, overseer of the poor, and brother-in-law to Customs Comptroller Benjamin Hallowell, epitomizes Boston's elite taking their place at the top of the social hierarchy, a hierarchy that would soon be challenged by new uses of consumer goods and by the growing importance of Whig-republican ideas. Eventually a new national culture with different relationships to material artifacts and different forms of polite gentility would emerge.[11] Ten years after Adams's visits, the Sons of Liberty

FIGURE 9. Nicholas Boylston, by John Singleton Copley, 1773. Painted at the request of the Harvard University Corporation, 1773. Courtesy of the Harvard University Portrait Collection.

would reign throughout Massachusetts and many of the Tories enjoying Boylston's table would be clinging to Georgian gentility as exiles in England.

Paradoxically, most eminent merchants supported the first Non-Importation Agreement, instituted in response to the Townshend Duties which placed taxes on a wide variety of foreign goods.[12] Non-importation favored John Rowe, Thomas Boylston, and others who depended on the (illegal) Dutch trade. It also aided others, like John Hancock, who through poor business practices owned overstocked inventories that they could unload at high prices during the ban.[13] As a result of the Non-Importation Agreement, English exports to New England in 1769 dropped by half, from over £400,000 to slightly more than £200,000. Consumption of necessary British goods—items like nails, pins, and the everyday cotton cloth being manufactured in the factories springing up across northern England—continued even though some Patriot leaders promoted a program of home manufacture for essential products like cloth. Boston's town meeting voted funds to construct four hundred spinning wheels and resurrect the Manufactory House designed to employ the poor in spinning and weaving. Samuel Adams even organized a spinning bee on Boston Common. Often hundreds of spectators would watch these Daughters of Liberty "vie with each other in skill and industry." Following Boston's lead, every family in Connecticut had "become a manufactory House." Whig politics succeeded in associating homespun with Patriotism and resistance to British policies. "Industry and frugality" were now the behaviors that exalted women's "character in the Eyes of the World." No longer did polite charms—dancing, needlework, painting, and speaking French—or fashionable dresses of imported silk and calico mark the "Paths of true Politeness."[14]

In 1770 when the Townshend Duties were repealed except for the tax on tea, many merchants wanted to end the Non-Importation Agreements while political leaders and a few traders pushed to continue the ban. John Tyler argues that this split the merchant community decisively. But divisions were not always clear-cut. Throughout much of the decade between 1765 and 1775, the portable culture of Georgian gentility brought together those with strong political differences. Nick Boylston and his brother Thomas, for example, would argue over non-importation and other matters at a dinner table that included both the Tory Lieutenant Governor Thomas Hutchinson and the Whig-leaning John Rowe, organizer of the non-importation movement. Until the closing of the Port of Boston in June of 1774 and then the departure of British troops in March 1776, the stance of many leading merchants and professionals seemed uncertain. The power of polite norms among the Boston and Salem elite muted differences over how to respond to British imperialism.

When pressured to publicly renounce the agreement in 1770, Nicholas Boylston and his partner Joseph Green replied that they "would not render themselves obnoxious [to the Patriots] when they had no assurance of protection." Hutchinson, having already sacrificed his house and furnishings five years earlier in the Stamp Act riots, observed in a letter that Boylston and Green "are afraid of their fine houses."[15] Another reminder of that time hit even closer to home when Boylston recalled the rioters' warnings—slashed portraits hanging askew—in his brother-in-law Hallowell's newly built mansion.

In spite of growing political differences the mercantile elite continued to socialize and do business with each other. Historians have offered several explanations for the seemingly contradictory behavior of Boston's and Salem's mercantile elite in the years leading up to the Revolution. Some scholars stress the economic motives that led New England merchants to temporarily jeopardize their own business in the Non-Importation Agreements of 1769–1770. Arthur Schlesinger, in his pioneering work on colonial merchants and the Revolution, maintained that traders subjected themselves to this short-term punishment for long-term gains, hoping to eliminate onerous British taxes. John Tyler suggests that the Non-Importation Agreement was financially beneficial to those merchants such as Hancock who viewed the situation from the doors of overstocked warehouses.[16]

But economic interests offer only a partial answer. Without taking into consideration the powerful influence of Georgian gentility in the socially constructed identities of the mercantile elite, the contradiction implied in John Adams's visit to the Sons of Liberty one night, and to the home of a wealthy Anglophile the next, is difficult to interpret. The function of polite society—to smooth over differences of religion and ethnicity—carried over to politics. During the tumultuous prerevolutionary years, gentlemen in Boston and Salem—"Patriots," "Tories," and British officers—continued to meet and dine together. Boston and Salem gentry invited British officers to their official "state" dinners held to celebrate civic occasions. For a number of years, the dictates of civility could contain political disagreements.

The prominent Boston merchant John Rowe, considered by most historians to be a Patriot, demonstrated his commitment to commercial and genteel values, in spite of a growing uncertainty about British motives. In a single not atypical day during the 1765 Stamp Act resistance, Rowe dined on board the *Jamaica*, a British man-of-war, with naval officers, customs officials including Hallowell, and several other leading merchants of Boston. He "came ashore about six of Clock and spent the Evening at the Coffee House" with a group of gentlemen who, within the decade, would take strong and visible positions on opposing sides of the revolutionary divide. Harrison Gray and the Boylston brothers would solidify their Tory sentiments, while others of the coffeehouse group, such as James Otis and William Mollineux, developed into famous Patriot leaders. Two days later, on 14 August 1765, Rowe described the turbulent events in Boston: "A Great Number of people assembled . . . this morning to see the Stamp Officer, merchant Andrew Oliver, hanged in Effigy." That evening, a crowd cut down the mannequin and "carried [it] in Triumph amidst the acclamations of many thousands." The crowd "pulled down" a new brick building and "did some mischief" to Oliver's house. Rowe, concerned about the disorder, felt the crowd was "much to blame." The populace, not constrained by the dictates of elite refinement, expressed their views forcefully.[17]

When Parliament repealed the Stamp Act the following year, Salem townspeople broke into "Rejoicings"; the whole "province was in a Rapture." Joyful celebrations sustained the possibility of rapprochement between Britain and Boston. At a festive dinner attended by several eminent merchants including John Rowe, the gentlemen showed their appreciation: "we drank fifteen Toasts and very Loyal they were." The evening continued with a grand illumination and fireworks. "The whole was much admired and the day Crowned with Glory & honour." During a similar dinner the following year, the group drank to the king, queen, and royal family, ministers, Parliament, "the Extension of Traded Commerce," and finally to "the United and Inseparable Interest of Great Britain and Her Colonies." These genteel rituals reasserted the Anglo-American identity of Massachusetts's mercantile elite. That summer, even the Sons of Liberty met at the Liberty Tree and "drank the King's Health!"[18]

British officers, absorbed into the merchant elite, enlivened the social scene. Refined gatherings generated good will and held a promise for continued Anglo-American alliance shaped by gentility and supported by commerce. In their scarlet coats, British soldiers brightened biweekly assembly dances and concerts; the first winter assembly of 1768 included "the Honorable the Commissioners of the Customs, Commodore Hood, Brigadier General Pomeroy, and most of the Gentlemen of the Army and Navy." It seemed that after the initial shock of seeing four thousand military men descend on their city in October, Bostonians, at least the upper echelon, welcomed the new faces of English gentlemen and their ladies.[19] The mixed gatherings continued amidst a climate of growing distrust and hostility in the streets. In January of 1771, not quite a year after the infamous Boston Massacre, "all the Best people in town" celebrated the queen's birthday with "a Very Grand Assembly" at the Concert Hall attended by the Governor, the Lieutenant Governor, the commodore and captains of the British Navy, colonels and captains of the army, customs commissioners, and the gentlemen and ladies of Boston's high society. The event, in the view of one celebrant, marked a "Coalition so that Harmony Peace & Friendship will once more be Established." Polite manners and refined sociability were designed to create a common ground among a certain class. Participants understood this, observing that "Very good Dancing & Good Musick" enhanced good will.[20]

When General Gage came to Salem as governor in May of 1774 just after the hated Boston Port Bill had closed the harbor, he was followed by a train of Boston gentry in carriages and greeted by a procession of Salem leaders. A few days later, the Salem mercantile elite of "110 Gentlemen, as Many Ladies," marked the king's birthday and Governor Gage's arrival with a ball at their Assembly Hall. As one local historian noted, "things began to be gay in town for the Tory element" as British officers in their military attire magnified the gaiety of local parties.[21]

As the local gentry and British officials danced, other events gradually undermined the bases of Anglo-American polite and commercial culture. Impaired economic opportunity emerged as one of the major developments that intensified the growing divide between British sympathizers and Patriot supporters. Business became increasingly difficult as British policies and actions continued to erode the economic cooperation that supported the merchant class in England and America. Merchants agreed on a non-importation policy without recognizing its potential to erode the foundation of their cultural capital. They did not realize that their policy marked the beginning of the end of Georgian gentility and the Anglo-American polite and commercial culture. Activities during the non-importation period introduced new associations and meanings for the fashionable dress and imported luxuries that had been leading consumer goods and important markers of gentility. After British forces closed the port of Boston in reaction to the Tea Party, the hope that class connections and a shared culture would continue to bridge political differences between Massachusetts and Britain, and between Tories and Whigs, seemed increasingly hollow.

Through the diary entries of one leading member of Massachusetts's polite and commercial elite, we can view the declining power of Georgian gentility and the growth of an alternative culture. The written record of John Rowe's activities and his responses to critical events reveal the complex interactions of economic, cultural, and political pressures. Events in the spring and summer of 1774 exerted escalating economic burdens on merchants like Rowe and Boylston in Boston and Timothy Orne III and Benjamin Pickman III, grown sons of Salem's wealthiest merchants. The cessation of overseas trade at Boston, and two years later the exodus of British troops, became fundamental turning points in the lives of Massachusetts's mercantile elite. First, the edict closing Boston's port to all ships in June 1774, created a serious problem for local merchants. As news of the Boston Port Bill reached the Province in the late spring of 1774, the pace of meetings and committees stepped up as many realized that their livelihoods were at stake. Rowe met with town committees and merchants as they shaped their response to "the Distressing Situation of the Town." Rowe understood that closing the Harbor would "be a Great Evil." Anticipating events, he welcomed General Gage's arrival with a silent prayer, "God Grant his Instructions be not severe as I think him to be a Very Good Man." A few days later, Rowe paid a polite call on the general, "who Received me very Cordially."[22]

During this period Boston's committee of correspondence attempted without much success to get merchants to recall their orders for fall imports from Britain and sign a strict non-importation agreement called the Solemn League and Covenant. Rowe still tried to straddle the fence by meeting with the Patriot group—John and Samuel Adams, Thomas Cushing, William Mollineux, and Dr. Joseph Warren—one day and joining "a prominent minority" calling on Gage the next. As he grew increasingly despondent for "Poor Unhappy Boston," Rowe continued to hew to the middle way, consulting with the general in the morning and attending town meeting in afternoon, where "Nothing done by Harangue."[23] As Rowe met with merchants and rebels and supped with gentry of all persuasions, Boston Harbor emptied of commercial vessels. On a Sunday walk "round the Wharffs" he mourned, "tis impossible to describe the Distressed Situation of this Poor Town—not one Topsail Merchantman to be seen." As trading vessels departed, British troop transports took their place, disgorging regiment after regiment, often watched by large gatherings of townspeople. At one point, as many as four regiments camped on Boston Common. In mid-June eight hundred "Tradesmen of the Town" (not to be confused with the more select mer-

chant group that continued to meet at the Crown Coffee House) gathered to "Consult on the Distress of this Place" but like others, "they did
nothing, being much divided in Sentiment."[24]

Economic distress increased pressures for a strong political response.
Two days later another general town meeting, searching for "a sympa-
thetic replacement for an absent Samuel Adams," chose first James
Bowdoin who refused to be moderator, and then John Rowe who also refused. Rowe explains in his diary, "I was much engaged and therefore did
not accept." Clearly he wanted to avoid controversy and postpone any ir-
revocable commitment to Tory or Whig principles. Believing that "the
people at present seem very averse to Accommodate Matters," he continued to hope that "they will Repent of their Behavior sooner or later."
Meanwhile, John Adams stood in as moderator. For two more days, 27
and 28 June, the town meeting continued "very warm on both sides" as
they debated the activities of the committee of correspondence. Samuel
Adams, Dr. Warren, William Mollineux, and several others spoke on behalf of the committee's work. Those against included future Loyalists
Harrison and Thomas Gray, John Amory, and Ezekial Goldthwait, all
from wealthy merchant families. The restrictive non-importation agreement of the Solemn League and Covenant underlay the contentious
meeting, which had turned into a vote of confidence for continuance of
the committee of correspondence. Rowe stayed on the sidelines but in
private he said, "I think they [the committee] are wrong . . . in the matter
the Merchants have taken up against them, they have in my Opinion exceeded their Power." The town disagreed, three-quarters of those present supporting the committee, but in the face of opposition from Whig
and Tory merchants alike, the Solemn League and Covenant did not
pass. Rowe opined that "this affair will cause much evil one against the
other" and consoled himself by dining on turtle at the Peacock with
forty-three Ladies and Gentlemen who "spent the afternoon agreeably
and were very merry."[25]

Scholarly interpretations of the episode of the Solemn League and
Covenant differ. Earlier historians viewed this as a key moment, when
merchants withdrew their support for the Patriot movement. In his recent study of Boston merchants on the eve of the Revolution, John Tyler
suggests that the merchant community had been deeply divided from
the boycotts of the late 1760s and the divisions over the Solemn League
created an opportunity for radical Whigs as it "catalyzed revolutionary
sentiments." Richard D. Brown argues that rather than consolidating the
power of the Patriot group, this episode demonstrated that the commit-

tee of correspondence could only enact those measures "grounded on a broad consensus."[26]

The turning point for most leading merchants, I believe, did not come from their opposition to the Solemn League and Covenant, nor from their early responses to non-importation. Instead, their continued sharing of economic ventures and polite sociability demonstrated the persistence of strong cultural ties. But British policies made it increasingly difficult to carry on business—closing the port and decimating Boston's commerce, compelling the townsmen to support more and more British troops, and forcing Bostonians to do their business through the smaller port of Salem. These pressures strengthened the bond between Whig merchants in Massachusetts's two largest ports, and they found it ever more onerous to accept British actions.

Each trader had to form opinions on issues that now drastically impacted their own families' well-being. For John Rowe, a changing attitude did not immediately translate into political action. While avoiding leadership positions that would publicly proclaim his Patriot or Tory allegiance, he continued to hope that reason, civility, and order would produce acceptable solutions. Although he promptly called on newly appointed Governor Gage and developed a warm family friendship with the British admiral and his wife and daughter, he did not sign a welcoming address offered to the new Governor by the Hutchinsonian faction. As a "sober man" he condemned crowd actions such as the tarring and feathering of John Malcom as "outrageous Violence." In July, following the contentious town meetings, a number of ministers recommended a fast day "on Account of the Miserable Situation of this Town." Rowe expressed frustration: "I should much rather the People would do Justice and Recommend the Payment for the Tea instead of losing a Day by fasting." During this period he conducted his business in Salem where his ships entered and departed for London, Portugal, and other Atlantic ports. Frequently he stayed with the Salem merchant and loyalist Colonel Benjamin Pickman Jr. in his family home decorated with gilded carvings of codfish. Rowe also enjoyed the hospitality of the colonel's brother, Clark Gayton Pickman, who had married heiress Sarah Orne and lived in a modish home built the same year (1763) and in a similar style as that of his father-in-law Timothy Orne. Less than a year later, the Pickman family would be split by political beliefs. In March 1775, Benjamin Pickman Jr. departed for Bristol, remaining in exile for ten years as his wife and his brother maintained the family property.[27]

A decisive blow to a shared transatlantic culture came in March 1776 when British troops under General Howe evacuated Boston. This was the final point of decision. Loyalists who wanted to preserve their cultural, economic, and political connections with England departed with the troops. Those who identified with the emerging American culture stayed. Rowe chose to remain even though the "Distress of this Unfortunate Town," fired on from "Every Quarter"—by both colonial and British troops during the first days of March—"alarmed us very much." The notice that the British troops intended to evacuate "put the Inhabitants . . . into Great Disorder, Confusion and much Distress." Both the soldiers and the Loyalist families that hoped to leave with them had very little time to gather their effects and load them aboard vessels. Rowe described "nothing but hurry and Confusion, every Person," including several of his friends and in-laws, "striving to get out of this Place." On their last few days in town, the British troops, presumably under orders, behaved "very Insolently and with Great Rapacity" repeatedly breaking open warehouses, stealing two thousand six hundred pounds of his inventory as Rowe stood by unable to "hinder their Destruction of my Goods." The British continued "making havoc in every house and Destruction of all kinds of Furniture" for several days as "Continual Fire from both sides" rained down on Boston. Rowe seemed horrified and outraged, taking particular note of an attack on Mrs. Hooper's house where several officers broke a looking-glass worth twenty Guineas. When British officers, one a social acquaintance, approached Rowe, demanding wine, he refused and the British "Damned me and swore they would take it by Force." Officers and gentlemen violated the norms of polite sociability and the ideology of private property on which it was based; ties between British and American gentry ruptured in the midst of "Such Barbarous Treatment."[28]

The British officers and Massachusetts gentlemen had dishonored an important ideological and cultural tenet: a respect for the ownership of mobile property—ships, trading goods, bills of credit. In a society constructed by an Anglo-American mercantile elite, "notions of refinement and politeness" as J. G. A. Pocock argues, "were crucial elements in the ideology of eighteenth-century commerce." As gentility broke down during these chaotic days, Rowe's allegiance to Britain was finally and completely severed. Destroying property, committing mayhem for days on end while never asking "who is the Owner," so violated Rowe's conception of order and civility that he made a choice—to forsake his British attachments in favor of an American identity.[29]

The rise of a culture of homespun eroded the clear connection between fashionable possessions and privileged status. Owning and using material possessions had become an integral part of constructing individual and group identity in the mid-eighteenth-century polite and commercial culture then holding sway in the Atlantic ports. But, during the later 1760s and 1770s, crowds and political groups in England and America began to appropriate and use elite objects for alternative political expressions. Multiplying the possible meanings of important cultural symbols created components for shaping a new identity. In revolutionary Massachusetts, homespun cloth replaced fashionable fabrics, a silver punch bowl became an icon of liberty, and imported tea steeped in the harbor waters. Altering the uses of genteel possessions and the messages they conveyed, enabled Patriots to distinguish themselves from the Anglo-American elite, to communicate political beliefs, and to devise new modes of self-fashioning.

During and following the non-importation period between 1767 and 1770, fashionable goods acquired additional political meanings defined and expressed in the language and ideology used by the opposition party in Britain. Whig Country Party ideology had been as avidly imported to the colonies during the same decades as Georgian gentility and British "baubles." Goods already spoke a latent political message by denoting status and power, particularly for the merchants and their allies who dominated social and economic life in Boston and Salem. When the revolutionary leaders Samuel and John Adams brought together non-importation and non-consumption agreements with opposition ideology, imported finery came to represent both dangerous economic obligations to British traders and a "decay of virtue."[30] Many colonists now recognized "the riches and luxuries of the East," which bedecked Nicholas Boylston and had so beguiled the Higginson clan and their neighbors in early Salem, as debilitating and enervating substances that would deplete individual vigor, virtue, and independence. Some Americans insisted that in the home country, "luxury has arrived to a great pitch; and it is a universal maxim that luxury indicates the declension of a state."[31] In 1767, the Boston town meeting, believing that the contagion had spread across the Atlantic, decried "the distressed Circumstances of this Town, by means of the amazing growth of Luxury." Samuel Adams repeatedly reminded them that "luxury and extravagance are . . . destructive of those virtues which are necessary for the preservation of liberty and the happiness of the people." The allure evident in Nicholas Boylston's portrait and furnishings seemed to confirm the potential seductiveness of luxury.[32] For many, the only solution to preserving American liberties was a return to homespun.

Prominent merchants supported the first embargo on British imports during the 1760s primarily for economic reasons. Boston merchants, vowing to use "every Legal Measure of freeing the Country from the present Embarrassments [the Townshend Duties]," developed a plan similar to the town meeting's. Traders called for what amounted to a committee of correspondence to enlist the aid of merchants in other towns and provinces. They had no wish to overturn British rule or end colonial dependence on imported goods; they simply wanted to eliminate new taxes and recover their profitable place within the pre-war imperial system.[33] In August 1764, Boston merchants agreed to discard laces and ruffles and to forgo elaborate and expensive mourning rituals associated with funerals of well-to-do gentlemen. Ten years later, the Continental Association incorporated a pledge that "on the death of any relative or friend, none of us . . . will go into any further mourning-dress than a black crape or ribbon on the arm or hat, for gentlemen and a black ribbon and necklace for ladies." Signers throughout the colonies also vowed to "discontinue the giving of gloves and scarves at funerals." The very rituals carried out to honor the wealthy Boston merchant Samuel Shrimpton in 1697 and continued by the merchant elite in Massachusetts were now proscribed throughout the new nation. Revolutionary values had inverted the connection between character and display that elaborate funerals betokened. In the 1760s, graduates at Harvard, Yale, and the College of Rhode Island appeared at commencements sporting suits made of homespun cloth. For a new generation, homespun was in vogue.[34]

The famous Liberty Bowl offers another clear example of appropriating high-style goods for political purposes. Boston's Sons of Liberty commissioned member Paul Revere, a noted silversmith, to design and craft a silver punch bowl to celebrate "the Rescinders" or the "Massachusetts Ninety-two," whose actions constituted an important moment in the forming of Patriot resistance. In February 1768, the Massachusetts General Court voted to send a circular letter to other provincial assemblies calling for another intercolonial caucus like the Stamp Act Congress in 1765. Lord Hillsborough, then in charge of American affairs, ordered the governor to instruct the Assembly to rescind the circular letter; he believed it was "calculated to inflame the Minds" of colonists who might assemble in "unwarrantable Combination" to "subvert the True Principles of the Constitution." On 13 June 1768 the Massachusetts legislature voted on Hillsborough's command. As one Boston merchant recorded, "This day the General Court behaved very steadily and according to the Approbation of most Good People who have any Regard for their Country and Posterity." Ninety-two mem-

bers voted not to rescind the letter, and seventeen "were so mean spirited to vote away their Blessings as Englishmen, namely their Rights,
Liberty and Properties" by voting yea. In retaliation, Governor
Barnard dissolved the General Court. By that fall, the merchants had negotiated another non-importation agreement, British troops had marched
through the streets of Boston, and Paul Revere had fashioned a silver
punch bowl celebrating the Rescinders' decision.[35]

The bowl displayed the ninety-two names of the men who defied
Hillsborough's order and it carried an inscription condemning "the in-
solent Menaces of Villains in Power." It also had a conspicuous reference
to "Number 45," the issue of *North Briton* that made John Wilkes a fugi-
tive and cause célèbre in England. Revere, reached for materials close at
hand and created an artifact that projected double messages. In crafting
the Liberty Bowl of a durable substance—many punch bowls from this
era were made in ceramic—he ensured its lasting quality. By using a
costly material long associated with elite possessions to celebrate
American resistance to British control, he transformed the meaning of a
significant status marker from Georgian gentility to Patriot virtue. In
using a punch bowl for a political message, Revere adapted a practice
emerging in the Wilkite culture of Britain in the late 1760s.

John Wilkes, a somewhat disreputable journalist and member of the
House of Commons, burst on the international scene in the early 1760s
after his arrest for libeling the king in issue No. 45 of his periodical *North
Briton*. He was arrested under a general warrant for search and seizure,
expelled from Parliament, imprisoned for a time in the infamous Tower
of London, and eventually fled to France. His name and "Number 45"
became a rallying cry for protest against general warrants and ministerial tyranny. By late 1766, Parliament had repealed the Stamp Act and a
British court had declared general warrants illegal. Wilkes returned
from exile as a celebrity and was reelected to and then expelled from
Commons four times in 1768. Each reelection was greeted with large
demonstrations and raucous celebrations. Wilkes was jailed again and
kept at King's Bench Prison during his trial. When the next session of
Parliament opened on 10 May 1768, thousands of Wilkes's supporters
gathered in St. George's Field outside the prison while British troops attempted to keep order. Events got out of hand; the troops fired on the
crowd, killing several and wounding others. Accounts of the St.
George's Field Massacre reached Massachusetts in July. That news, combined with the Townshend Duties and rumored imposition of British
troops, confirmed the fears of the Sons of Liberty.[36]

Wilkes's celebrity in England and America, fostered by continual ref-

FIGURE 10. Sons of Liberty Bowl showing No. 45 in honor of John Wilkes.
Paul Revere, 1768. Gift by Subscription and Francis Bartlett Fund, 1949.
Courtesy of Museum of Fine Arts, Boston.

erences to the numbers 45 and 92—Charleston's artisans met under a
Liberty Tree trimmed with forty-five lights, then toasted with forty-five
bottles of wine and ninety-two glasses while Maryland supporters sent
forty-five hams and forty-five hogsheads of tobacco to Wilkes and
Bostonians supplied him with turtles for feasting weighing forty-five
and forty-seven pounds for a total of ninety-two—spread through "a
novel form of political controversy" and an alternative use of material
goods. A radical political culture developed its own types of dress, its
own consumer goods, and its own modes of celebration. Producers immediately capitalized on the new sentiments and responded with goods
that inspired consumer demand and political participation. Clubs and
benevolent societies throughout Britain organized celebrations and
protests on behalf of Wilkes; sometimes calling themselves Sons of
Liberty, they ordered inexpensive ceramic mugs, punchbowls, and
medals sporting the number 45 or slogans like "Wilkes For Ever." The
refined Whig could purchase an expensive porcelain figure of Wilkes or
fine teapots and snuff boxes adorned with "45" or "Wilkes and Liberty."
and even a Wilkite wig with forty-five curls. "Wilkes' Head Inns," and
"Forty-five Taverns" sprouted everywhere, and the traditional festivity

of May Day became a Wilkite fair in Bristol.[37] Buying and displaying these new commodities furnished one very visible means of identifying with the Whig cause.

American resisters borrowed from British radical politics, especially the movement around John Wilkes, in organizing American resistance to what was increasingly seen as a ministerial and Parliamentary tyranny. In June 1768, as the Massachusetts legislature voted not to rescind its circular letter, Boston's Sons of Liberty began a direct correspondence with Wilkes. At a huge dinner for 350 held by Boston's Sons of Liberty, the diners drank forty-five toasts. John Adams acknowledged that "Festivals" like this "render the People fond of their Leaders in the Cause" and "impregnate them with the sentiments of Liberty." British and American radicals shared a general but diffuse goal of "liberty." However, Americans, such as the Sons of Liberty in Massachusetts, moved beyond British activities to develop their own methods—committees of correspondence and tarring and feathering—and their own goals which included weaning Americans from British consumer goods. Civility and order retained importance for many, but elegant fashion no longer demonstrated the highest social values.[38]

The Boston Tea Party episode provides another view of revolutionary resistance as it complicated or multiplied the meaning(s) associated with consumer goods. The genteel behaviors and imported wares used in brewing, serving, and drinking this warm and stimulating beverage had evolved into a significant ritual of Anglo-American polite and commercial culture. Peter Faneuil demonstrated his membership in Boston's mercantile elite at elaborate tea ceremonies in his elegant parlor. For Mary Holyoke, a physician's wife popular among Salem's elite, drinking tea became a central activity in her social calendar. In November 1761, while visiting Boston for a few days, her diary recorded a busy round of dinners and teas with leading merchant families. On the fifth, she "Drank tea at Mrs. Fitch." The following day she "Drank tea and spent the evening" with her aunt and uncle. On the seventh, she drank tea at Mrs. Allen's and on the eighth with Mrs. Davis. Back in Salem she invited guests for tea in her own home and visited others to enjoy this polite ritual. These social exchanges of afternoon tea, served with elaborate silver and porcelain ware, helped to define the professional and commercial gentry of Salem and Boston.[39]

But during the non-importation movement of the late 1760s–1770s, imported tea and resistance to British tyranny intertwined in a manner that heightened the political meaning of the social practice. A broadside issued in New York and addressed "to the tea-drinking ladies" bore the title *The Female Patriot no. I*. Three years later, when the British refused to repeal the tax on tea and limited exports to the East India Company and its assigned dealers/merchants, protests quickly transformed foreign tea into a central symbol of resistance. As the first shipments of Company tea began to arrive in port, Bostonians and inhabitants from nearby towns met in Faneuil Hall to "determine the most proper and effectual method to prevent the unloading, receiving, or vending the detestable tea sent out by the East-India Company." "The Body" or "The People," one to two thousand strong, met again the following day and resolved to ignore the governor's edict and return the tea to England. This placed many leading merchants in a difficult position. During the furor, John Rowe reluctantly accepted a committee position "much against [his] will" but felt he "dare not say a word." Even after he was chosen to represent the resisters, Rowe was called before "The Body" to explain his association with a Captain Bruce whose ship had just entered the harbor with a shipment of tea on board. Rowe agreed to "prevail on [the captain] to act with Reason in this Affair" and not unload the tea, admitting privately that "it hath given me great Uneasiness." "The Body" continued meeting, determined not to permit any tea to come on land. On the night of 16 December a group concealed in "Indian Dresses" boarded three ships, "hoisted out the Tea and flung it overboard" observed by a crowd of over two-thousand. The "party" worked quickly and methodically to dump over ninety-thousand pounds of tea worth about nine thousand pounds and "made a Tea Pot of the Harbor of Boston."⁴⁰

Contemporary reactions to what has become an American myth varied. John Adams praised the action, saying, "there is a Dignity, a Majesty, A Sublimity in the last Effort of the Patriots." Rowe, caught up in these events as both a potential importer of tea and an enforcer of "The Body's" prohibition against it, insisted he knew "nothing of the Matter nor who were concerned in it" and expressed his sincere sorrow for the destruction of the tea. He noted with regret "I would rather have lost five hundred Guineas than [Captain] Bruce should have taken any of this Tea on board his Ship." Peter Oliver, a disgruntled Tory, later described meetings of "The Body" as "hissing and clapping, cursing and swearing of the Rabble." To him, the "Deeds of Darkness" that evening constituted "Acts of Treason and Rebellion."⁴¹

For most, the Tea Party complicated the meaning of an elite ritual. Mocking the polite performance at the tea table by dressing as Indians—the "partiers" inverted a high-style ceremony by making a teapot of Boston Harbor where, in the words of one scornful Loyalist, "the fish had the whole Regale to theirselves [*sic*]." Earlier, gathering the fruits of foreign trade and performing the ritual of afternoon tea had allowed colonists of varying ethnicity such as Peter Faneuil to proclaim themselves as English gentleman. The Tea Party, by turning that process on its head and discarding imported tea into the murky waters along Boston's docks, revised opinion about the value and significance of India tea. To refuse it, meant to be an American, to imbibe it, un-American.[42]

Adding a new layer of meaning to the message that imported tea communicated to elites and commoners did not eliminate the earlier ritual. It did make the choice to participate a significant message about political and cultural affiliations. Elite Loyalist sympathizers like the Paine family of Worcester or the Ornes of Salem showed an unwavering commitment to Anglo-American politics and politeness by ordering an elaborate silver tea service just a few months after the episode in Boston. When genteel physician Dr. Edward Holyoke sent his wife to safety on Nantucket after the conflicts at Lexington and Concord, she joined many other Salem and Boston families as they quickly began an active round of dining and drinking tea. The Massachusetts Loyalists who fled to England such as Benjamin Pickman, Judge Peter Oliver, and the Hutchinson and Hallowell families, also continued their polite customs, often meeting over tea in London, Bristol, and other provincial cities. Adhering to former political allegiances and social customs, the Loyalists proclaimed themselves British, not American.[43]

Anglo-American polite culture built on business connections and shaped by a particular relationship to consumer goods came under assault from British policies and radical politics. British policies and behaviors, particularly the closing of Boston's harbor, stood directly in the way of overseas trade and thus undermined the sense of belonging to a shared transatlantic commercial and genteel culture. Consumer goods and genteel rituals were a fundamental part of constructing an Anglo-American polite and commercial culture. As the meaning of goods and rituals changed it became more and more difficult to override differences between Britain and America and between Patriots and Loyalists.

Boston and Salem merchants who attempted to continue business and pleasure as usual experienced difficult circumstances. At least two of Timothy Orne's children, progeny of one of Salem's wealthiest merchants at midcentury, found themselves subject to Patriot discipline during the revolutionary period. Just a few years after her father's and mother's premature death, Lois Orne, possessor of a substantial inheritance, married into Worcester's prominent Paine family. The wedding announcement referred to the bride's financial qualifications, calling her "a young Lady in Possession of a large Fortune." The elite nature of the Orne-Paine alliance was embodied in a forty-five-piece silver tea service bearing the Orne coat of arms and the bride's initials "L.O." The service included tea and coffee pots, porringers, one creamer, two butter boats, tongs, and eighteen silver spoons. Commissioned by the groom in honor of the upcoming nuptials, the pieces were crafted by the Patriot silversmith Paul Revere. The patron-client relationship inherent in the production of high-style consumer goods could still, for the moment, bridge diverging political sympathies.[44]

The opulence accompanying the couple's marriage may have helped draw the attention of revolutionary crowds to the Paine family. In August of 1774, not quite a year after the Orne-Paine marriage, a crowd of thousands gathered in Worcester.[45] Drawn from town and the surrounding hamlets, people began assembling at 7 A.M. Led by their officers, militia units practiced formations on the common while a small group walked to the Paine house to confront Timothy Paine, the family patriarch. The delegation hoped to convince Paine to resign as a royally appointed councillor, warning him that they could not "answer for the consequences of refusal."[46] Paine, unable to convince the delegation to withdraw, agreed to issue a statement that "my appointment was without my solicitation" and agreed not to "take a seat . . . unless it is agreeable to the Charter of this province." He was then forced to walk bareheaded, "cap in hand," through a crowd to deliver his resignation. Paine noted the emotions of that day in a letter to General Gage, observing that "the people's spirits are so raised they seem determined to risk their lives and everything dear to them in the opposition."[47] No longer feeling protected by an elite position, Lois's husband William, a devoted British sympathizer, left for England shortly after the confrontation.[48]

As the culture of homespun gained influence and power, other elite families found it expedient to leave Massachusetts. They departed to escape retribution for continuing to display both luxury and Loyalism. Thomas Hutchinson, after being replaced as governor by General Gage, left Boston with his family on 31 May 1774, the last day before the Boston Port Bill shut down incoming shipping. Hutchinson, joined by his Oliver relatives, became the acknowledged leader of the expatriate group. Loyalist Colonel William Browne, of Salem's leading mercantile family, departed for England via Halifax a year later. He left his wife and children in Salem to guard the family holdings from confiscation by Patriot leaders. When Browne became a distinguished officer in the British Army two years later, his family joined him in England. Subsequently he garnered an appointment as governor of Bermuda. Colonel Benjamin Pickman Jr. likewise left his wife to guard the family estate until his return to Salem in 1785. John Rowe's close friend and relative George Inman of Cambridge sailed for England with Rowe's daughter and son-in-law. Soon, other leading merchant families, such as the Clarkes and Ervings, joined their fellow political refugees.[49]

Attempting to recreate their social cohesion, refined lifestyle, and privileged position, the exiled Loyalists congregated at the New England Coffeehouse in London and established a New England Club that dined weekly at the Adelphi in the Strand. A number of Massachusetts merchants were assisted and entertained by partners in British merchant houses. Colonel Pickman, upon arriving in Bristol in 1775, dined almost immediately with the America merchant Mr. Griffiths who dealt with several prominent overseas traders from Salem. Griffiths arranged introductions to London dignitaries including a member of Parliament. In London, Pickman found his early weeks filled with "seeing the Curiosities of London," visiting with Hutchinson's circle, and enjoying dinners in this "gay city." Members of Lane, Son, and Fraser, London's premier firm trading with New England, often entertained Colonel Pickman. Lane and Fraser frequently dined with other exiled Massachusetts merchants such as Peter Frye, George Erving, and Harrison Gray during their wartime exile.[50] Bristol, the second largest port in the kingdom, attracted eighteen Massachusetts refugee families, including Rowe's relative George Inman. Many of them noted with longing Bristol's similarity to Boston. In London and Bristol Loyalists formed genteel social groups of merchants and professional families just as they had done in Boston and Salem. No longer at home in Massachusetts, Anglo-American polite and commercial culture persisted in the streets and parlors of England.

After their initial enthusiasm, transplanted New Englanders found it difficult to enjoy England's polite and commercial culture without easy access to goods or credit. Once they were cut off from their supplies of farm products and fish and, in many cases, from the means to continue shipping goods for others, the financial underpinnings of their gentility and elite status disintegrated. The British government provided an annual pension of one hundred pounds to each loyalist family but in the expensive environs of London, this provided for few of the elegancies that had become necessities for colonial elites. Colonel Pickman observed that "Many of my Countrymen have applied to [the British] Government for Assistance and have received it." More fortunate than most, Pickman explained to his wife that "My friends Messrs Lane Son &

Fraser are willing to supply me till I can receive money from you." Perhaps because his two brothers in Salem carried on the family business, Pickman could maintain his credit for a longer period than many Massachusetts exiles. Even so, Pickman grew tired of London, "the Rumbling of the Coaches, the Jostling in the Streets, the Fog, Smoke and Dirt of the Town, appear inexpressibly odious." Yet when he attended the theater or concerts he could understand why people flocked to the metropolis.

Prominent Loyalists continued to cling to class distinctions, refusing to mingle with British-sympathizing artisans and laborers who also fled New England. Demonstrating their persistent status concerns, exiles such as Samuel Curwen of Salem complained vociferously about misbehavior of common people at the theater and other public venues. As the war in America dragged on, many were forced to abandon London for cheaper locations in provincial towns and smaller villages. No doubt homesickness intensified as their exile continued and the decline of their fortunes and position at the top of the social hierarchy became increasingly evident.[51]

The few British sympathizers who remained in Boston or Salem but refused to accommodate to the culture of homespun did not fare well. Lois Orne's brother, Timothy Orne III, married to the daughter of his father's friend and fellow clubman William Pynchon, chose to stay. He barely escaped being tarred and feathered for suspected Loyalist leanings. Pynchon, long a respected attorney for Salem merchants, found his windows broken by a mob that doubted his Patriotism. Those among the Massachusetts merchant elite who adapted to the new political and social realities earned handsome profits from privateering during the war. From 1777 to 1780, Salem's fleet of armed vessels doubled from thirty to sixty. Local captains regularly brought British brigantines and schooners laden with flour, rum, and English goods into port to auction off the goods and share the profits among investors and owners. A few merchant families, including the Cabots, Derbys, and Rowes, found themselves in better financial circumstances when the war ended than when it began. In the 1790s, they would reinvest their capital in the China trade and later establish the textile industry in New England, becoming important figures in the new nation.[52]

Wealthy Patriot merchants who adopted republican ideals and homespun simplicity did not forsake all components of Georgian refinement. John Rowe, for instance, made a polite call on General Washington shortly after provincial troops entered Boston, and a few days later, the Rowes entertained Generals Greene and Putnam and several other officers at their home. But the integral connection between status and ownership of high-style British goods no longer lay at the center of polite society. Patriots of all levels endeavored to redefine the meaning of material goods and, in doing so, built the makings of an American identity.

Epilogue

My Lord is a Baniya. He conducts His commerce righteously.
Without scales and balances, He weighs the entire universe.
                    KABIR GRANTHAVALI, C. 1500

AFTER THE REVOLUTION, merchants in Boston and Salem
initiated direct trade with Asia, profiting mightily from a resurgence of
consumer demand and their ability to eliminate the British middleman,
particularly the East India Company which had drawn the ire of
Bostonians in 1773.[1] A few of the leading merchants in the China trade
were descendants of eighteenth-century mercantile families. Others, like
the Derbys of Salem, had been masters and ship captains for Timothy
Orne and other leading merchants. And new traders arrived from
Newburyport and other smaller communities north of Boston. But no
dominant mercantile elite emerged in the early republic. One prerevolutionary holdover, the merchant James Bowdoin, noted in 1783, "you will
scarcely see any other than new faces." The postwar merchants of
Boston "formed a diffuse assemblage of venturers" not an integrated
merchant community.[2]

Over time, families successful in accumulating profits in the China
trade began to seek other investments for their money. The Jeffersonian
embargoes and the War of 1812 demonstrated what earlier merchants
knew as well, that overseas trade was a risky business. In an effort to
find more secure and predictable sources of money for their families, the
new merchants formed the Boston Associates and established the textile
industry in Massachusetts. Gradually, an entrepreneurial elite, including families like the Cabots, Lawrences, Lowells, and Appletons,
emerged during the 1820s and 1830s. They pooled capital to found the
textile mills of Waltham, Lowell, and Lawrence, contributed funds to
build the Charles River Bridge and the Boston and Lowell Railroad, and
launched the Suffolk Bank and the Massachusetts Hospital Life (a kind
of investment bank).[3] In a manner similar to the eighteenth-century merchant elite they used money derived from global business connections

for local improvements rather than national endeavors. Joining in public philanthropic projects, they helped to establish the Massachusetts General Hospital and the McLean Asylum. They shared a variety of ventures through friendship and intermarriage, developing new businesses, charity works, and cultural institutions. Like their predecessors, they used philanthropy to demonstrate class distinction.[4] And, not surprisingly, some of them looked fondly back to the Boston and Salem of a century before.

Amos Lawrence, one of the Boston Associates, had traded a merchant's livelihood based on calculation and risk for a textile entrepreneur's steady income and philanthropic pursuits. Lawrence sought to escape the rapidly growing towns of industry and immigrants that he had helped to initiate. He looked back to what he imagined was a more homogeneous world in his benefactions to rural academies and colleges (Lawrence Academy in Groton, and Williams College) and revolutionary monuments (Bunker Hill). In a portrait by Chester Harding done in 1846, Lawrence fashioned his image for posterity by posing in a silk dressing gown (a banyan) and velvet cap in imitation of Copley's painting of wealthy Boston merchant Nicholas Boylston in the 1760s (see figure 9, p. 150). Lawrence may have seen Boylston's portrait at annual exhibitions of the "Great Masters" held at the Boston Athenaeum—he was a founding member—or at the Philosophy Room at Harvard where the full-length likeness, crafted by Copley after Boylston's death,[5] shows the merchant's feet encased in dark leather slippers. Lawrence chose velvet slippers. In portraying himself as a colonial merchant, Lawrence perhaps evoked a simpler time when society seemed more rooted in social "brotherhood."[6] Or was he reminding himself, his family, and his society that much of the consumer demand that engendered Massachusetts industry had been produced by the exploits of Boston and Salem's merchant princes?

The one hundred years between 1660–1763 may have been "the golden age of commerce" for colonial merchants. By the turn of the century leading traders in Boston and Salem began in earnest to adopt Georgian gentility and refigure their identity based on purchased goods and acquired manners. In pursuing economic goals and proclaiming personal status, they used wealth derived from global trading connections to reshape local environs. To gain increasing control over the production and distribution of economic resources, including foodstuffs and the fisheries, they rebuilt their towns, widening and straightening streets, enlarging docks, and constructing rows of warehouses to facilitate the flow of goods in and out of port. They erected urban villas and gardens patterned after British bourgeois styles and filled them with the latest cos-

FIGURE 11. Amos Lawrence costumed like Nicholas Boylston. Portrait of
Amos Lawrence, Benefactor by Chester Harding, 1846. Courtesy of Williams
College Museum of Art.

mopolitan furnishings. New Georgian-style public buildings, churches, assembly rooms, and market halls materialized in Boston and Salem through the largess of merchant families.

Not only did merchants change the built landscape and improve the economic infrastructure, they also transformed the social order in these port cities, eclipsing the Puritan elite that had governed Massachusetts in the previous century. Men who made their living from gathering, counting, valuing, packing, and shipping goods came to place increasing weight on the meaning of material things. They and their families adopted cosmopolitan manners and high-style possessions to define themselves individually and as a group. They shared mercantile ventures, developed new kinds of leisure pursuits, and devoted interest, money, and time to investing in consumer wares and acquiring refined behaviors. Consumption at this level demanded time and effort to learn the methods of preparing and serving beverages like tea, coffee, and chocolate, and to select the new assemblage of teapots, cups and saucers, sugar bowls, waste bowls, and spoons, all necessary to the tea table. The ability and willingness to invest in consumption distinguished the merchant elite from those less able or disposed to participate in fashionable living.

A culture based on goods and manners offered a pathway into the gentry for successful traders and professionals from other European ethnic groups. Notable among these immigrants who refashioned themselves into Georgian gentlemen were the Cabot family from the Channel Islands, Jacob Wendell of Dutch ancestry, the French Huguenot Faneuil family, and the German-speaking Crowninshields. All acquired their wealth from trading ventures and each joined the mercantile elite in Boston or Salem, by adopting English manners and building Georgian-style homes.

Other developments flowed from the individual and group practices of Boston and Salem merchants and their strong influence on cultural values in provincial Massachusetts. An increase in religious toleration, required by the new Massachusetts Charter of 1691, gained support from cultural change that emphasized outward appearances, signaled in fashionable clothes, expensive houses, and refined manners rather than spiritual conversion as evidence of character and value. Even John Adams, on seeing Nicholas Boylston's opulent home, had to conclude that it was "a Seat for a noble Man."[7] Gradually, Bostonians and Salemites began to accept that value and character could be acquired by those of various Protestant faiths—Huguenots, Dutch Reformed, Anglicans—and began to include them among the "best men."

A culture constructed around material acquisitions and sociable gatherings produced an explosion in demand for new articles at all levels. While the families studied here demonstrated an intense involvement in consumer goods and polite graces, even the middling and lower sort demanded their tea.[8] Increasing consumer demand, we can see in retrospect, was the next step in a massive expansion of capitalism. While most histories of the Industrial Revolution have concentrated on changes in production, scholars of the Consumer Revolution argue that it was the demand associated with the growth and expansion of the "world of goods" that called forth new methods and structures of production.[9] Although neither the Faneuils nor the Ornes could foresee the coming of industry to Massachusetts, their activities contributed an important link in that chain of development.

The whole enterprise of this study combines an exploration of material culture and the built landscape with an investigation of economic, social, and cultural practices in two Atlantic ports. Only through studying consumption along with production can we more fully understand the broad developments and the crucial role played by the merchant elite in Massachusetts. The creation of a "polite and commercial" culture on this side of the Atlantic and its connections to and differences from Britain only become clear when we examine the material world, see the adoption of Georgian architecture and fashions, observe the rebuilding of cities for economic and cultural purposes, and learn of new leisure pursuits, all means by which this new class came together. Case studies of merchant families demonstrate how the practices and decisions of individuals created a new culture. We learn, for example, how French merchants like Peter Faneuil transformed themselves into English gentlemen by an astute deployment of high-style goods and rituals. Through a consideration of the material world, we can see how a culture used possessions to communicate economic power, group membership, and personal identity.

We are familiar with the existing paradigm of "Puritan to Yankee," based on small-town Connecticut, and often take it to be the story of New England as a whole.[10] But, in Atlantic ports like Boston and Salem, historical change followed a different pattern. In the eighteenth century a merchant elite arose that transformed the cultural landscape of Boston and Salem from a Puritan community into a social marketplace of polite graces and consumer goods. To negotiate that bazaar required a new strategy, a transformation from Puritan planter to Georgian gentleman. With the emergence of revolutionary politics, goods again took on new meanings in the hands of the Sons of Liberty and their followers.

Numbers of the mercantile elite clung to their attachment to fashionable possessions and Anglo-American gentility, leaving Massachusetts for English settlements in Canada or transplanting themselves and their families to London or provincial capitals in Britain. Many of Boston and Salem's Georgian gentlemen used the changing attitudes toward material goods to transform their culture once again and shape a new identity as Patriots and Americans.

For over two-thirds of the eighteenth century the mercantile elite in Boston and Salem, using money derived from their connections to worldwide trade, exerted strong economic and cultural influence over their local settings. After 1774–5, with their influence overturned by revolutionary ideals, their possessions ransacked by mobs or British troops, and their families scattered, few of the merchant elite of early Boston and Salem retained their important positions. Descendants of some, like the Cabot family, immigrants from the French culture of the Channel Islands to Georgian Salem, or the Jacksons in Newburyport, continued merchant activities amassing fortunes in the China trade that sprang up in the 1790s. They intermarried with newer entrepreneurial families like the Appletons and Lawrences. By the 1830s and 1840s another entrepreneurial elite coalesced and exerted a cultural hegemony over Massachusetts and through Whig political activities broadcast their values onto the national stage. They looked back to Boston and Salem merchants as exemplars. Like their presumed forefathers from mid-eighteenth-century ports, they little resembled the Yankee traders of literary construction. The way they spent their wealth defined them as much as the means by which they gained it. Their character, so they hoped, could be read through their portraits, possessions, and philanthropic gestures. From the quiet high-ceilinged rooms of the Boston Athenaeum to the brick walls confining the mad at the McLean Asylum, the Boston Brahmins—named after India's highest caste and the Hindu spirit from which all being emanates and returns—like the Georgian gentlemen who preceded them, could be known best by the goods they acquired and the gifts they gave.

.

Notes

Introduction. "Emporium for the World"

1. Alexander Pope, quoted in Mark Girouard, *The English Town: A History of Urban Life* (New Haven, Conn.: Yale University Press, 1990), 38. The phrase taken as the title of my introduction is based on contemporary usage. In the *Spectator*, in 1711, Joseph Addison called London "a kind of Emporium for the Whole Earth." A century later the English National Census claimed that London was "the greatest Emporium in the known world." Both quoted in Roy Porter, *London: A Social History* (Cambridge, Mass.: Harvard University Press, 1995), 99. Boston and Salem served the same role for the hinterlands of colonial New England.

2. Daniel Defoe, *A Tour through the Whole Island of Great Britain* (London: G. Strahan, 1724; reprint ed., London: Penguin Books, 1986), 316.

3. Dr. Alexander Hamilton, visiting the Northeast in 1744, said, "Boston is the largest town in North America, being much about the same extent as the city of Glasgow in Scotland." *The Itinerarium of Dr. Alexander Hamilton, 1744*, ed. Carl Bridenbaugh (Pittsburgh: University of Pittsburgh Press, 1948), 144.

4. James Birket, *Some Cursory Remarks Made by James Birket in His Voyage to North America, 1750–1751* (New Haven: Yale University Press, 1916), 19, quoted in Marcus Rediker, *Between the Devil and the Deep Blue Sea: Merchant Seaman, Pirates, and the Anglo-American Maritime World, 1700–1750* (Cambridge: Cambridge University Press, 1987), 62.

5. Ibid.; Hamilton, *Itinerarium*, 145; James Duncan Phillips, *Salem in the Eighteenth Century* (Salem, Mass.: Essex Institute, 1969), 77–78; Captain Nathaniel Uring, *Voyages and Travels*, 112, 113, quoted in Phillips, *Salem*, 85.

6. Paul Langford, *A Polite and Commercial People: England 1727–1783* (Oxford: Clarendon Press, 1989), 168.

7. Langford, *A Polite and Commercial People*, 168–70; John J. McCusker and Russell R. Menard, *The Economy of British America, 1607–1789* (Chapel Hill: University of North Carolina Press, 1985), 39–42. Also see Ralph Davis's many works on English shipping and foreign trade, especially *The Rise of the English Shipping Industry in the Seventeenth and Eighteenth Centuries* (London: Macmillan, 1962) and *The Rise of the Atlantic Economies* (Ithaca: Cornell University Press, 1973).

8. See McCusker, *Economy of British North America*, 39–45, for a discussion of the arguments over the importance of the slave trade to the growth of capitalism and the industrial revolution initiated by Eric Williams in *Capitalism and Slavery* (Chapel Hill: University of North Carolina Press, 1944).

9. Joyce Oldham Appleby, *Economic Thought and Ideology in Seventeenth-Century England* (Princeton, N.J.: Princeton University Press, 1978) provides a detailed discussion of economic writings in the seventeenth century.

10. David Hancock finds London merchants "relatively indifferent to national borders" and mildly opposed to state intervention and management of commerce. David Hancock, *Citizens of the World: London Merchants and the Integration of the British Atlantic Community, 1735–1785* (Cambridge: Cambridge University Press, 1995), 38.

11. See Hancock, *Citizens of the World*; Langford, *A Polite and Commercial People*, and Lawrence Stone and Jeanne C. Fawtier Stone, *An Open Elite? England, 1540–1880* (Oxford: Clarendon Press, 1984).

12. Thomas Haskell suggests that capitalism produced a new "cognitive style," "a heightened sense of personal effectiveness created by the possession and use of powerful recipes . . . Made powerful . . . in part by the growing calculability of a market society." The market taught one "to attend to the remote consequences of one's acts." That led in turn to an expanded sense of responsibility toward humanitarian concerns. Thomas Haskell, "Capitalism and the Origins of the Humanitarian Sensibility, Part 1," and "Capitalism and the Origins of the Humanitarian Sensibility, Part 2," in *The Antislavery Debate: Capitalism and Abolitionism as a Problem in Historical Interpretation*, ed. Thomas Bender (Berkeley: University of California Press, 1992), 111, 151. See also Lorraine Daston in *Classical Probability in the Enlightenment* (Princeton, N.J.: Princeton University Press, 1988).

13. Evidence indicates that most eighteenth-century Massachusetts merchants studied here maintained positive credit balances with their British correspondent firms. I saw no evidence that they had to scramble to repay their English creditors, as has often been assumed about colonial merchants.

14. Stone and Stone, *Open Elite?* 10, 7.

15. Ibid., 212–21. The suburban villa is an example of a housing form designed to meet the needs of the wealthy commercial classes. Its size, purpose, layout, and decoration varied greatly from those of the country seats of the landed elite. On the evolution of the villa see John Summerson, *Architecture in Britain, 1530–1830* (New Haven, Conn.: Yale University Press, 1953), 346–48.

16. On Puritan economic culture see Stephen Innes, *Creating the Commonwealth: The Economic Culture of Puritan New England* (New York: Norton, 1995).

17. Albert O. Hirschman explores this changing outlook or worldview in *The Passions and the Interests: Political Arguments for Capitalism before Its Triumph* (Princeton, N.J.: Princeton University Press, 1977).

18. Max Weber, *The Protestant Ethic and the Spirit of Capitalism*, trans. Talcott Parsons (New York: Scribner, 1958). Subsequent scholars have discussed Weber's complex thesis. See Thomas Nipperdey, "Max Weber, Protestantism, and the Context of the Debate around 1900," in *Weber's Protestant Ethic: Origins, Evidence, Contexts*, ed. Hartmut Lehmann (Washington, D.C.: Cambridge University Press for the German Historical Institute, 1993), 74–75. See also Ernst Troeltsch, *Protestantism and Progress: A Historical Study of the Relation of Protestantism to the Modern World*, trans. W. Montgomery (Boston: Beacon Press, 1958); R. H. Tawney, *Religion and the Rise of Capitalism* (New York: Harcourt Brace, 1926); H. M. Robertson, *Aspects of the Rise of Economic Individualism: A Criticism of Max Weber and his School* (Cambridge: Cambridge University Press, 1933). More recent work includes Gordon Marshall, *In Search of the Spirit of Capitalism: An Essay on Max Weber's Protestant Ethic Thesis* (New York: Columbia University Press, 1982); John Patrick Diggins, *Max Weber: Politics and the Spirit of Tragedy* (New York: Basic Books, 1996).

19. Weber, *The Protestant Ethic*, 158, 160, 166, 171, 121, 154, 69, 71.

20. Perry Miller, *The New England Mind: From Colony to Province*, (Cambridge: Harvard University Press, 1953) 41.

21. Richard Mather, quoted in Perry Miller, *The New England Mind: The Seventeenth Century* (New York: Macmillan Company, 1939; reprint ed., Boston: Beacon Press, 1961).

22. Ibid., 44, 50.

23. Reverend John Higginson, quoted ibid., 36. On the Higginson family see Higginson Letters, *Collections of the Massachusetts Historical Society 3rd* ser. 7 (1838): 197–217. Miller, *The Seventeenth Century*, 40, 52.

24. Ibid., 171, 170. On Mather's *Political Fables* and polite learning see Harry S. Stout, *The New England Soul: Preaching and Religious Culture in Colonial New England* (New York:

Oxford University Press, 1986), 132. On the decline of providential thinking and Cotton Mather as a transitional figure, see Michael P. Winship, *Seers of God: Puritan Providentialism in the Restoration and Early Enlightenment* (Baltimore: Johns Hopkins University Press, 1996).

25. Works on capitalism in early New England include Stephen Innes, *Labor in a New Land: Economy and Society in Seventeenth-Century Springfield* (Princeton, N.J.: Princeton University Press, 1983), and *Creating the Commonwealth*; John Frederick Martin, *Profits in the Wilderness: Entrepreneurship and the Founding of New England Towns in the Seventeenth Century* (Chapel Hill: University of North Carolina Press, 1991).

26. T. H. Breen, "An Empire of Goods: The Anglicization of Colonial America, 1690–1776," *Journal of British Studies* vol. 25 no. 4 (October 1986): 475; John J. McCusker and Russell R. Menard, *The Economy of British America, 1607–1789* (Chapel Hill: University of North Carolina Press, 1985). Many Provincial officials from Massachusetts could devote themselves to civic duty because they had economic support from a family engaged in long-distance trade. The mercantile elite included high-level government leaders, and many customs officials appointed by the crown. By 1750, the growing prestige of attorneys and physicians vaulted them into Boston and Salem's elite.

27. Richard L. Bushman, *From Puritan to Yankee: Character and the Social Order in Connecticut, 1690–1765* (Cambridge, Mass.: Harvard University Press, 1967), 25; Breen, "Empire of Goods," 491, 497.

28. Bushman, *Puritan to Yankee*, 124–25; *Boston Gazette* for the year 1720; Bernard Bailyn and Lotte Bailyn, *Massachusetts Shipping, 1697–1714: A Statistical Study* (Cambridge, Mass.: Harvard University Press, 1959), tables 17 and 18 (102–9), and table 26 (127).

29. Hancock, *Citizens of the World*.

30. Richard L. Bushman, *The Refinement of America: Persons, Houses, Cities* (New York: Knopf, 1992), xvii, 465.

31. Weber, *The Protestant Ethic*, 71.

32. For a detailed discussion of Peter Faneuil and his gentry status, see chapter 4.

33. Peter Faneuil to Samuel and William Baker, 10 June 1738. "Peter Faneuil Letterbook," New England Historical and Genealogical Society, Boston, Massachusetts.

34. William Luscomb and John Pickering subscribers, 31 January 1763. Timothy Orne Papers, Phillips Library, Peabody and Essex Museum (hereafter Orne Papers).

Chapter 1. Piety and Profit in Puriton Boston

1. The epigraph of John Hull, "Some Passages of God's Providence About Myself and in Relation to Myself: Penned Down that I May be the More Mindful of, and Thankful for, all God's Dispensations Toward Me" (1624–1680), published as "Diary of John Hull," *American Antiquarian Society Transactions and Collections* 3 (1857): 156 (hereafter Hull's "Diary").

2. John Winthrop, "Common Grevances Groaninge for Reformation," quoted in Darrett Rutman, *Winthrop's Boston: Portrait of a Puritan Town, 1630–1649* (Chapel Hill: University of North Carolina Press, 1965), 6.

3. John Winthrop, "A Modell of Christian Charity," reprinted in *Puritanism and the American Experience*, ed. Michael McGiffert (Reading, Mass.: Addison-Wesley, 1969), 31.

4. John Winthrop, quoted ibid., 32, 33.

5. Joan Thirsk, *Economic Polity and Projects: The Development of a Consumer Society in Early Modern England.* (Oxford: Clarendon Press, 1978), 1.

6. Richard Saltonstall to Emmanuel Downing, 4 February 1631, in *The Saltonstall Papers, 1607–1815* vol. 1, *Massachusetts Historical Society Collections* vol. 80 (Boston: Massachusetts Historical Society, 1972), 117.

7. Ibid.

8. Two important articles that represent this precapitalist viewpoint are James A. Henretta, "Families and Farms: *Mentalité* in Pre-industrial America," *William and Mary*

Quarterly (hereafter *WMQ*), 3rd ser., 35 (1978): 3–32; and Daniel Vickers, "Competency and Competition: Economic Culture in Early America," ibid., 47 (January 1990): 3–29. See also Kenneth A. Lockridge, *A New England Town: The First Hundred Years* (New York: Norton, 1970). Two significant recent entries in the transition to capitalism debate are Christopher Clark, *The Roots of Rural Capitalism: Western Massachusetts, 1780–1860* (Ithaca: Cornell University Press, 1990) and Winifred Barr Rothenberg, *From Market Places to a Market Economy: The Transformation of Rural Massachusetts, 1750–1850* (Chicago: University of Chicago Press, 1992), both of whom suggest that rural New Englanders were not fully involved in the "spirit of modern capitalism" until the mid- to late eighteenth century.

9. Stephen Innes, *Creating the Commonwealth: The Economic Culture of Puritan New England* (New York: Norton, 1995), 42, 44, 45.

10. Ibid., 56. Innes refers to Robert Brenner who argues that the growth of commercial agriculture in England produced an early transition to capitalism. Brenner argues, in short, that English capitalism developed "within an aristocratic landlord framework" and not through a Marxian bourgeois revolution. Robert Brenner, "Bourgeois Revolution and Transition to Capitalism," in *The First Modern Society: Essays in English History in Honour of Lawrence Stone*, ed. A. L. Beier, David Cannadine, and James M. Rosenheim (Cambridge: Cambridge University Press, 1989), 303–4. See also *The Brenner Debate: Agrarian Class Structure and Economic Development in Preindustrial Europe*, ed. T. Aston and C. H. E. Philpin (Cambridge: Cambridge University Press, 1985).

11. Innes, *Creating the Commonwealth*, 47, 51, 209, 206.

12. Ibid., 101, 208, 312, 251.

13. On the connections among magic, wonder literature, Providential thinking, and Puritan beliefs see especially David D. Hall, *Worlds of Wonder, Days of Judgment: Popular Religious Belief in Early New England* (Cambridge: Harvard University Press, 1990), chap. 2, "A World of Wonders," 71–116. On wonder literature in England see J. Paul Hunter, *Before Novels: The Cultural Contexts of Eighteenth-Century English Fiction* (New York: Norton, 1990), chap. 8, " 'Strange, but True': Fact, Certainty, and the Desire for Wonder," 195–224.

14. Hull, "Diary," 215, 214, 207, 189, 230, 218.

15. John Hull to Mr Thomas Buckham and Mr Daniell Allin, 29 October 1672, from "Letterbook of John Hull," manuscript and typescript in the collections of American Antiquarian Society, Worcester, Massachusetts (hereafter Hull Lbk). The letterbook contains copies of letters Hull sent to his business correspondents.

16. Hull, "Diary," 149, 223.

17. Ibid., 242, 242–43; John Hull to John Harwood, 6 August 1677, Hull Lbk.

18. Ibid., 218, 220, 176, 187.

19. Perry Miller indicates that in Puritan thought "the rewards of industry were not consequences of industriousness, nor of the state of the market or of rates of exchange," rather, the "gifts were from God." Perry Miller, *The New England Mind: From Colony to Province* (Cambridge, Mass.: Harvard University Press, 1953), 41.

20. Hull, "Diary," 154, 154–55, 156.

21. See, for example, Perry Miller, *Errand into the Wilderness* (New York: Harper & Row, 1964); Sacvan Bercovitch insists that in Cotton Mather's *Magnalia Christi Americana*, "the idea of national election takes on a literalness undreamed of by Luther or Foxe. . . . The New England Puritans gave America the status of visible sainthood. The subsequent impact of their concept cannot be overestimated." Sacvan Bercovitch, *The Puritan Origins of the American Self* (New Haven, Conn.: Yale University Press, 1975), 108.

22. Keith Thomas, *Religion and the Decline of Magic* (New York: Scribner, 1971), 91; Hull, "Diary," 167, 168.

23. Hull, "Diary," 147.

24. John Hull, orders to John Harris, 20 September 1677, Hull Lbk; John Hull to Edward Hull, 20 May 1680, Hull Lbk.

25. David Hall eloquently expresses the feeling of uncertainty and the desire for protection that recurs in Samuel Sewall's diary. "It is this yearning for protection that, from start to finish, unifies the diary and emerges as the substance of religion." Hall, *Worlds of Wonder*, chap. 5, "The Mental World of Samuel Sewall," 224, 214.

26. On the merchants' role in alleviating the depression see Darrett Rutman, *Winthrop's Boston: Portrait of a Puritan Town, 1630–1649* (Chapel Hill: University of North Carolina Press, 1965), 186.

27. Hull, "Diary," 142. Hull may have received his training from his stepbrother Richard Storer who served an apprenticeship in London. See Albert S. Roe and Robert F. Trent, "Robert Sanderson and the Founding of the Boston Silversmith's Trade," in *New England Begins: The Seventeenth Century*, ed. Jonathan L. Fairbanks and Robert F. Trent, vol. 3 (Boston: Museum of Fine Arts, 1982), 3:482.

28. For information on Hull's work as a silversmith see Roe and Trent, "Founding of the Boston Silversmith Trade," 480–500; Kathryn C. Buhler, *American Silver, 1655–1825 in the Museum of Fine Arts Boston*, 2 vols. (Boston: Museum of Fine Arts, 1972), 1:4–10; Kathryn Buhler and Graham Hood, *American Silver: Garvan and Other Collections in the Yale University Art Gallery*, 2 vols. (New Haven, Conn.: Yale University Press, 1970), 1:2–9; Martha Gandy Fales, *Early American Silver* (New York: Dutton, 1973), 4–12; Graham Hood, *American Silver: A History of Style, 1650–1900* (New York: Praeger, 1971), 12–45; and Samuel Eliot Morison, *Builders of the Bay Colony* (Boston: Houghton Mifflin, 1930), 154. Barbara McLean Ward and Gerald W. R. Ward's *Silver in American Life* (Boston: David R. Godine, 1979) is helpful on eighteenth-century silver in colonial America but has little to say about John Hull.

29. See Hood, *American Silver*, 12, on the social significance of owning silver pieces or "plate" as it was often called; Roe and Trent, "Founding of the Boston Silversmith's Trade," 480, 485.

30. See Fales, *Early American Silver*, 4–5, and Robert F. Trent, "The Concept of Mannerism" in Fairbanks and Trent, *New England Begins: The Seventeenth Century*, 368–412. See also, Buhler's stylistic analysis of possible Dutch influence through England and colonial New York on Hull and Sanderson's work in *American Silver*, 1:2–9.

31. Roe and Trent, "Founding of the Boston Silversmith's Trade," 486. See also Hood, *American Silver*, 37.

32. Roe and Trent assert that Hull's responsibilities as a banker and broker took precedence over his craft activities. Sanderson however, continued to train apprentices and produce stylish silver objects. Roe and Trent, "Founding of the Boston Silversmith's Trade," 480, 484.

33. In Puritan New England, marriage was considered a civil agreement not a religious sacrament. Governor Winthrop probably performed the marriage because Judith was the daughter of Edmund Quincy, an influential early settler. Quincy received a several hundred-acre land grant at Mount Wollaston (later the site of the town of Quincy) and is classed among the middling gentry by Rutman in *Winthrop's Boston*, 73. By marrying Judith, Hull allied himself to an important family.

34. Hull, "Diary," passim; Laurel Thatcher Ulrich, *Good Wives: Image and Reality in the Lives of Women in Northern New England, 1650–1750*, 1st ed. (New York: Knopf, 1982).

35. See David Cressy, *Coming Over: Migration and Communication between England and New England in the Seventeenth Century* (Cambridge: Cambridge University Press, 1987), 269–91; Bernard Bailyn, *New England Merchants in the Seventeenth Century* (Cambridge: Harvard University Press, 1955), 35–36, 87–91, 134–37; and Ian K. Steele, *The English Atlantic, 1675–1740: An Exploration of Communication and Community* (New York: Oxford University Press, 1986).

36. Hull, "Diary," 145.

37. Pence, shillings, and pounds made up the basic units of the English monetary system. Twelve pence equaled one shilling, and twenty shillings equaled one pound. The English pound or pound sterling traded at a discount to colonial currency. That is to say,

the colonial units were usually worth less than the British units. To further complicate matters, these units usually represented units of account rather than specific coins. The most frequently circulated coins were Spanish dollars or pieces of eight. For data that demonstrate the rapid inflation of the 1730s and 1740s, see John McCusker, *Money and Exchange in Europe and America, 1600–1775: A Handbook* (Chapel Hill: University of North Carolina Press, 1978).

38. Hull, "Diary," 120. Hull may have chosen Sanderson as his partner in the mint but this seems unclear, judging by the paucity of references to Sanderson in Hull's manuscripts.

39. Bailyn, *New England Merchants,* 87.

40. John Hull to Mountsier James De la Ronde, 22 January 1675; John Hull to Mr. de La Ronde, 31 March 1676; John Hull to Mr. Solomon Delyon, 12 March 1672; John Hull to Samuel Bradstreet, 27 September 1687; all Hull Lbk.

41. See Vickers, "Competency and Competition." James Henretta in his "Introduction" to *The Origins of Capitalism in America: Collected Essays* (Boston: Northeastern University Press, 1991) insists that "capitalist practices and values were not central to the lives of most of the inhabitants of British North America before 1750" (xxi).

42. On tenant farms in early New England, see John Frederick Martin, *Profits in the Wilderness: Entrepreneurship and the Founding of New England Towns in the Seventeenth Century* (Chapel Hill: University of North Carolina Press, 1991), 32–33; Stephen Innes, *Labor in a New Land: Economy and Society in Seventeenth-Century Springfield* (Princeton, N.J.: Princeton University Press, 1983); and Daniel Vickers, *Farmers and Fishermen: Two Centuries of Work in Essex County, Massachusetts, 1630–1850* (Chapel Hill: University of North Carolina Press, 1994), 77–83.

43. Hull, "Diary," 149; Martin, *Profits in the Wilderness,* 32; John Hull to Richard Collicott, June 10, 1675, Hull Lbk; Hull, "Diary," 187. See Martin, *Profits in the Wilderness,* 106–7, on Hull's lumber mill in Maine, and ibid., 73–79, on Hull's investment in land in Rhode Island where he raised horses for export to Barbados.

44. Darrett B. Rutman, "The Social Web: A Prospectus for the Study of the Early American Community," in *Insights and Parallels: Problems and Issues of American Social History,* ed. William L. O'Neil (Minneapolis: Burgess Publishing Co. 1973), 57–89.

45. Cotton Mather, *A Christian at His Calling; Two Brief Discourses, One Directing a Christian in his General Calling; Another Directing Him in His Personal* (Boston, 1701) reprinted in McGiffert, *Puritanism and the American Experience,* 126, 122–24; Hull, "Diary," 154, 146.

46. Walter Muir Whitehill, *Boston: A Topographical History,* 2d. ed. (Cambridge, Mass.: Harvard University Press, 1968), 6, 15, 9; *Report of a French Protestant Refugee, in Boston, 1687,* trans. E. T. Fisher (Brooklyn, N.Y., 1868), 14.

47. For detail on the spatial development of early Boston see Rutman, *Winthrops's Boston,* 240–41, and Whitehill, *Boston,* 8–9.

48. John Josselyn, *Two Voyages to New-England* (London, 1674), reprinted as *John Josselyn, Colonial Traveler* (Hanover, Mass.: University Press of New England, 1988), 114–15; Whitehill, *Boston,* 14–15; see also Rutman, *Winthrop's Boston,* 241–42.

49. Bailyn, *New England Merchants,* 98; Robert Keayne, quoted ibid., 97. See also Whitehill, *Boston,* 13.

50. See Mark Girouard, *Cities and People: A Social and Architectural History* (New Haven, Conn.: Yale University Press, 1985), 152–56.

51. Henry Shrimpton, Inventory, 24 July 1666, Docket no. 406, Suffolk County Probate Records, Judicial Archives, Massachusetts Archives; Bailyn, *New England Merchants,* 192.

52. James A. Henretta, "Economic Development and Social Structure in Colonial Boston," *WMQ* 22 (January 1965), 80. See also Gloria L. Main and Jackson T. Main, "Economic Growth and the Standard of Living in Southern New England, 1640–1774," *Journal of Economic History* 48 (March 1988): 27–43; Darrett Rutman, in

Winthrop's Boston, asserts that by the second generation, "men of more than average means—constituted a gentry and dominated the town economically, socially, and politically" (246). Yet Henry Shrimpton, one of Boston's wealthiest men, did not figure in gentry circles or hold any major political positions. Rutman may be underestimating the continuing importance of religious affiliation and English, especially East Anglian origins.

53. Robert Blair St. George, "Bawns and Beliefs: Architecture, Commerce, and Conversion in Early New England," *Winterthur Portfolio* 25, no. 4 (Winter 1990): 266–71; St. George argues that merchants used forms that invoked "benevolent images" of monasteries and inns as built metaphors "to mask private interest" (269–70).

54. On this transitional material culture see Cary Carson, "The Consumer Revolution in Colonial British America: Why Demand?" in *Of Consuming Interests: The Style of Life in the Eighteenth Century*, ed. Cary Carson, Ronald Hoffman, and Peter Albert (Charlottesville: University Press of Virginia, 1994), 554, 580.

55. Bailyn, *New England Merchants*, 192.

56. Hall describes Samuel Sewall's response to returning home as a "feeling of transition from a zone of danger to one of safety." Hall, *Worlds of Wonder*, 217. For descriptions and plans of these first-period houses see Abbott Lowell Cummings, *The Framed Houses of Massachusetts Bay, 1625–1725* (Cambridge, Mass.: Harvard University Press, 1979).

57. Shrimpton Inventory, 1666.

58. Peter Thornton, *Seventeenth-Century Interior Decoration in England, France, and Holland* (New Haven, Conn.: Published for the Paul Mellon Center for Studies in British Art by Yale University Press, 1978), 7–8.

59. Ibid., 104, and Shrimpton Inventory.

60. Bailyn, *New England Merchants*, 35; Shrimpton Inventory. See also Shrimpton Family Papers, Massachusetts Historical Society.

61. These purchases are recorded in the Thwing Catalogue at Massachusetts Historical Society.

62. Thornton, *Seventeenth-Century Interior Decoration*, 109.

63. Edgar de N. Mayhew and Minor Meyers, Jr., *A Documentary History of American Interiors from the Colonial Era to 1915* (New York, Scribner, 1980), 7, 23. Mayhew notes that during the period 1675–1715, "window curtains remained rare, confined only to chambers in fashionable houses." Lorna Weatherill, *Consumer Behavior and Material Culture in Britain, 1660–1760* (London: Routledge, 1988), 8 and table 2.2.

64. Perhaps Shrimpton's lack of civic prominence explains why historians have overlooked him. Perry Miller mentions him only once in *The New England Mind* and conflates him with his son Samuel. Only Bernard Bailyn has more than a passing reference to this extremely successful trader. Bailyn, *New England Merchants*, 35, 135, 192–93.

65. Rutman claims that as early as the second decade of settlement (the 1640s) wealth could buy status. The example of Henry Shrimpton calls that assertion into question. Rutman, *Winthrop's Boston*, 248.

66. Whitehill, *Boston*, 14–15. On Keayne see Bernard Bailyn, ed., *The Apologia of Robert Keayne* (Boston: Colonial Society of Massachusetts, 1964). On the just price in colonial New England see Innes, *Creating the Commonwealth*, 124–25, 160–62.

67. John Hull to Mr. Daniell Allin, 23 August 1672, Hull Lbk.

Chapter 2. Much Commerce and Many Cultures

1. Peter Stallybrass and Allon White, *The Politics and Poetics of Transgression* (Ithaca: Cornell University Press, 1986), 27.

2. The three most important treatments of witchcraft in New England are Paul Boyer and Stephen Nissenbaum, *Salem Possessed: The Social Origins of Witchcraft* (Cambridge, Mass.: Harvard University Press, 1974); Carol F. Karlsen, *The Devil in the Shape of a Woman: Witchcraft in Colonial New England* (New York: Norton, 1987); and John Demos, *Entertaining Satan: Witchcraft and the Culture of Early New England* (New York: Oxford University Press, 1982).

3. On the urban environment as an expression of culture see Edward T. Hall, *The Hidden Dimension* (Garden City, N.Y.: Doubleday, 1966), 2.

4. Stephen Innes, *Creating the Commonwealth: The Economic Culture of Puritan New England* (New York: Norton, 1995), 71.

5. On English joint-stock companies and the Dorchester Company in particular see John Frederick Martin, *Profits in the Wilderness: Entrepreneurship and the Founding of New England Towns in the Seventeenth Century* (Chapel Hill: University of North Carolina, 1991), 134–35, 137–38.

6. Richard P. Gildrie, *Salem, Massachusetts, 1626–1683: A Covenant Community* (Charlottesville: University of Virginia Press, 1975), 2, 8, 19.

7. They followed Williams to escape not only religious persecution but also depressed economic conditions. Innes, *Creating the Commonwealth*, 73.

8. Gildrie, *Salem*, 27, 28; Christine Heyrman, *Commerce and Culture: The Maritime Communities of Colonial Massachusetts, 1690–1750* (New York: Norton, 1984), 33, 35; Stephen Foster, *The Long Argument: English Puritanism and the Shaping of New England Culture, 1570–1700* (Chapel Hill: University of North Carolina Press, 1991), 139. Some of the "strange" ways practiced by Roger Williams's congregation included women wearing veils and lay prophecy during church meetings by both men and women.

9. On the differences between the ports and towns of East Anglia, origin of the largest group of early Salem arrivals, and the farms and villages of the "Old Planters" from the West Country see David Grayson Allen, *In English Ways: The Movement of Societies and the Transferral of English Local Law and Custom to Massachusetts Bay in the Seventeenth Century* (Chapel Hill: University of North Carolina Press, 1981), 66, 70, 89. See also Roger Thompson, *Mobility and Migration: East Anglian Founders of New England, 1629–1640* (Amherst: University of Massachusetts Press, 1994), 14–20. The term "imagined community" is drawn from Benedict Anderson, *Imagined Communities: Reflections on the Origin and Spread of Nationalism*, rev. ed. (New York: Verso, 1991).

10. David Hackett Fischer also characterizes the differences between the farming villages and commercial ports of East Anglia and the larger manor holdings and landed gentry (and aristocracy) that dominated the West Country. David Hackett Fischer, *Albion's Seed: Four British Folkways in America* (New York: Oxford University Press, 1989), 42–49, 241–47; Gildrie, *Salem*, 33, 55, 36.

11. Gildrie, *Salem*, 46, 61, 49; For a short biography of Curwen see Joseph B. Felt, *Annals of Salem* (Boston, 1845), 274. Darrett Rutman, *Winthrop's Boston: Portrait of a Puritan Town, 1630–1649* (Chapel Hill: University of North Carolina Press, 1965), 118–36.

12. See Innes, *Creating the Commonwealth*, 113; Peter had a wide popularity in England: he preached to a crowd of six or seven thousand people at St. Sepulchre's in London. Rutman, *Winthrop's Boston*, 14. In the 1640s Peter returned to England as chaplain to Oliver Cromwell and gave his life for the Puritan cause. See Innes, *Creating the Commonwealth*, 228; Gildrie, *Salem*, 51.

13. Innes, *Creating the Commonwealth*, 288. In these early years of settlement, the colony arranged or sponsored the building of at least two 300 ton ships. Most ships plying the Atlantic and owned by New England merchants during the next hundred years and more were half that size or less. Ocean-crossing vessels could be as small as 40 tons and some were as large as 200 tons, but most ranged between 80 and 150 tons.

14. For Innes the problem centered on social mobility. "The Puritan economic ethic . . . contained features that subverted the social order it was designed to sustain—in particular a degree of economic mobility inconsistent with the ideal of an ordered social hierar-

chy." Ibid., 101. In my interpretation, cultural differences among groups drawn to Massachusetts by Puritan economic plans posed the most difficult problem. Social mobility among established Puritans from eastern England was welcomed, as witnessed by the careers of Simon Bradstreet and John Hull.

15. Gildrie, *Salem*, 52–53; Perry Miller, *The New England Mind: The Seventeenth Century* (Cambridge, Mass.: Harvard University Press, 1939), 439. Innes says, "few leaders of Winthrop's generation appear to have realized that many of their own policies were fostering this social mobility." Nor, I argue, did they recognize that they were fostering cultural pluralism. Innes, *Creating the Commonwealth*, 105.

16. Boyer and Nissenbaum, *Salem Possessed*, 39, 37; Gildrie, *Salem*, 61, 57. For a discussion of tenant farms and tenancy in Essex County, not widely recognized as an important feature of early New England, see Daniel Vickers, *Farmers and Fishermen: Two Centuries of Work in Essex County, Massachusetts, 1630–1850* (Chapel Hill: University of North Carolina Press, 1994), 53–54, 77–83.

17. Gildrie, *Salem*, 123, 153. Constables were charged with keeping order and collecting taxes in their assigned neighborhoods.

18. Ibid., 71.

19. Ibid., 61, 110.

20. Heyrman, *Commerce and Culture*, 214 and passim; Boyer and Nissenbaum, *Salem Possessed*, 49, 39, 40–42; Gildrie, *Salem*, 26, 67, 103, 113, 67–70.

21. Miller points out that "the saints did not need to be a majority if only they held the power," as they did, for the most part, in Salem. Miller, *Colony to Province*, 53.

22. Ibid., 87; Felt, *Annals of Salem*, 238, 252; Gildrie, *Salem*, 107, 109, 138; Bernard Bailyn, *New England Merchants in the Seventeenth Century* (Cambridge, Mass.: Harvard University Press, 1955), 135–36; Boyer and Nissenbaum, *Salem Possessed*, 87.

23. Boyer and Nissenbaum, *Salem Possessed*, 87; Gildrie, *Salem*, 138; Vickers, *Farmers and Fishermen*, 91–94; Harold A. Pinkham, Jr., "Winter Island, Salem: Its Use and Abuse," *Essex Institute Historical Chronicles* 118 (1982): 189; Heyrman, *Commerce and Culture*, 209–11; Bailyn, *New England Merchants*, 77.

24. Vickers, *Farmers and Fishermen*, 96, 97, 139; David Thomas Konig, *Law and Society in Puritan Massachusetts: Essex County, 1629–1692* (Chapel Hill: University of North Carolina Press, 1979), 75–76; Richard P. Gildrie, "Taverns and Popular Culture in Essex County, Massachusetts, 1678–1686," *EIHC* 124 (1988): 165–67.

25. Pinkham, "Winter Island," 190; Vickers, *Farmers and Fishermen*, 130–31; Heyrman, *Commerce and Culture*, 213.

26. Rutman, *Winthrop's Boston*, 183–84; Bailyn, *New England Merchants*, 45–47.

27. "Quintal" means "hundredweight" and equals one hundred pounds though in practice the amount could vary considerably. Vickers, *Farmers and Fishermen*, 98–100; Bailyn, *Merchants*, 78.

28. Gildrie, *Salem*, 61, 103, 106–7, 111; manuscript guide, Curwen Family Papers, Phillips Library, Peabody Essex Museum; Richard D. Pierce, ed., *The Records of the First Church in Salem, Massachusetts, 1629–1736* (Salem, Mass.: Essex Institute, 1974), 9, 27; Boyer and Nissenbaum, *Salem Possessed*, 119; Sidney J. Perley, *The History of Salem, Massachusetts*, 4 vols. (Salem: Sidney Perley, 1929), 2:221; Felt, *Annals of Salem*, 279, 274.

29. Felt, *Annals of Salem*, 274; Gildrie, *Salem*, 61, 103; Konig, *Law and Society*, 76–77; manuscript guide, Curwen Family Papers.

30. Bailyn, *New England Merchants*, 77, 80–81; Vickers, *Farmers and Fishermen*, 45, 108–13, 112.

31. This reconstruction of the exchange cycle in the fishing industry is built upon Vickers's study and my own examination of merchants' papers and account books. For an excellent discussion of the importance of the fish trade to Massachusetts, see James G. Lydon, "Fish for Gold: The Massachusetts Fish Trade with Iberia, 1700–1773," *New England Quarterly*, 54, no. 4 (December 1981): 539–82.

32. Vickers, *Farmers and Fishermen*, 133, 139, 135, 138; Cotton Mather, *The Fisher-mans Calling* (Boston, 1712), 12–20, 42–43.

33. Nathaniel B. Shurtleff, ed., *Records of the Governor and Company of Massachusetts Bay in New England*, (Boston: W. White, 1853–54) 2:553; Heyrman, *Commerce and Culture*, 213; Vickers, *Farmers and Fishermen*, 127.

34. Gildrie, *Salem*, 117, 130, 133; Carla Pestana, *Quakers and Baptists in Colonial Massachusetts* (New York: Cambridge University Press, 1991), 25, 27 n. 4, 27–28, 29, 36–37, 42; Christine Heyrman, "Specters of Subversion, Societies of Friends: Dissent and the Devil in Provincial Essex County, Massachusetts," in *Saints and Revolutionaries: Essays on Early American History*, ed. David D. Hall, John M. Murrin, and Thad W. Tate (New York: Norton, 1984), 48.

35. See Jonathan M. Chu, "The Social Context of Religious Heterodoxy: The Challenge of Seventeenth-Century Quakerism to Orthodoxy in Massachusetts," *EIHC* 118 (April 1982): 119–50.

36. Pestana, *Quakers and Baptists*, 41; James Duncan Phillips, *Map of Salem 1700* (Salem: Essex Institute, 1930); Heyrman, *Commerce and Culture*, 126–30. Springer v. Vittum, 1712, quoted in Heyrman, "Specters of Subversion," 62.

37. Perley, *History of Salem*, 3:28; A. G. Jamieson, ed. *A People of the Sea: The Maritime History of the Channel Islands* (New York: Methuen, 1986), 272; Vickers, *Farmers and Fishermen*, 111, 114; Phillips, *Map of Salem 1700*.

38. See Salem Tax Lists, transcribed by WPA, in the Salem Town Records, Phillips Library, Peabody Essex Museum (hereafter Salem Tax Lists). Also see Gildrie, *Salem*, passim, on the merchant elite in Salem.

39. A. G. Jamieson, ed. *A People of the Sea: The Maritime History of the Channel Islands.* (New York: Methuen, 1986), xxx, xxxii.

40. Philip Falle, *An Account of the Isle of Jersey, The Greatest of Those Islands that are now the only Remainder of the English Dominions in France with A New and Accurate Map of the Island.* (London: John Newton, 1694), 60; Jamieson, *People of the Sea*, xxx–xxxii.

41. Jamieson, *People of the Sea*, xxx–xxxii; Falle, *Isle of Jersey*, 56, and preface.

42. Jamieson, *People of the Sea*, xxx, xxxv; J. C. Appleby, "Neutrality, Trade, and Privateering, 1500–1689," ibid. 61–74; Falle, *Isle of Jersey*, Preface.

43. Rosemary E. Ommer, *From Outpost to Outport: Structural Analysis of the Jersey-Gaspe Cod Fishery, 1767–1886* (Montreal: McGill-Queen's University Press, 1991), 12; Appleby, "Neutrality, Trade, and Privateering," 60; Jamieson, *People of the Sea*, xxxvi; F. B. Tupper, *The History of Guernsey and Its Baliwick*, 2nd ed. (London: Simpkin, Marshall, 1876), 132, quoted in Appleby, "Neutrality, Trade, and Privateering," 61; Lord Hatton, Governor of Guernsey, quoted ibid., 69, 71, 75, 78, 85.

44. G. R. Balleine, *A History of the Island of Jersey* (London: Holder & Stoughton, 1950), 225, quoted in Ommer, *Outpost to Outport*, 15; Appleby, "Neutrality, Trade, and Privateering," 89, 86, 94.

45. Appleby, "Neutrality, Trade, and Privateering," 77, 85, 87; This production was accomplished by a total population of about twenty-five thousand; therefore per capita production equaled about one hundred stockings annually. Ommer, *Outpost to Outport*, 13, 18.

46. Falle, *Isle of Jersey*, 84, 85–86; See Robert A. Gross, *The Minutemen and Their World* (New York: Hill and Wang, 1976), 76 and chap. 4, passim.

47. A. G. Jamieson, "The Channel Islands and Overseas Settlement, 1600–1900," *People of the Sea*, 273–74; Falle, *Isle of Jersey*, 83–84. See Marcus Rediker, *Between the Devil and the Deep Blue Sea: Merchant Seamen, Pirates, and the Anglo-American Maritime World, 1700–1750* (Cambridge: Cambridge University Press, 1987), chap. 1, "The Seaman as Man of the World: A Tour of the North Atlantic, c. 1740."

48. General information about Philip English and Salem is drawn from local histories cited above and below. On English's first appearance in Salem see Bailyn, *New England Merchants*, 144, 146; George F. Cheever, "A Sketch of Philip English—A Merchant in

Salem from about 1670 to about 1733–4," *EIHC* 1, no. 5 (November 1859): 158; letter of indebtedness between Philipe L'Anglois and Sieur Cennaud Cou?id, merchant, 20 April, 1677 (typed translation), English Family Papers in the English/-Touzel/Hathorne Papers, Phillips Library, Peabody Essex Museum (hereafter English Family Papers).

49. Philip English to Major John Pilgrim, 28 January, 1695, English Family Papers; account page, 1705–7, English Family Papers. Both Osnabrigs and Holland Duck are kinds of sturdy cloth.

50. See English Family Papers and Konig, *Law and Society,* 70–71; Jamieson, *People of the Sea,* 237; Phel. Gaudin to Philippe L'Anglois, indenture, 7 January 1675; Jean Binet to Philippe L'Anglois, indenture, 5 February 1675 (originals in French), English Family Papers.

51. Not all of Philip English's documents survived and other brief references, like Josiah Cotton's remark quoted below, indicate that English played an important role in supplying Salem and Marblehead with "French" labor.

52. Josiah Cotton, quoted in Heyrman, *Commerce and Culture,* 245.

53. *Records and Files of the Quarterly Courts of Essex County, Massachusetts,* 8 vols. (Salem: Essex Institute, 1911), 6:347, 348, 346–48.

54. Ibid., 9:198; Konig, *Law and Society,* 71. For a discussion of the material goods and economic prospects of resident fishermen (often from Jersey) in seventeenth-century New England, see Vickers, *Farmers and Fishermen,* 135.

55. Konig, *Law and Society,* 70; David Konig, "A New Look at the Essex 'French': Ethnic Frictions and Community Tensions in Seventeenth-Century Essex County, Massachusetts," *EIHC* 110, no. 3 (July 1974): 165–80; Heyrman, *Commerce and Culture,* 245. The cultural differences were so persistent that even in the third decade of the eighteenth century there existed a climate of mutual hostility between poor Jerseyans and other Essex County families. See ibid., 299–300.

56. Falle, *Isle of Jersey,* 118, 137, 141, 136, 141.

57. Richard P. Gildrie, "Taverns and Popular Culture in Essex County, Massachusetts, 1678–1686," *EIHC* 124 (1988): 171–72; Felt, *Annals of Salem,* 262; Vickers, *Farmers and Fishermen,* 156–57; Heyrman, *Commerce and Culture,* 213.

58. Gildrie, "Taverns," 161–62; Peter Clark, *The English Alehouse: A Social History, 1200–1830* (London: Longman, 1983), 44–45.

59. Reverend John Higginson, quoted in Gildrie, "Taverns," 163. In his study of public houses in Massachusetts, David Conroy found that by the 1680s, "tavern crowds became perhaps the most visible and chronic contradiction of Puritan social ideals . . . ever more disturbing because of the decline in applicants for church membership." David W. Conroy, *In Public Houses: Drink and the Revolution of Authority in Colonial Massachusetts* (Chapel Hill: University of North Carolina Press, 1995), 56.

60. *Records and Files of the Quarterly Courts* 7:1, 110, 246–47; B. B. James and J. Franklin eds., *Journal of Jasper Danckaerts, 1679–80* (New York, Scribners, 1913), 274.

61. See Gildrie, "Taverns," table 2, and pp. 164, 168; Vickers, *Farmers and Fishermen,* 133.

62. See English Family Papers; Cheever, "Sketch of Philip English," 160.

63. Salem Tax Lists. In 1690 English and Samuel Gardner were each assessed six pounds, Major Redford ten pounds, and Major William Browne thirty-six pounds.

64. James Duncan Phillips, *Salem in the Seventeenth Century* (Boston: Houghton Mifflin, 1933), 323, xviii, 296; Cheever, "Sketch of Philip English," 160; In his diary, Reverend William Bentley, noted intellectual and bibliophile, describes a visit to English's house in 1790. "It was the largest in Town and he was a merchant having 24 sail of vessels. . . . Went over the well known house of English near the neck gate. The Cellars are completely finished. The Stone wall is built of as large stones as are now in use which contradicts the opinion that they generally built of small stones of choice, at that age. There is an hearth, very large oven, and all conveniences. The Rooms are the largest in Town. The floors are laid in plank, and are sound at this day. . . . the upper part of the house among the Peeks have curious partitions and very much Room. Even the Cellars are plastered." Bentley's editor, Edward S. Waters, adds a note about the house: "It was taken down

before 1840 and was then known as the 'forty peaked house.' " William Bentley, *The Diary of William Bentley: Pastor of the East Church Salem, Massachusetts,* 4 vols. (reprint ed., Gloucester, Mass.: Peter Smith, 1962), 248.

65. For observations on the neighborhood where English built his "Great House," see Phillips, *Salem in the Seventeenth Century,* 180–81, 314, 322, and James Duncan Phillips, *Salem in the Eighteenth Century* (1937; reprint ed., Salem: Essex Institute, 1969).

66. On the geographic and social marginalizing of merchants, markets, and exchange, see Jean-Christophe Agnew, *Worlds Apart: The Market and the Theater in Anglo-American Thought, 1550–1750* (Cambridge: Cambridge University Press, 1986), 21–23. On the Liberties outside the walls of London as a site of production and exchange beyond the control of guilds see ibid., 50.

67. Steven Mullaney, "Civic Rites, City Sites: The Place of the Stage," in *Staging the Renaissance: Reinterpretations of Elizabethan and Jacobean Drama* (New York: Routledge, 1991), 22.

68. Susan G. Davis, *Parades and Power: Street Theater in Nineteenth-Century Philadelphia* (Berkeley: University of California Press, 1986), 78. Stuart Blumin also characterizes Philadelphia's Northern Liberties as an area with few merchants and professionals and many unskilled workers. It was among the "least attractive and least convenient parts of the city," where "municipal services were poorly performed." Stuart M. Blumin, *The Emergence of the Middle Class: Social Experience in the American City, 1760–1900* (Cambridge: Cambridge University Press, 1989), 48.

69. Gildrie, "Taverns," 171; *Town Records of Salem, Massachusetts,* 3 vols. (Salem: Essex Institute, 1869, 1913, 1934), 2:257–58.

70. Daniel King to Philip English, 1688, English Family Papers.

71. Ms. account pages, 1688 and 1689, English Family Papers; Perley, *History of Salem, Massachusetts,* 4:317.

72. Salem Tax Lists.

73. See David Lovejoy, *The Glorious Revolution in America* (New York: Harper and Row, 1972) and J. M. Sosin, *English America and the Revolution of 1688: Royal Administration and the Structure of Provincial Government* (Lincoln: University of Nebraska Press, 1982) on the Mason and Gorges claims.

74. Konig, *Law and Society,* 159, 161, 160–63, 162–64.

75. Ibid., 162–63. For a discussion of the ideal of "competency" or "a degree of comfortable independence" as the goal for most colonists see Daniel Vickers, "Competency and Competition: Economic Culture in Early America," *William and Mary Quarterly,* Vol. 47 no. 1 (January 1990): 3–29.

76. Heyrman, "Specters of Subversion," 56.

77. N. I. Bowditch, quoted in Walter Muir Whitehill, *Boston: A Topographical History,* 2d ed. (Cambridge, Mass.: Harvard University Press, 1968), 35.

78. John Allin, Joshua Moody, and Samuel Willard, *The Principles of the Protestant Religion Maintained* (Boston: Richard Pierce, 1690), preface.

79. Heyrman, *Devil and Dissent,* 56–57; See Gary Nash, *The Urban Crucible: Social Change, Political Consciousness, and the Origins of the American Revolution* (Cambridge, Mass.: Harvard University Press, 1979), 50–52, on George Keith in Philadelphia.

80. Allin et al., *Principles of the Protestant Religion,* preface.

81. See Lovejoy, *The Glorious Revolution in America.*

82. Bradstreet's first wife, also named Ann, who was New England's first published poet, died in 1672. The Gardner/Bradstreet "mansion," a Tudor-style house, stood on what are now the grounds of the Essex Institute of the Peabody Essex Museum in Salem.

83. See Boyer and Nissenbaum, *Salem Possessed,* 108, on the problem of weak institutions in New England during this period.

84. On witchcraft in seventeenth-century England and America, see Demos, *Entertaining Satan;* Keith Thomas, *Religion and the Decline of Magic* (New York: Scribner, 1971); Karlsen, *The Devil in the Shape of a Woman;* and David D. Hall, *Worlds of Wonder,*

Days of Judgment: Popular Religious Belief in Early New England (Cambridge, Mass.: Harvard University Press, 1990). On witchcraft in Salem the best full-length treatment is Boyer and Nissenbaum, *Salem Possessed.*

85. John Demos, cited in Boyer and Nissenbaum, *Salem Possessed,* 31, 11–12; Demos, *Entertaining Satan,* 11–12, 13.

86. Boyer and Nissenbaum, *Salem Possessed,* 31; Demos, *Entertaining Satan,* 10; Paul Boyer and Stephen Nissenbaum, ed. *The Salem Witchcraft Papers: Verbatim Transcripts of the Legal Documents of the Salem Witchcraft Outbreak of 1692.* 3 vols. (New York: Da Capo, 1977), 1:313–21.

87. Demos, *Entertaining Satan,* 93. See also Boyer and Nissenbaum, *Salem Possessed,* 204–8.

88. Boyer and Nissenbaum, *Salem Possessed,* 21; *Salem Witchcraft Papers,* 1:317–19, 317–18.

89. *Salem Witchcraft Papers,* 318–19, quoted in Heyrman, *Commerce and Culture,* 220, 216.

90. *Records and Files of the Quarterly Courts,* 5:90–92.

91. See Boyer and Nissenbaum, *Salem Possessed,* 187, 191. In his recent reworking of the Salem trials, Peter Hoffer emphasizes the role of the judges. "A defendant might ask a question of the accusers, and the accusers might add to their stories, but everything was initiated, generated, controlled, and limited by what the judges asked and where they wanted to go with the answers." Peter Charles Hoffer, *The Devil's Disciples: Makers of the Salem Witchcraft Trials* (Baltimore: Johns Hopkins University Press, 1996), 160, 192, 187.

92. See map 5, "The Ipswich Road, 1692," in Boyer and Nissenbaum, *Salem Possessed,* 95, 147, 200.

93. Konig, *Law and Society,* 55, 68; William Hubbard, *A General History of New England from the Discovery to MDCLXXX* (1684; reprint ed., Cambridge, Mass.: Hillard & Metcalfe, 1815), xiv; Cotton Mather, *Memorable Providences Relating to Witchcrafts and Possessions* (Boston, 1690).

94. Cheever, "Sketch of Philip English," 162; Konig supports this interpretation of English as a vulnerable outsider. Philip English "possessing vast property, privileges denied to others, and a certain 'arrogance of manner,' " was, Konig notes, "the preeminent symbol of the Jersey community that his English neighbors regarded suspiciously and enviously." Konig, *Law and Society,* 74.

95. Konig, *Essex French,* 171–73; Heyrman, *Commerce and Culture,* 214; Falle, *Account of the Isle of Jersey,* 111. I am greatly indebted to David Konig's work on the Essex French for providing support for my understanding of the ethnic "other" in Salem.

96. In Jersey, bankruptcy laws required creditors to assume all of a debtor's outstanding debts to recover just their own loss. Konig, *Essex French,* 173–74.

97. Philip English in *Masury v. Bridges, Records and Files of the Quarterly Courts,* 7:111. Konig explains that the judicial system on Jersey and Guernsey differed in important ways from the system of Quarterly Courts used in the Massachusetts Bay Colony. However, Konig perhaps goes too far in stressing the difference between Massachusetts and Channel Island's debt collection practices. The records of Essex Quarterly Court reveal that rapid and ruthless debt collection was not confined to those of French origin. For example, in a single court session in 1655, the wealthy Ipswich merchant William Payne, member of the local gentry and benefactor of the grammar school in Ipswich, evicted three separate impecunious defendants from their lands for overdue debts and even seized the corn crop of one of the debtors who subsequently disappeared from the town records. Konig also refers to English's willingness to sue his father-in-law's estate as a breach of Bay Colony procedures, but in Boston at about the same time, the leading Puritan merchant Peter Sergeant initiated a suit against the settlement of his father-in-law's estate. The suit embroiled Sergeant and his brother-in-law, Samuel Shrimpton, inheritor of the Shrimpton fortune, in a legal battle that lasted for years. Therefore, while the Channel Islanders' willingness to resort to legal measures might have exceeded that of other Salem figures, it represented only an incremental addition to the practices of an

already litigious society. Rapid debt collection in itself would not account for the marginalization of a successful trader like Philip English. Coupled with his French origins and accent, and his Anglican beliefs, however, it added to difference against which Puritan merchants defined themselves.

98. Heyrman, *Commerce and Culture*, 214; Brock's case (1672), *Records and Files of the Quarterly Courts*, 5:90–92; *Beadle v. Best* (1683), and *Ketville v. Tucker* (1681), ibid., quoted in Konig, *Essex French*, 174–75, 171, 172, 171.

99. Perley, *History of Salem*, 3:321. Sir Edmund Andros and Philip English were both from the Channel Islands but in spite of this intriguing connection I could find no evidence of any direct relationship between them.

100. Linda Colley, *Britons: Forging the Nation 1707–1837* (New Haven, Conn.: Yale University Press, 1992), 23, 26, 6. For other discussions of anti-French feeling and the complicated relationship between British identity and France, see Gerald Newman, *The Rise of English Nationalism: A Cultural History, 1740–1830* (1987) and Jeremy Black, *Natural and Necessary Enemies: Anglo-French Relations in the Eighteenth Century* (Athens, Ga.: University of Georgia Press, 1987).

101. *Salem Witchcraft Papers*, 3:989–91, 1044.

102. Cheever, "Sketch of Philip English," 166.

103. Invoice to Philip English, 11 July 1695, English Family Papers; Benjamin Marston to Philip English, power of attorney 23 November 1700, English Family Papers.

104. Salem Tax Lists. Historians debate over the correlation between wealth and assessed values for tax purposes. By 1699 Salem included three categories in the total assessment, polls, house and land, and goods, thereby making certain that merchants' trade goods did not escape their notice. Therefore I believe these Salem tax assessments provide a good indicator of relative wealth.

105. For an interpretation that positions the "Jerseymen" of Salem as outside the local power structure see Konig, "Essex 'French,' " 165–80.

106. Mary Douglas, *Purity and Danger: an Analysis of the Concepts of Pollution and Taboo* (London: Ark Paperbacks, 1966), 96, 99.

107. Heyrman, *Commerce and Culture*, 267.

108. William, the older son, was by all accounts a talented mariner. One account from 1712 details a voyage to Surinam by the sloop *Mary* with "William English Commander." Three years later, at twenty-five, William English died. Philip Jr. had a more difficult time mastering the skills required, from careful accounting to aggressive bargaining and from supervising cargo to plotting an ocean course by sun and stars. See Cheever, "Sketch of Philip English" 174; numerous account pages show John Touzel sailing for Philip English and, later, on his own account. Touzel Family Papers, Subgroup 3 of the English/Touzel/Hathorne Papers.

109. Philip English to John Touzel, deed of land, 1720. English Family Papers.

110. Guardianship of Philip English, 3 July 1732, English Family Papers; Cheever, "Sketch of Philip English," 176. Note on back of summons to Philip English, 1733, English Family Papers; summons to Philip English, 1733, English Family Papers.

111. Account page of Philip English Jr. to his father's estate, 1732–37, English Family Papers. On the mirage of a Ship of Fools sometimes forced to sail forever outside the bounds of civilized society, see Michel Foucault's *Madness and Civilization: A History of Insanity in the Age of Reason*, trans. Richard Howard (New York: Vintage Books, 1965).

112. See especially Boyer and Nissenbaum, *Salem Possessed*.

113. Salem Tax Lists. The Brownes—William, Samuel and their sons—consistently ranked first, second and third on Salem tax assessments for decades. Their assessments were often several multiples greater than those of English and other merchants ranking fourth, fifth, and sixth.

114. This is supported by Richard Gildrie in *Salem*.

115. Boyer and Nissenbaum, *Salem Possessed*.

116. See Heyrman, *Commerce and Culture*; also Stephen Innes, especially *Labor in a New Land: Economy and Society in Seventeenth-Century Springfield* (Princeton, N.J.: Princeton University Press, 1983); Bailyn, *New England Merchants*; and Martin, *Profits in the Wilderness*.

Chapter 3. Puritans, the Polite, and the Impolite

1. Paul Langford traces the growing influence of social rituals and refined behavior on English society in *A Polite and Commercial People: England 1727–1783* (Oxford: Clarendon Press, 1989); Lawrence and Jeanne Stone noted the rise of an urban patriciate in eighteenth-century England identified by genteel norms and suburban villas and distinct from the landed elite. In American ports like Boston and Salem, in the absence of an inherited land-based nobility, a similar "commercial aristocracy" developed. Lawrence Stone and Jeanne C. Fawtier Stone, *An Open Elite? England 1540–1880* (Oxford: Clarendon Press, 1984) 252–54, 404–5.

2. According to Bernard Bailyn, "by 1687 he [Shrimpton] was the richest man in Boston. In that year he paid the town's largest tax. His assessed wealth in trade was 1.7 per cent of the total assessed mercantile property in Boston: his estimated real estate holdings in that town alone totaled 6 percent of the entire value of the principality's land and buildings." Bernard Bailyn, *The New England Merchants in the Seventeenth Century* (Cambridge, Mass.: Harvard University Press, 1955), 192.

3. Peter Barbour, Anna Peacock, and John Roulston (14 February), Thomas Walker (12 February), William Mumford, Savill Simpson (25 December), John Egberd (21 February), bills to the estate of Col. Samuel Shrimpton, 1698; Roger Killcup, account page, 1687–98; Shrimpton Family Papers, Massachusetts Historical Society (hereafter Shrimpton Papers); Mark Girouard, *Life in the English Country House: A Social and Architectural History* (New Haven, Conn.: Yale University Press, 1978), 90. Girouard describes how the courtyard, entrance facade, stairs, and rooms leading to the coffin were draped in black cloth for funerals. For aristocrats, the coffin room was draped in black velvet.

4. Samuel Sewall, *The Diary of Samuel Sewall, 1674–1729*, 2 vols., ed. Thomas Halsey (New York: Farrar, Straus, and Giroux, 1973), 1:387.

5. For a typical Puritan funeral see David E. Stannard, *The Puritan Way of Death: A Study in Religion, Culture, and Social Change* (New York: Oxford University Press, 1977).

6. Sewall, *Diary*, 1:121, 150–51.

7. Peter Barbour, account pages 1694–97, Shrimpton Papers.

8. Samuel Shrimpton, Jr., inventory, 22 January 1704, Suffolk County Probate Records, File 2826, Massachusetts Archives; Dressing boxes first appeared in New England inventories in the 1670s, while the term "dressing table" only appears in inventories after 1700. Cary Carson, "The Consumer Revolution in Colonial British America: Why Demand?" in *Of Consuming Interests: The Style of Life in the Eighteenth Century*, ed. Cary Carson, Ronald Hoffman, and Peter J. Albert (Charlottesville: University Press of Virginia, 1994), 575–89. See also Kevin M. Sweeney, "Furniture and the Domestic Environment in Wethersfield, Connecticut, 1639–1800," in *Material Life in America, 1600–1860*, ed. Robert Blair St. George (Boston: Northeastern University Press, 1988), 276–77; Richard Sennett, *The Fall of Public Man* (New York, Knopf, 1977); Jean Christophe Agnew, *Worlds Apart: The Market and the Theater in Anglo-American Thought, 1550–1750* (Cambridge: Cambridge University Press, 1986), 154, 155. Jonathan Belcher to Richard Waldron, April 1734, Belcher Letterbooks, Massachusetts Historical Society, 4:88, quoted in Michael C. Batinski, *Jonathan Belcher, Colonial Governor* (Lexington: University Press of Kentucky, 1996), 85.

9. On the importance of visible details in creating valid experience see Barbara Stafford, *Voyage into Substance: Art, Science, Nature, and the Illustrated Travel Account,*

1760–1840 (Cambridge, Mass.: MIT Press, 1984). See also Simon Schaffer, "A Social History of Plausibility: Country, City, and Calculation in Augustan Britain," in *Rethinking Social History: English Society 1570–1920 and Its Interpretation* (Manchester: Manchester University Press, 1993), 128–57.

10. See Neil McKendrick, John Brewer, and J. H. Plumb, *The Birth of a Consumer Society: The Commercialization of Eighteenth-Century England* (Bloomington: Indiana University Press, 1982); Lorna Weatherill, *Consumer Behaviour and Material Culture in Britain, 1660–1760* (London: Routledge, 1988).

11. Nicholas Barbon, *A Discourse of Trade* (London, 1690) quoted in James Raven, *Judging New Wealth: Popular Publishing and Responses to Commerce in England, 1750–1800* (Oxford: Clarendon Press, 1992), 161. On capitalism's "need to stimulate consumption through the mobilization of fashion and style as artificial marks of social distinction" see David Harvey, "Money, Time, Space and the City," in *The Urban Experience* (Baltimore: Johns Hopkins University Press, 1989), 193.

12. John Brewer, " 'The Most Polite Age and the Most Vicious': Attitudes towards Culture as a Commodity, 1660–1800," in *The Consumption of Culture 1600–1800: Image, Object, Text*, ed. Ann Bermingham and John Brewer (London: Routledge, 1995), 341–45.

13. Norbert Elias, *The Civilizing Process: The Development of Manners*, trans. Edmund Jephcott (New York: Urizen Books, 1978), 144, 147, 148. See sections "On Spitting" (153–60) and on "Natural Functions" (130, 132, 153–60, 129–42).

14. *The Spectator*, ed. Donald F. Bond, 5 vols. (Oxford: Clarendon Press, 1965), 5:156–57.

15. Ibid., 159, 52, 158, 91; Lawrence E. Klein, "Politeness for Plebes: Consumption and Social Identity in Early Eighteenth-Century England," in Bermingham and Brewer, *Consumption of Culture*, 367–71, 378–80.

16. Carrie Rebora, Paul Staiti, Erica E. Hirshler, Theodore E. Stebbins, Jr., and Carol Troyen, *John Singleton Copley in America* (New York: Metropolitan Museum of Art, 1995), 224, 228–29; *Spectator*, 5:56, 183.

17. Charge book, Social Library Records in the Salem Athenaeum Records, Phillips Library, Peabody Essex Museum (hereafter Social Library Records); *New England Courant*, March 19–26 1722.

18. On trade and smuggling with "foreign" islands see Thomas Barrow, *Trade and Empire: The British Customs Service in Colonial America, 1660–1775* (Cambridge, Mass.: Harvard University Press, 1967), 134, 143–52. Barrow cites evidence that Peter Faneuil, Thomas Hancock, and Timothy Orne were all involved in illegal trade in proscribed items from "foreign" (not British-controlled) ports in Europe and the West Indies, and in avoiding customs duties. See Philip English, miscellaneous account pages, English Family Papers in the English/Touzel/Hathorne Papers, Phillips Library, Peabody Essex Museum.

19. Account pages and correspondence found in the letterbook of John Hull and the papers of Philip English, Samuel Shrimpton, Peter Faneuil, Timothy Orne, and Frances Cabot all provide evidence of transatlantic trade. "Wine Islands" is a contemporary term that refers to Madeira and usually includes the Azores as well.

20. Warehouses owned by George Curwen of Salem appear in a sketch of Merchants Row, "To the Children of Robert Gibbs, Henry Gibbs and the children of Mr. George Corwin," 19 January 1726, Miscellaneous Boston Town Records, Manuscript Collection, Boston Public Library. Peter Faneuil's business letters document his efforts to construct a wharf and warehouse in Canso, Nova Scotia, to increase his supply of fish for export. Peter Faneuil Papers, New England Historical and Genealogical Society, Boston (microfilm, Massachusetts Historical Society) (hereafter Faneuil Papers).

21. Vigo is on the Atlantic coast of Spain north of Portugal; Bilbao is a port on the Bay of Biscay in northern Spain; Placentia is a port in Newfoundland; the Bay of Campeche, where merchants took on mahogany and logwood (used to dye fabric), is off the coast of the Yucatán Peninsula. Cayenne is a port in the French West Indies; Ceuta is located in Spanish

territory on the coast of North Africa across from Gibraltar; Cowes is the main port on the Isle of Wight off the southern coast of England; and Providence Island is in the western Caribbean and was settled by a group of Puritan entrepreneurs in the seventeenth century.

22. Benedict Anderson, *Imagined Communities: Reflections on the Origin and Spread of Nationalism*, rev. ed. (New York: Verso, 1991), 46, 22, 24–25. Kathleen Wilson, "The Good, the Bad, and the Impotent: Imperialism and the Politics of Identity in Georgian England," in Bermingham and Brewer, *Consumption of Culture*, 240.

23. John Higginson Jr. to Nathaniel Higginson, 20 August 1697, "Higginson Letters," *Collections of the Massachusetts Historical Society* 3rd ser., 7 (1838): 202, 196 (hereafter *MHSC*). On the Higginson family and John Sr.'s career see James Duncan Phillips, *Salem in the Eighteenth Century* (Salem, Mass.: Essex Institute, 1969), 64–65; map, "The East India Company's settlements in the Indies 1660–1760," in K. N. Chaudhuri, *The Trading World of Asia and the English East India Company 1660–1760* (Cambridge: Cambridge University Press, 1978), 42.

24. Publication Committee, Introduction to the Higginson Letters, *MHSC*, 196; Rev. John Higginson to Nathaniel Higginson, 18 July 1692, Letters, ibid., 199; John Higginson Jr. to Nathaniel Higginson, 20 August, 1697, ibid., 202; Nathaniel Higginson to John Higginson Jr. 6 October 1699, ibid., 214; John Higginson Jr. to Nathaniel Higginson, 29 August 1700, ibid, 218; Nicholas Noyes to Nathaniel Higginson, 3 August 1699, ibid., 213; John Higginson Jr. to Nathaniel Higginson, 16 April 1699, ibid., 205.

25. John Higginson, *Our Dying Saviour's Legacy of Peace to His Disciples in a Troublesome World*, quoted in David Thomas Konig, *Law and Society in Puritan Massachusetts: Essex County, 1629–1692* (Chapel Hill: University of North Carolina Press, 1979), 107–8.

26. Throughout 1720, stock prices for the Bank of England, East India Company, South Sea Company, and Royal African Company were published in the *Boston Gazette* with a two to three month time delay. On some occasions, several prices for each stock, especially the South Sea Company, indicated a wildly fluctuating market.

27. *Boston Gazette*, 29 February–7 March 1720; 16–23 May 1720. In late July 1720 the *Boston Gazette* detailed the expansive plans for a new house that John Law was building in Paris. ibid., 25 July–1 August 1720.

28. *Boston Gazette*, 20–27 June 1720; 25 July–1 August 1720; 15–22 August 1720.

29. The information in the next three paragraphs is based on *The Town of Boston in New England*, map by John Bonner, 1722, reprint by George G. Smith (Boston, 1835), Massachusetts Historical Society; Walter Muir Whitehill, *Boston: A Topographical History*, 2d ed. (Cambridge, Mass.: Belknap Press of Harvard University Press, 1968); and William Price, *View of the Great Town of Boston in New England in America* (Boston, 1743), American Antiquarian Society.

30. Richard Bushman notes that "merchants whose wealth gave them a claim to positions at the top of colonial society" were the first to build "new mansions" at the end of the seventeenth century. Richard L. Bushman, *The Refinement of America: Persons, Houses, Cities* (New York: Knopf, 1992), 112.

31. John Summerson, *Architecture in Britain 1530–1830*, 9th ed. (New Haven, Conn.: Yale University Press, 1993), 142–56. For a discussion of the transitional artisan-mannerist style architecture in the colonies, see Cary Carson, "The Public Face of Architecture in the American Colonies," a slide lecture presented at the Fortieth Williamsburg Antiques Forum, 31 January–5 February 1988. The artisan-mannerist style had a sculptural character and was spread by craftsmen like the aptly named mason Nicholas Stone, who trained in Holland with Hendrick de Keyser, master mason and sculptor to the City of Amsterdam, rather than with court architects like Inigo Jones; hence the term "artisan." Summerson, *Architecture*, 143–45.

32. Whitehill, *Boston*, 17–18, 19–20.

33. *A Report of the Record Commissioners of the City of Boston*, 22 vols. (Boston: Rockwell and Churchill, 1876–90), 8:154–55 (hereafter *Boston Records*). On the concept of "creative

destruction" see David Harvey, *The Urban Experience* (Baltimore: Johns Hopkins University Press, 1989), 83, 191.

34. *Boston Records*, 8:47, 48.

35. Ibid., 66, 567.

36. See Whitehill, *Boston*, 39–40. For church steeples as an eighteenth-century design feature, see Bushman, *Refinement of America*, 172–74; W. T. Baxter, *The House of Hancock: Business in Boston, 1724–1775* (Cambridge, Mass.: Harvard University Press, 1945), 96.

37. *Spectator*, 5:159; Salem did not develop into a major twentieth-century city like Boston, so that more early homes are still standing or remained intact long enough to be captured in pen and ink (English) or in a photograph (Orne).

38. Roy Porter, *London: A Social History* (Cambridge, Mass.: Harvard University Press, 1995), 168, 174. Celia Fiennes, *The Journeys of Celia Fieness*, ed. C. Morris (London: Cresset, 1949), 340, cited in Peter Borsay, *The English Urban Renaissance: Culture and Society in the Provincial Town 1660–1770* (Oxford: Clarendon Press, 1990), 175–76; *Boston News Letter*, 3 May 1714.

39. *Spectator*, 5:183; Borsay, *Urban Renaissance*, 273; See also J. H. Plumb, *Georgian Delights* (Boston: Little, Brown, 1980), 33–34. Karin Calvert concurs that "for the eighteenth-century gentlemen, the moment when his costume, manner, grace, ease, and mastery of the general accomplishments would most likely and most often come under public scrutiny was on the dance floor." Karin Calvert, "The Function of Fashion in Eighteenth-Century America," in Carson, *Of Consuming Interests*, 272.

40. On the importance of dancing see Rhys Isaac in *The Transformation of Virginia, 1740–1790* (New York: W. W. Norton & Co., 1982), 81–87. For one example of an illustrated self-help books see Kellom Tomlinson's *The Art of Dancing, Explained by Reading and Figures* (London, 1735) discussed in Carson, "Why Demand?" 644–47.

41. George Brownell, account page, 1715, Shrimpton Papers. David Shields believes that "in the provinces the dancing masters rose to be the most effective agents in the instruction of youth and manners." David S. Shields, *Civil Tongues and Polite Letters in British America* (Chapel Hill: University of North Carolina Press, 1997), 38. See also Bushman, *Refinement of America*, 50.

42. Porter declares that in the metropolis, "the nobs wanted to see and be seen, chic London loved holding the mirror up to itself." Porter, *London*, 179.

43. See N. B. Harte, "State Control of Dress and Social Change in Pre-Industrial England," in *Trade, Government and Economy in Pre-Industrial England: Essays Presented to F. J. Fisher*, ed. D. C. Colman and A. H. John (London: Weidenfeld and Nicolson, 1976), 132–65; Carole Shammas, *The Pre-Industrial Consumer in England and America* (New York: Oxford University Press, 1990), 216–19; Phyllis Hunter, "Oh What a Tangled Web We Weave: Multiple Discourses in Early Massachusetts Sumptuary Laws," paper presented at the American Studies Association Annual Meeting, Boston, 4–7 November 1993.

44. Elizabeth Shrimpton, account page, 21 August 1684, Shrimpton Papers.

45. Elizabeth Roberts to Samuel Shrimpton Jr., 17 July 1697, Shrimpton Papers.

46. For the importance of advertisements in educating affluent urban residents and spreading the desire for genteel goods see Richard L. Bushman, "Shopping and Advertising in Colonial America" in Carson, *Of Consuming Interests*, 233–51, and T. H. Breen, " 'Baubles of Britain': The American and Consumer Revolutions of the Eighteenth Century," in Carson, *Of Consuming Interests*, 444–842.

47. *Boston News Letter*, 22 March 1714. Bushman emphasizes the dual role of shopkeeper as both tutor (in the new fashions) and servant (in meeting his customers' demand). Bushman, "Shopping and Advertising," 250.

48. *Boston Gazette*, 13–20 June 1720.

49. Ibid., 29 February–7 March 1720, 8–15 February 1720, 11–18 July 1720.

50. *Boston Gazette*, 29 February–7 March 1720, 16–23 May 1720, 18–25 January 1720, 4–11 April 1720. See also ibid., 20–27 June 1720, 11–18 July 1720.

51. Ibid., 20–27 June 1720, 25 July–1 August, 1720, 11–18 July 1720, 21 December 1719, 13–20 June 1720.

52. For a discussion of the "fashion pattern" and the exaggerated attention to novelty in fabric, style, and color of clothing, see McKendrick, *Birth of a Consumer Society*, passim.

53. *Boston News Letter*, 5 December 1720, 2 May 1734.

54. For a discussion of the role of artisans in transmitting genteel culture from London to provincial cities see Richard L. Bushman, "American High-Style and Vernacular Cultures," in *Colonial British America: Essays in the New History of the Early Modern Era*, ed. Jack Greene and J. R. Pole (Baltimore: Johns Hopkins University Press, 1984).

55. Mrs. Hatton's advertisement appeared in the *Boston Gazette*, 21 May 1733. For a treatment of fashion as a visual system of classification, and the "ongoing reformulation" of that code during the eighteenth century, see Calvert, "Function of Fashion," passim.

56. On stimulating recurrent desire see Janice A. Radway, *A Feeling for Books: The Book-of-the-Month Club, Literary Taste, and Middle-Class Desire* (Chapel Hill: University of North Carolina Press, 1997), 171; and Roland Marchand, *Advertising the American Dream: Making Way for Modernity, 1920–1940* (Berkeley: University of California Press, 1985).

57. Sewall, *Diary*, 1:440–42.

58. Ibid., 609, 601, 609.

59. Daniel Neal, *The History of New England . . .* (London, 1720); Sewall, *Diary*, 2:600, 947.

60. Sewall, *Diary*, 1:448–49, 2:245–46. On the use of wigs in colonial America see Calvert, "Function of Fashion," 263–70. On Sewall's black cap see *Diary*, 2:419 n. 28. The cap is clearly visible in Sewall's portrait painted by John Smibert in 1729.

61. Cotton Mather to Thomas Prince, 25 December 1719. Mather begins, "considering the Agitation in the Minds of people throughout the Countrey on our late Aurora Borealis, I knew not, but a Sheet given to the public upon it, might have some considerable Benefits attending of it." He then suggests that if Prince did not think it should be published as a broadside, it should be given to the newspapers. Letter printed in Cotton Mather, *Diary of Cotton Mather 1681–1724*, ed. M. Halsey Thomas (New York: Farrar, Straus and Giroux, 1973), 2:596.

62. Ibid., 606, 611, 607, 609.

63. Ibid., 560.

64. Kenneth Silverman, *The Life and Times of Cotton Mather* (New York: Harper & Row, 1984), 146.

65. Lydia George's father, Samuel Lee, received his clerical training at Oxford and had for a few years ministered to a church in Bristol, Rhode Island. As a young man, Cotton Mather took extensive notes on a series of sermons that Reverend Lee had preached in Boston. Silverman, *Cotton Mather*, 282–83.

66. Cotton Mather to Thomas Craighead, July 1715, reprinted in Mather, *Diary*, 2:321–22.

67. Mather, *Diary*, 22 March 1718, 2:517.; *Selected Letters of Cotton Mather*, comp. Kenneth Silverman (Baton Rouge: Louisiana State University Press, 1971), 90. See Thomas Prince's eulogy quoted ibid., 416; Anthony Boehm to Cotton Mather, 19 March 1717, Curwen Manuscripts, American Antiquarian Society; *Mather Letters*, 69, 165. On Mather as a transatlantic figure see Michael P. Winship, *Seers of God: Puritan Providentialism in the Restoration and Early Enlightenment* (Baltimore: Johns Hopkins University Press, 1996).

68. For an example see diary entry for 13 September 1718: "Among the Families arrived from Ireland, I find many and wondrous Objects for my compassions." Mather, *Diary*, 2:555, 528.

69. Cotton Mather to John Stirling, 26 June 1716, in Mather, *Letters*, 208–9.

70. Cotton Mather to John Stirling, 16 September 1715, Mather, *Letters*, 185–86. Silverman interprets Mather's wearing of a wig and supposed defense of wigs in sermons as part of his maturing personality; "hardly a trait of Mather's maturing personality is more striking than his preoccupation with seeming irreconcilables and his view of

himself as peacemaker between warring factions." Silverman refers to Mather's "twin attraction to the metropolitan world of London and the world of his grandfathers." Silverman, *Cotton Mather*, 145–46. On Mather's ambiguity about the new culture of politeness see Winship, *Seers of God*, 90–92. Mather's diary entry for 12 February 1718 reads: "I am determined, that I will never have my Picture drawn; and I repent, that I have heretofore satt for some Draughts of it;" *Diary*, 2:514.

71. Daniel Defoe in *Weekly Review*, 31 January 1708, quoted in Beverly Lemire, *Fashion's Favourite: The Cotton Trade and the Consumer in Britain, 1660–1800* (Oxford: Oxford University Press, 1991), 16, 12–23; Lemire states that between 1660 and 1683 the East India Company gave Charles II £324,150 in "voluntary contributions." In return the king promoted the fashionableness of Indian fabrics by wearing an "oriental-style waistcoat." From an East India Company dispatch book, 1687; quoted ibid., 16; John E. Willis, "European Consumption and Asian Production in the Seventeenth and Eighteenth Centuries," in *Consumption and the World of Goods*, ed. John Brewer and Roy Porter (London: Routledge, 1993), 136.

72. See McKendrick, *Birth of a Consumer Society*, 137.

73. Nicholas Barbon, *A Discourse of Trade* (London, 1690), quoted in James Raven, *Judging New Wealth: Popular Publishing and Responses to Commerce in England, 1750–1800* (Oxford: Clarendon Press, 1992), 161.

74. *Spectator*, 5:139; Marchand, *Advertising the American Dream*, 156; McKendrick, *Birth of a Consumer Society*, 41–57. Joyce Appleby discusses the attitudes and concepts popularized by Child, Barbon, and other writers on economic matters that created an understanding, if not acceptance, of the importance of home demand and consumption in driving foreign trade. Joyce Appleby, *Economic Thought and Ideology in Seventeenth-Century England* (Princeton, N.J.: Princeton University Press, 1978), 169–98.

75. Sylvia L. Thrupp, *The Merchant Class of Medieval London* (Ann Arbor: University of Michigan Press, 1948), 123; Grant McCracken, *Culture and Consumption: New Approaches to the Symbolic Character of Consumer Goods and Activities* (Bloomington: Indiana University Press, 1988), 13, 16. On the aristocratic power base and its ties to local reputation and manor lands as opposed to urban elites developing in the seventeenth and eighteenth centuries see Stone and Stone, *An Open Elite?* 252–54, 404–05.

76. Radway notes in her study of the Book-of-the-Month Club that by "associating books with phrases such as 'the au courant' and 'the-up-to-date' and invoking the fear of becoming a cultural laggard," the club's founder, Harry Scherman, both relied on and contributed to "this new discourse that helped to sever the connection between value and longevity, age, or permanence." Radway, *A Feeling for Books*, 376–77 n.53. Radway is exploring what appears to be the first application of these methods of producing desire to marketing books. Most studies of "modern" consumption emphasize the difference between the patterns they document and an earlier pre-commodity culture and pre-mass-consumption society. I believe that rather than being a radical disjuncture, the transition from one to the other might better be conceived as a changing history of the categories of meaning placed on consumer goods and how alterations in meaning produced changes in identity formation and class divisions. See for example ibid., 161, 374–75.

77. On the concept of the *bricoleur* see Claude Lévi-Strauss, *The Savage Mind* (Chicago: University of Chicago Press, 1966), 16–33. See Willis, "European Consumption," 137; Lemire, *Fashion's Favourite*, 35–36.

78. Perhaps this news carried a Paris byline because many of the weavers were Huguenot refugees from France who congregated in various areas of London, including Spitalfields. *Boston Gazette*, 4–11 July 1720, 11–18 July 1720, 15–22 August 1720.

79. The Bailyns' statistical study of Massachusetts shipping in the early years of the new century confirms the growing concentration of shipping in the hands of fewer and fewer leading commercial families. Leading shipowners "owned an increasing portion of the province's shipping," especially the largest vessels that offered both the greatest risk

and the greatest opportunity. As a result, "the balance of holdings between the large and the small investors [in ships] was shifting significantly." Bernard Bailyn and Lotte Bailyn, *Massachusetts Shipping 1697–1714: A Statistical Study* (Cambridge, Mass.: Harvard University Press, 1959), 68.

80. Governor Dudley to the Board of Trade, 8 April 1712, *Calendar of State Papers, Colonial Scenes* (1711–12), 258–60, quoted in Gary Nash, *The Urban Crucible: Social Change, Political Consciousness, and the Origins of the American Revolution* (Cambridge, Mass.: Harvard University Press, 1979), 60.

81. John Higginson Jr. to Sir Josiah Child, governor of the East India Company, London, 18 July 1692, "Higginson Letters," [*MHSC*], 199.

82. Cotton Mather, *The Bostonian Ebenezer* (Boston, 1698), quoted in Nash, *The Urban Crucible*, 60.

83. They "agreed that the market Appointed by Law should be kept at one place at Present viz in and about the Town house and that the market be opened on the 11th day of Aug'st., next." *Boston Records*, 7:224.

84. Ibid. See also Karen J. Friedmann, "Victualiing Colonial Boston," *Agricultural History* 47 (1973): 194.

85. Many localities restricted peddling; for example the Lord of the Market in Woodbridge, England, threatened to prosecute " 'persons who come to this town with fish, fowl, fruits, butter, cheese, eggs' . . . and who carry these things from house to house in stead of taking a stand or stall in the market." Ipswich and East Suffolk County Record Office, V 5 / 9 / 6-3 (3), quoted in E. P. Thompson, "The Moral Economy Reviewed," *Customs in Common: Studies in Traditional Popular Culture* (New York: The New Press, 1993), 316 n. 1.

86. The selectmen and constables of each town kept the official weights and measures. An Act for Due Regulation of Weights and Measures, *The Acts and Resolves, Public and Private, of the Province of the Massachusetts Bay. . . .*, 21 vols. (Boston: Potter & Wright, 1869–1922), 1:69–79; *Boston Records*, 7:207. Cotton Mather estimated that a fifth of his congregation were widows; Batinski, *Jonathan Belcher*, 20. The problem of poor widows in Boston continued. In 1742, a tax census enumerated one thousand two hundred widows, "1,000 whereof are in low circumstances" out of a total population of 16,382. Eric Nellis suggests that for "several hundred women, full-time spinning and periodic charity were the major sources of their material support." Eric G. Nellis, "The Working Poor of Pre-Revolutionary Boston," *Historical Journal of Massachusetts* 17 (Summer 1989): 137–59, 156, 157.

87. The law required the monthly publication of prices after 1701. Freidman, "Victualing Colonial Boston," 193–94, 194 n. 23; Thompson, "The Moral Economy Reviewed," 290.

88. Thompson and other historians refer to the Assize of Bread, and to elements of what Thompson defines as "the moral economy" as "traditional," thereby implying that merchants' efforts to control the market were "modern." These terms serve to generalize and confuse the specific historical contexts of the Boston market controversy.

89. G. B. Warden, *Boston, 1689–1776* (Boston: Little, Brown, 1970), 52; Nash, *Urban Crucible*, 56–57, offers a brief biographical sketch of Andrew Belcher.

90. Michael Batinski confirms that Andrew Belcher "not only dominated the town's grain supply but in collusion with the town's bakers controlled bread production." Of Belcher he says, "Andrew could not imagine a limit to his ambitions." Batinski, *Jonathan Belcher*, 20, 19, 20–22.

91. Ibid., 20–22; See petition (submitted by bakers) to the General Court for an increase in the prices of bread, 16 September 1709. Miscellaneous Bound Manuscripts (Misc. Bd.), Massachusetts Historical Society.

92. There are several accounts of this incident. See Warden, *Boston*, 64–67; Nash, *Urban Crucible*, 76–78; Batinski, *Jonathan Belcher*, 21. See Thompson, "The Moral Economy Reviewed" regarding the precision with which crowds selected their targets. Thampson, "The Moral Economy Reviewed," 340.

93. Nash, *Urban Crucible*, 77; Batinski, *Jonathan Belcher*, 22. Belcher was the most prominent merchant during this period. From 1697 to 1714 he owned shares in 137 vessels, more than any other Massachusetts trader; 22 of these he owned outright. Bailyn and Bailyn, *Massachusetts Shipping*, table 27, 128–29.

94. Thompson, "The Moral Economy Reviewed," 340 et passim.; E. P. Thompson, "The Moral Economy of the English Crowd in the Eighteenth Century," in *Customs in Common*, 185–258. In a recent article Barbara Clark Smith offers a brief review of the literature on the moral economy. See Barbara Clark Smith, "Food Rioters and the American Revolution," *William and Mary Quarterly* 51, no. 1 (January 1994): 3–38.

95. I am indebted to my colleague Nan Enstad for this observation.

96. In discussing New England leaders' views of these disorders, Batinski says of the elite, "They could not hear the voices from below affirming their right to rule. If the voices became audible, they heard a raucous and irreverent democracy." Batinski, *Jonathan Belcher*, 82.

97. Thompson explains that English immigrants brought with them to America a "bunch of beliefs, usages, and forms associated with the marketing of food in time of dearth." Thompson, "The Moral Economy Reviewed," 338. On cultural transmission and the baggage settlers from England brought with them, see David Cressy, *Coming Over: Migration and Communication between England and New England in the Seventeenth Century* (Cambridge: Cambridge University Press, 1987); and David Hackett Fischer, *Albion's Seed: Four British Folkways in America* (New York: Oxford University Press, 1989).

98. Sewall, *Diary*, 1:123–24; *Weekly Rehearsal* (Boston), 20 May 1734; *New England Weekly Journal*, 22 June 1736. Regarding the role of the "Anglican renaissance" and the impact of bells on the aural landscape of colonial America, see Jon Butler, *Awash in a Sea of Faith: Christianizing the American People* (Cambridge, Mass.: Harvard University Press, 1990), 110–12.

99. Harriet Silvester Tapley, *St. Peter's Church in Salem Massachusetts before the Revolution* (Salem: Essex Institute, 1944), 7–11. I am indebted to Mark Nystedt of Salem for drawing my attention to English's key role in founding St. Peter's Church.

Chapter 4. The Work of Gentility in the Provinces

1. J. G. A. Pocock, *Virtue, Commerce, and History: Essays on Political Thought and History, Chiefly in the Eighteenth Century* (Cambridge: Cambridge University Press, 1985), 108–9; John Brewer, "Commercialization and Politics," in *The Birth of a Consumer Society: The Commercialization of Eighteenth-Century England*, ed. Neil McKendrick, John Brewer, and J. H. Plumb (Bloomington: Indiana University Press, 1982), 197. Colin Bonwick confirms that when elite Americans traveled to England "they mixed among the middle ranks of society, not among the aristocracy." Colin Bonwick, *English Radicals and the American Revolution* (Chapel Hill: University of North Carolina Press, 1977), 34–35. I am expanding the application of the term "Georgian" to include the reign of Queen Anne as well as the reigns of the Hanoverian kings George I, II, III. The term is also used to denote a style of furniture and architecture popular during the Georgian period.

2. John Brewer, " 'The Most Polite Age and the Most Vicious': Attitudes towards Culture as a Commodity, 1660–1800," in *The Consumption of Culture 1600–1800: Image, Object, Text*, ed. Ann Bermingham and John Brewer (London: Routledge, 1995), 351; Rodris Roth, "Tea-Drinking in Eighteenth-Century America: Its Etiquette and Equipage," in *Material Life in America 1600–1860*, ed. Robert Blair St. George (Boston: Northeastern University Press, 1988), 439–62.

3. Neil McKendrick, "Commercialization of Fashion," in McKendrick et al., *Birth of a Consumer Society*, 52, 49, 15; Daniel Miller, ed., *Acknowledging Consumption: A Review of New Studies* (London: Routledge, 1995), 181.

4. An eighteenth-century visitor to Annapolis, quoted in T. H. Breen, " 'Baubles of Britain': The American and Consumer Revolutions of the Eighteenth Century," in *Of Consuming Interests: The Style of Life in the Eighteenth Century*, ed. Cary Carson, Ronald Hoffman, and Peter J. Albert (Charlottesville: University Press of Virginia, 1994), 459; Alexander Hamilton, *Gentleman's Progress: The Itinerarium of Dr. Alexander Hamilton, 1744*, ed. Carl Bridenbaugh (Chapel Hill: University of North Carolina Press, 1948), 146; *Boston News Letter*, 19 April 1714.

5. On assemblies in English provincial towns see Peter Borsay, *The English Urban Renaissance: Culture and Society in the Provincial Town 1660–1770* (Oxford: Clarendon Press, 1990), 150–62. The word "assembly" was used to designate the event, the building, and / or the gathering. In reporting his tour of Britain, Daniel Defoe commented on "that new-fashion'd way of conversing by assemblies." Daniel Defoe, *A Tour Through the Whole Island of Great Britain* (London, 1724–26; reprint ed., London: Penguin, 1971), 214, 76, 518.

6. Roy Porter, *London: A Social History* (Cambridge, Mass.: Harvard University Press, 1995), 106.

7. Borsay, *Urban Renaissance*, 151–52, 154, 158–59.

8. Frances Drake, quoted in Mark Girouard, *The English Town: A History of Urban Life* (New Haven, Conn.: Yale University Press, 1990), 137; Shareholders of the York Assembly Rooms could receive annual dividends but rarely collected them so that in less than ten years the venture accumulated over five-hundred pounds. Borsay, *Urban Renaissance*, 160, 151–52, 154, 158–59; *Boston Gazette*, 8 January 1733. For a detailed discussion of assembly rooms and gatherings in provincial England see Girouard, *English Town*, 127–44.

9. James Duncan Phillips, *Salem in the Eighteenth Century* (Salem, Mass.: Essex Institute, 1969), 182; Mrs. Mary (Vail) Holyoke, *The Holyoke Diaries, 1709–1856* (Salem: The Essex Institute, 1911), 49, 51, 59; Gerald W. R. Ward, "The Assembly House," vol. 111 no. 4 *Essex Institute Historical Chronicle* (October 1975), 242; "A Historic Ball Room," ibid., 31:80.

10. *Essex Gazette*, 28 November 1769, quoted in Ward, "The Assembly House," 245; Holyoke, *Diaries*, passim; Phillips, *Salem*, passim. Turtles were a kind of feast centered around the cooking of a sea turtle that had been towed or transported from warmer waters.

11. Quoted in Kathleen Wilson, "The Good, The Bad, and The Impotent: Imperialism and the Politics of Identity in Georgian England," in Bermingham and Brewer, *The Consumption of Culture*, 243.

12. Clifford K. Shipton, *Biographical Sketches of Those Who Attended Harvard College*, 14 vols. (Cambridge, Mass.: Harvard University Press, 1933–75), 4:384. Belcher himself wed a wealthy merchant's widow and his five daughters married into the Lynde, Oliver, Noyes, and Stoddard trading families of Boston and the Vaughans of Portsmouth, New Hampshire. Michael C. Batinski, *Jonathan Belcher, Colonial Governor* (Lexington: University Press of Kentucky, 1996), 8.

13. Perry Miller notes that Anthony Stoddard the grandfather was a Puritan merchant, one of those who "humble themselves by public profession before the congregation" and who were able to "combine profits with search of soul." Perry Miller, *The New England Mind: From Colony to Province* (Cambridge, Mass.: Harvard University Press, 1953), 255. This demonstrates, in three generations of one family, the shift from Puritan to cosmopolitan that took place in Boston and Salem. Stoddard came from a staunch Puritan family yet aligned himself culturally with the provincial elite.

14. Ibid., 385; "Articles of Agreement" (re Stoddard lands in Connecticut) 1 May 1741, Miscellaneous Bound Manuscripts, Massachusetts Historical Society.

15. "Articles of Agreement"; Walter Muir Whitehill, *Boston: A Topographical History*, 2d ed. (Cambridge, Mass.: Belknap Press of Harvard University Press, 1968), 21.

16. Anthony Stoddard Estate Settlement Suffolk County Probate Records, Judicial Archives Massachusetts Archives, Docket no. 8959. Anthony Stoddard Inventory, 22 September 1748, Massachusetts Archives. Samuel Shrimpton's daughter Elizabeth married Anthony's brother David Stoddard.

17. In building his Boston mansion on Beacon Hill in 1735, Thomas Hancock instructed his gardener to "layout the upper garden allys," "Trim the beds," "Gravel the Walks," and "Sodd the Terras." Quoted in Richard L. Bushman, *The Refinement of America: Persons, Houses, Cities*. (New York: Knopf, 1992), 129. On the English habit of fashionable walks through landscaped gardens, see Porter, *London*, 173, and Girouard, *English Town*, 145–54.

18. Carole Shammas in *The Pre-Industrial Consumer in England and America* (New York: Oxford University Press, 1990) charts the decline in the importance of household linen, brass, and pewter, 172 and tables 6.3 and 6.4.

19. See Otto Mayr, *Authority, Liberty, and Automatic Machinery in Early Modern Europe* (Baltimore: Johns Hopkins University Press, 1986); David S. Landes, *Revolution in Time: Clocks and the Making of the Modern World* (Cambridge, Mass.: Harvard University Press, 1983).

20. Thomas Hancock to Wilks & Rowe, 10 July 1739, Thomas Hancock Letterbook, Baker Library, Harvard University.

21. Stoddard's high chest and other furniture may have been made in Boston. For a detailed examination of the adaptation of English furniture styles by colonial craftsmen see Margaretta Markle Lovell, "Boston Blockfront Furniture" in *Boston Furniture of the Eighteenth Century* (Boston: Colonial Society of Massachusetts, 1974), 77–135. Like much of the Georgian architecture coming into being in Boston, blockfront furniture was, according to Lovell, characterized by "a richness, rationality, classic proportions, and an uncompromising symmetry" (78).

22. Stoddard Inventory. On the custom of relaxed dressing in a gown and silken cap see Karin Calvert, "The Function of Fashion in Eighteenth-Century America," in Carson, *Of Consuming Interests*, 267–68.

23. See Janice A. Radway, *A Feeling for Books: the Book-of-the-Month Club, Literary Taste, and Middle-Class Desire* (Chapel Hill: University of North Carolina Press, 1997), 174.

24. Thomas Cushing, David Jeffries, Thomas Hancock, Jacob Wendell, Edward Bromfield, Andrew Oliver, John Wheelwright, and two of the Hutchinson family held positions as selectmen, or overseers of the poor. The town of Boston chose Cushing, Bromfield, Thomas Hutchinson, and James Allen (another local merchant), as their representatives to the General Court in 1740. The Council also included Jeffries, Wendell, Anthony Stoddard, John Cushing, and Edward Hutchinson of Boston. Stoddard and Hutchinson also acted as judges of the Suffolk County Court of Common Pleas. The Episcopal Charitable Society included Peter Faneuil, a Wendell, Charles Apthorp, Nathaniel Greene, a Bromfield, and Stephen Deblois. Besides Hallowell, several of the merchant gentlemen named above, along with the merchants John Wheelwright and John Goldthwait, participated in the Ancient and Honorable Artillery Company. "At a Meeting of the Lincolnshire Company," 15 January 1723, Price Family Papers, Massachusetts Historical Society; Purchasers of Long Wharf to Oliver Noyes, 26 January 1715, Price Family Papers, MHS; Robert Francis Seybolt, *The Town Officials of Colonial Boston, 1634–1775* (Cambridge, Mass.: Harvard University Press, 1939), 1740; William H. Whitmore, *The Massachusetts Civil List for the Colonial and Provincial Periods, 1630–1774* (Baltimore: Genealogical Publishing Company, 1969), 1740; Boston Episcopal Charity Society, 1726. Quincy, Wendell, Holmes and Upham Family Papers, Massachusetts Historical Society. Oliver Ayer Roberts, *History of the Military Company of the Massachusetts Now Called the Ancient and Honorable Artillery Company of Massachusetts, 1637–1888* vol. 2 (Boston: Alfred Mudget & Son, 1895), 474.

25. See Porter, *London*, 96–115; Roy Porter, *English Society in the Eighteenth Century*, rev. ed. (London: Penguin, 1990), 46; Borsay, *Urban Renaissance*, 75.

26. Defoe, *Whole Tour*, 286.

27. Porter, *London*, 99–119; Defoe, *Whole Tour*, 297.

28. Quoted in Porter, *London*, 100–102; See David S. Shields, *Civil Tongues and Polite Letters in British America* (Chapel Hill: University of North Carolina Press, 1997), 182 n. 11.

29. Girouard, *English Town*, 57, 82, 160–61; Porter, *London*, 102, 112–20, 120–23, Porter, *Eighteenth Century*, 46.

30. Whitehill, *Boston*, 30, 40–41. See Betsy Blackmar, "Rewalking the 'Walking City': Housing and Property Relations in New York City, 1780–1840," in *Material Life in America 1600–1860*, ed. Robert Blair St. George (Boston: Northeastern University Press, 1988), 371–84.

31. Porter, *Eighteenth Century*, 45; Joyce Ellis, "A Dynamic Society: Social Relations in Newcastle-upon-Tyne, 1660–1760," in *The Transformation of English Provincial Towns*, ed. Peter Clark (London: Hutchinson, 1984), 198; Borsay, *Urban Renaissance*, 295.

32. Hull often used the fact that his home was located "out of the way of trade" to explain his inability to sell some of the goods shipped to him by his family connections in London. John Hull to Mr. Daniell Allin, 23 August 1672, Letterbook of John Hull, manuscript and typescript in the collections of the American Antiquarian Society.

33. Girouard, *English Town*, 44; Whitehill, *Boston*, 35; Carrie Rebora, Paul Staiti, Erica E. Hirshler, Theodore E. Stebbius Jr., Carol Troyen, "Accounting for Copley," in *John Singleton Copley in America* (New York: Metropolitan Museum of Art, 1995) 32; Whitehill, *Boston*, 44.

34. W. T. Baxter, *The House of Hancock: Business in Boston, 1724–1775* (Cambridge, Mass.: Harvard University Press, 1945), 96; Bushman, *Refinement of America*, 129.

35. Staiti, "Copley," 38–39; For examples of Georgian chimney breasts and balusters see Dan Cruickshank and Neil Burton, *Life in the Georgian City* (London: Viking, 1990), 256–65; Roger G. Kennedy, *Architecture, Men, Women, and Money in America, 1600–1860* (New York: Random House, 1985) 107–8. On "standard" housing see Shammas, *Pre-Industrial Consumer*, 167, and Edward Chappell, "Housing a Nation: The Transformation of Living standards in Early America" in Carson, *Of Consuming Interests*, 208.

36. Under a "List of Inhabitants of Salem 1754," Orne enumerates "3,464 inhabitants, 372 houses, 205 widows, 1505 families, and 123 Negroes." Civic Papers, Timothy Orne Papers, Peabody Essex Museum; Hamilton, *Gentleman's Progress*, 122; James Birket, *Some Cursory Remarks Made by James Birkett in his Voyage to North America* (New Haven: Yale University Press, 1916), 15–16, quoted in Hamilton, *Gentleman's Progress*, 278, 239.

37. "Capt. Francis Goelet in 1750," *Two Centuries of Travel in Essex County Massachusetts: A Collection of Narratives and Observations Made by Travelers, 1605–1799*, comp. George Francis Dow (Topsfield, Mass.: Topsfield Historical Society, 1921), 75.

38. Phillips, *Salem*, 169, 319.

39. Girouard, *English Town*, 168; Borsay, *Urban Renaissance*, 74–79, 98.

40. Girouard notes that "many of the finest Georgian town houses were built by commercial families." *English Town*, 109.

41. Stoddard Inventory.

42. Shammas demonstrates the direct connection between the rising importation of tea and the diffusion of ceramic tableware required to handle hot beverages. Shammas, *Pre-Industrial Consumer*, 78–83, 187.

43. In discussing the role of consumer goods in England, Paul Langford concludes that "the middleclass which benefited so markedly by the economic changes of the eighteenth century was a class defined by material possessions." Paul Langford, *A Polite and Commercial People: England 1727–1783* (Oxford: Clarendon Press, 1989), 121.

44. According to Langford, contemporaries in eighteenth-century England "were struck by the extent to which the pursuit of politeness submerged rather than exposed distinctions" and led to a decline of regional differences. Ibid., 116–17, 121, 464.

45. Kathleen Wilson, "Imperialism and the politics of Identity," 242; see also 248, 250, 253.

46. B. F. Browne, memorandum book, quoted in Phillips, *Salem*, 246, 247; Holyoke, *Diaries*, 49, 50, 52, 54, 55, 59, 60, 62, 63, 64, 65, 67, 68, 69, 72, 75.

47. In the 1670s the Faneuil family in France sent trade goods to Boston via an agent named William Taylor. Bernard Bailyn, *The New England Merchants in the Seventeenth Century* (Cambridge, Mass.: Harvard University Press, 1955), 145.

48. For an account of French families' arrival in Boston see Justin Winsor, *A Memorial History of Boston* 4 vols. (Boston: J. R. Osgoods, 1868–1874), 2:249–53. Jon Butler's *The Huguenots in America: A Refugee People in New World Society* (Cambridge, Mass.: Harvard University Press, 1983) offers a general account of Huguenot settlements in America but is too broad to be useful here.

49. Probably they came via Rotterdam where a branch of the family had settled. See J. F. Bosher, "Huguenot Merchants and the Protestant International in the Seventeenth Century," *William and Mary Quarterly*, 3d ser., 52 (January 1995): 91, and unpaginated genealogy of "The Faneuil Family, with Relatives," Ibid.

50. Thwing Catalogue, Massachusetts Historical Society; Bosher, "Huguenot Merchants," 90. The Bank of England was established to supply William III with funds to carry on war with France. In July 1694, the *London Gazette* announced a meeting at Mercer's Hall in Cheapside where commissioners would accept subscriptions of five-hundred pounds or more. Each subscriber, Thomas Bureau among them, became a member of the Company of the Bank of England. Porter, *London*, 146.

51. For information on similar trading networks maintained by Huguenot merchants who settled in Charlestown, South Carolina, see Bertrand van Ruymbeke, "Kin, Social, and Regional Networks and the Integration of the South Carolina Huguenots," paper delivered at the OIEAHC Conference, Winston-Salem, North Carolina, 6–8 June 1997.

52. Thwing, Catalogue; Bosher, "Faneuil Family, with Relatives."

53. Abram English Brown, *Faneuil Hall and Faneuil Hall Market or Peter Faneuil and His Gift* (Boston: Lee and Shepard, 1900), 12–13.

54. Thwing Catalogue.

55. Thwing Catalogue; Whitehill, *Boston*, 26. The Bunch of Grapes Tavern later became a place to discuss Whig political ideas and a meeting place for the Sons of Liberty. Conroy, *Public Houses*, 257–58.

56. The purchase from Davie is recorded in the Thwing Catalogue. Several sources mention Faneuil's mansion.

57. *The Town of Boston in New England*, map by John Bonner, 1722, reprint by George G. Smith (Boston, 1835), Massachusetts Historical Society; Eliza S. M. Quincy, *Memoir of the Life of Eliza S. M. Quincy*, quoted in Winsor, *Memorial History*, 259; Whitehill, *Topographical History*, 35; Brown, *Faneuil Hall*, 15.

58. Bosher, "Huguenot Merchants"; *Boston News Letter*, 23 February 1738, quoted in Winsor, *Memorial History*, 261; Brown, *Faneuil Hall*, 23, 27.

59. Peter Faneuil, inventory, 28 March 1743, Suffolk County Probate Records, File 7877, Massachusetts Archives. See Gary Nash, *The Urban Crucible: Social Change, Political Consciousness, and the Origins of the American Revolution* (Cambridge, Mass.: Harvard University Press, 1979), 118 and table 7, 400. Comparing the range of personal wealth in Boston and Philadelphia in pounds sterling, Nash lists the £7,557 as the top figure in Boston between 1736 and 1745. This figure corresponds to Nash's calculation of Peter Faneuil's inventory and most likely represents the highest estate valuation Nash encountered in Suffolk County wills during the ten-year period. Comparing Faneuil's wealth to the median personal wealth figure of £1,065 sterling of the richest 10 percent of Bostonians in Nash's sample, we can see that he probably maintained or improved on his uncle's position and remained the wealthiest man in Boston.

60. Ibid., 399.

61. Peter Faneuil to Samuel and William Baker, 10 June 1738. Peter Faneuil Letterbook, New England Historical and Genealogical Society (microfilm).

62. Samuel Grant, 29 May 1738, 4 August 1738, 14 August 1738, "Account Book, 1737–1745," American Antiquarian Society; Nash, *Urban Crucible*, table 6, 399. The easy chair was worth just slightly less than a Boston mariner's annual income in pounds sterling in the same year. Ibid., table 2, 392; Winsor, *Memorial History*, 260; Faneuil inventory.

63. This scene is recreated from the details in the Faneuil inventory.

64. Timothy Orne memorandum books, 1763, 1764, 1765, 1766, Orne Papers.

65. Winifred Barr Rothenberg, *From Market-Places to a Market Economy: The Transformation of Rural Massachusetts, 1750–1850* (Chicago: University of Chicago Press, 1992), 130; John L. Brooke, *The Heart of the Commonwealth: Society and Political Culture in Worcester County Massachusetts, 1713–1861* (Cambridge: Cambridge University Press, 1989), 48; Timothy Orne memo book, 1765, Orne Papers.

66. Timothy Orne memorandum book, 1765, Orne Papers.

67. Timothy Orne memorandum book, 1765, Orne Papers; Brewer, "Commercialization and Politics," 198, 199.

68. Gordon S. Wood, *The Radicalism of the American Revolution* (New York: Random House, 1991), 63.

69. Timothy Orne ledger, 1738–53, Orne Papers. To assist in understanding Orne's relationship to the local and international economy I constructed a summary table of all 271 accounts initiated during the 1740s and recorded in the ledger, including location (noted when it is not Salem), occupation when given, balance and date of account when the account is balanced (sometimes after several years), and the most common items bought and sold.

70. Lorraine Daston, *Classical Probability, in the Enlightenment* (Princeton, N.J.: Princeton University Press, 1988) 115 and chap. 3, "The Theory and Practice of Risk," passim.

71. In the world of commerce much still depended on "specific, up-to-the-minute, . . . personal knowledge . . . to be sifted and weighed by an old hand in the business." Ibid., 112.

72. Christine Heyrman comes to the same conclusion about the phrase "objects of charity" and the process of distancing that occurred in eighteenth-century New England between donor and recipient or between wealthy elites and the poor and unfortunate. "More and more the poor were alluded to in passing only as the 'objects' of charity." Christine Leigh Heyrman, "The Fashion among More Superior People: Charity and Social Change in Provincial New England, 1700–1740," *American Quarterly* 34 (summer 1982): 107–24. In contrast, Conrad Edick Wright, in *The Transformation of Charity in Postrevolutionary New England* (Boston: Northeastern University Press, 1992), 20–23, stresses the benevolent and brotherly aspect of charity in colonial Massachusetts.

73. See Miller, *From Colony to Province*, 171, who says that as "the ethic of success" came to predominate, "Merchants who took advantage of the market learned to control congregations despite the clerics."

74. On the earlier reciprocal view of charity see Stephen Innes, *Creating the Commonwealth: The Economic Culture of Puritan New England* (New York: Norton, 1995), 71–72.

75. On Colman's background and his installation at Brattle Street Church, see Miller, *From Colony to Province*, 226, 241–44. Colman was "the single figure who marks the turn toward elegance in New England letters," and he learned his polite skills trading "epigrams with polite Christian ladies at Bath," Shields, *Civil Tongues and Polite Letters*, 67, 224.

76. Benjamin Colman, *The Merchandise of a People: Holiness to the Lord.* (Boston: J. Draper, 1736), ii–iii, 11. Colman delivered part of this sermon at "a private Meeting for Charity to the Poor" in 1726; Bernard Bailyn, "The *Apologia* of Robert Keayne," WMQ 3d ser., 7 (1950): 568–87.

77. Miller refers to "a smug acceptance of economic inequality . . . where lesser grades had no other function in the cosmos than to let their benefactors be instruments of heaven." Miller, *From Colony to Province*, 401.

78. Cotton Mather, *Durable Riches* (Boston: John Allen, 1695), 23.

79. According to Perry Miller, "the real thread of the story . . . becomes not . . . a growth of toleration, but rather a shedding of the religious conception of the universe." Miller, *From Colony to Province*, 171.

80. On dual motivations for charity see Eric G. Nellis, "The Working Poor of Pre-Revolutionary Boston," *Historical Journal of Massachusetts* 17 (summer 1989): 137–59.

81. See Robert Francis Seybolt, *The Town Officials of Colonial Boston, 1634–1775* (Cambridge, Mass.: Harvard University Press, 1939), passim.

82. Overseers of the poor were also responsible for orphans and children of destitute parents. Nellis, "Working Poor," 155.

83. See Stephen E. Wiberley Jr., "Four Cities: Public Poor Relief in Urban America, 1700–1775" (Ph.D. diss., Yale University, 1975).

84. 10 February 1735, Boston Town Records, Manuscript Collection, Boston Public Library. In January 1707 a meeting of the "Justices, Select men & Overseers of the Poor" agreed to "Visit the Familyes of this Town" once every quarter "in Order to prevent & redress disorders." The merchants acting as overseers for the year included Elisha Hutchinson, John Clark Esq., Thomas Brattle, Samuel Lynde, Thomas Hutchinson, Thomas Palmer, Eliakim Hutchinson, Simeon Stoddard, and Edward Bromfield—all from important merchant families.

85. Heyrman, "The Fashion among More Superior People," 107–24.

86. *A Report of the Record Commissioners of the City of Boston* 22 vols. (Boston: Rockwell and Churchill, 1876–90), 8:55 (herafter *Boston Records*); John Rowe recorded numerous visits to the poor and schools in John Rowe, *Letters and Diary of John Rowe, Boston Merchant, 1759–1762, 1764–1779* (Boston: W. B. Clarke, 1903), 101, 136, 152, 155, 168, 189. See also John Tudor, "The Diary of Deacon John Tudor" typescript, Massachusetts Historical Society, 23–24 July 1752, 2 August 1760. On outdoor relief and the selection of well-to-do townsmen as overseers, see Wiberley, "Four Cities," 76–77, 166–67, and table 6.1, "Rank of Boston Overseers of the Poor in Assessment List of 1771," 163; *Boston Records*, 12:55–56; Benjamin Colman, *The Merchandise of a People: Holiness to the Lord*. (Boston: J. Draper, 1736), 11.

87. See Karin Calvert, "The Function of Fashion in Eighteenth-Century America," in Carson, *Of Consuming Interests*, 252–83.

88. Tudor, "Diary," 2 August 1760; Rowe, *Diary*, 101; Heyrman, "The Fashion Among More Superior People," 107–24.

89. Tudor, "Diary," 2 August 1760; William Pencak, "The Social Structure of Revolutionary Boston: Evidence from the Great Fire of 1760," *Journal of Interdisciplinary History* vol. 10 no. 2 (autumn 1979): 272; Carl Bridenbaugh, "The High Cost of Living in Boston, 1728," *New England Quarterly* vol. 15 no. 3 (October 1932), 805–08, 802; G. B. Warden, "The Distribution of Property in Boston, 1692–1775," *Perspectives* 10 (1976): 86.

90. Pencak, "Revolutionary Boston," 273, 274; James A. Henretta, "Economic Development and Social Structure in Colonial Boston," *WMQ* vol. 22 no. 1 (January 1965): 85, 90; Allan Kulikoff, "The Progress of Inequality in Revolutionary Boston," ibid., vol. 28 no. 3 (July 1971): 381; Richard J. Morris, "Social Change, Republican Rhetoric, and the American Revolution: The Case of Salem, Massachusetts," *Journal of Social History* vol. 31 no. 2 (winter 1997): 422; Orne memorandum books, 1763, 1764, 1765, 1766, Orne Papers.

91. Rowe, *Diary*, 80, 185, 196, 332.

92. See Nellis, "Working Poor," passim; Warden, "Distribution of Property in Boston," 85–86. On middle-class entrepreneurs in Boston, see Barbara McLean Ward, "Boston Artisan Entrepreneurs of the Goldsmithing Trade in the Decades before the Revolution," 23–38, and Patricia Cleary, " 'Who shall say we have not equal abilitys with the Men when Girls of 18 years of age discover such great capacitys?': Women of Commerce in Boston, 1750–1776," 39–62, in *Entrepreneurs: The Boston Business Community, 1700–1850*, ed. Conrad Edick Wright and Katheryn P. Viens (Boston: Massachusetts Historical Society, 1997). Michael Batinski asserts that "New England's leaders sensed the gulfs." Batinski, *Jonathan Belcher*, 82.

93. *Boston News Letter*, 16–23 May 1734; *Weekly Rehearsal*, 20 May 1734; *Essex Gazette*, 22–29 November 1768.

94. Rowe, *Diary*, 67–68, 114, 194; John Adams, *Diary and Autobiography of John Adams*, vol. 1: *Diary 1755–1770*, ed. L. H. Butterfield (Cambridge Mass.: Harvard University Press, 1961), 321; Alfred F. Young, "English Plebeian Culture and Eighteenth-Century American Radicalism," in *The Origins of Anglo-American Radicalism*, ed. Margaret C. Jacob and James R. Jacob (Atlantic Highlands, New Jersey: Humanities Press International, 1991), 198; Nash, *Urban Crucible*, 260–61; G. B. Warden, *Boston, 1689–1776* (Boston: Little, Brown, 1970), 152.

95. For discussions of early markets see Jean-Christophe Agnew, *Worlds Apart: The Market and the Theater in Anglo-American Thought, 1550–1750* (New York: Cambridge University Press, 1986), 20–21, and 29; Fernand Braudel, *Civilization and Capitalism, 15th–18th Century*, vol. 2: *The Wheels of Commerce*, trans. Sian Reynolds (New York: Harper & Row, 1982), 27–60, 43, 45; and Girouard, *English Town*, 9–30, 22, 18–24.

96. Dorothy Davis, *Fairs, Shops, and Supermarkets: A History of English Shopping* (Toronto: Toronto University Press, 1966), quoted in Braudel, *Civilization and Capitalism,* 2:38. See Borsay, *Urban Renaissance*, 104–109.

97. John Winthrop, *Winthrop's Journal*, "History of New England" 1630–1649, 2 vols. ed. James Kendall Hosmer (New York: Scribner's, 1908), 1:215, quoted in Bailyn, *New England Merchants*, 41; Robert Keayne, *The Apologia of Robert Keayne* (Gloucester, Mass.: P. Smith, 1970).

98. Braudel, *Civilization and Capitalism*, 2:38.

99. *Boston Records*, 7:224 et passim. See also Karen J. Freidman, "Victualing Colonial Boston," *Agricultural History* 47 (1973): 194.

100. Warden, *Boston*, 117.

101. Ibid.; *Boston Records*, 12:57; Seybolt, *Town Officials of Colonial Boston*, 186; *Boston News Letter*, 15 March 1733. Fitch, Hutchinson, and Wendell were also selected to serve on several other committees, including a group to consider "the most convenient Places in this Town, for Fortifications."

102. Shipton, *Biographical Sketches*, 9:365.

103. John Mico (who trained Jacob Wendell) was one of the merchants who played a key role in founding the Brattle Street Church. Miller, *From Colony to Province*, 241.

104. Extant Wendell documents are to be found dispersed throughout several reels of the microfilm edition of the Quincy, Wendell, Holmes, and Upham Family Papers, Massachusetts Historical Society, together with the Quincy, Wendell, Holmes, and Upham Family Papers in the Collection of Hugh Upham Clark of Arlington, Virginia. Microfilm. Massachusetts Historical Society.

105. Jacob Wendell's first son to attend Harvard, who graduated in 1733, was ranked fifth in his college class, which indicated a high social standing. When Wendell's second son entered Harvard he was ranked first in the Class of 1747—a clear indication of the high social rank his father had achieved. See Shipton, *Biographical Sketches* 5:110, 6:408–09; 9:365–67; 12:367–74, 17:218–19.

106. *Boston Records*, 12:69, 72.

107. *At a Meeting of the Freeholders . . .* (Boston: Samuel Gerrish, 1734), 4. See also the earlier version of market regulations, *At a publick Town-Meeting . . .* (Boston, 1733), 3, 5.

108. *Some Considerations Against the Setting up of a Market in this Town* 5, 1, 3.

109. *Boston Records*, 12:46. See also the account of this meeting in *Boston News Letter*, 31 May 1733.

110. *Boston News-Letter*, 28 June 1733; *Boston Records*, 12:48–49. Warden, *Boston*, says that "country people who made their living by selling in Boston vehemently opposed any restriction on trade,"(117) but also goes on to interpret the conflict as one between Elisha Cooke's popular party and the supporters of Governor Belcher, 118–20. Nash, in *Urban Crucible*, 130–36 rightly emphasizes economic problems and focuses on crowd action as a response to those problems.

111. *Boston Records*, 12:69. The scheme was apparently approved by acclamation, since no vote totals appear. *Boston Gazette*, 25 March 1734.

112. Warden suggests that the 1734 proposals passed easily because they "were so lenient and moderate that the whole point of the market scheme was essentially thwarted." Warden, *Boston*, 120. A comparison of the scheme printed for the town on 9 May, 1733 and the proposals printed 24 April 1734, which passed by acclamation, indicates that some fines were reduced from twenty to ten shillings and that "Apples, Onions, Turnips, and all sorts of Roots, Fruit and Herbs" were exempted from the 1734 regulations. *At a Meeting of the Freeholders*, 4–5; *Boston Records*, 12:61.

113. *Boston News Letter*, 6 June 1734; *Boston Gazette*, 14 June 1734.

114. *Some Considerations*, 2; *Boston Records*, 12:134, 164, 171, 172.

115. The assessors made sure that "None might be allow'd to Vote in the Affair, Excepting such as were Rated in the last Tax Two Shillings and One penny New Tenor." Petition, 2 July 1740, Original Papers, 2:63, in Boston City Clerk's office; quoted in Winsor, *Memorial History*, 2:263, and reprinted in *Boston Records*, 12:259. The best account of this meeting is ibid., 258–60. See also Winsor, *Memorial History*, 2:263–64; Brown, *Faneuil Hall*, 79–83, offers a colorful but somewhat dubious rendition of events surrounding the meeting. The town agreed to pay for "whatsoever Damage may happen to be done to the Pews, Seats &c." *Boston Records*, 12:259, 260, 264; petition, 2 July 1740.

116. In the early republic between 1800 and 1820, a whole new round of major public buildings was constructed in a neoclassical style by a succeeding generation of merchant families like the Appletons, Lawrences, and Lowells who garnered their wealth from trade with Asia.

117. For details on the market for prints and its links to the consumer revolution see Margaretta M. Lovell, "Painters and Their Customers: Aspects of Art and Money in Eighteenth-Century America," in Carson, *Of Consuming Interests*, 298–306.

118. The Royal Exchange was begun by Sir Thomas Gresham in 1566. Queen Elizabeth officially opened the exchange in 1571. After the great fire of 1666 the Royal Exchange was rebuilt preserving Gresham's courtyard design (and apparently the grasshopper weather vane as well) but adding a grand two-story arch over the entrance fashioned in the artisan-mannerist mode. This building also succumbed to fire in 1838. John Newman Summerson, *Architecture in Britain, 1530 to 1830* (New York: Penguin, 1997), 46, 171, 188, 189. I can find no information that suggests why the weather vane was made in the form of a grasshopper. One scholar suggested the possible association of the grasshopper with industrious effort in *Aesop's Fables*.

119. John Lovell, *A Funeral Oration Deliver'd at the Opening of the Annual Meeting of the Town . . . Occasion'd by the Death of the Founder, Peter Faneuil, Esq.* (Boston: Green, Bushell, and Allen for S. Kneeland and T. Green, 1743), 7, 9, 10, 14.

120. Brown, *Faneuil Hall*, 90, 94.

121. *Report of a French Protestant Refugee, in Boston, 1687*, trans. E. T. Fisher (Brooklyn, N.Y., 1868), 25–26.

122. Jürgen Habermas, *The Structural Transformation of the Public Sphere: An Inquiry into a Category of Bourgeois Society*, trans. Thomas Burger (Cambridge, Mass.: MIT Press, 1989).

123. On coffeehouses see Shields, *Civil Tongues and Polite Letters*, 98.

124. *The Spectator*, ed. D. F. Bond, 5 vols (Oxford: Oxford University Press, 1965) quoted in John Brewer, "Commercialization and Politics"; McKendrick, *Birth*, 222, 218–223; Rules of the Civil Society 25 February 1745, Salem Miscellaneous Papers, Phillips Library, Peabody Essex Museum; Brewer, "Commercialization," 217; *Spectator*, no. 10, quoted in Agnew, *Worlds Apart*, 171.

125. Civil Society account, Salem Miscellaneous Papers, Phillips Library, Peabody Essex Museum; Rowe, *Diary*, passim; Hamilton, *Gentleman's Progress*, xix, 115–16, 133. See also Shields, *Civil Tongues and Polite Letters*, chapt. 6, "The Clubs," 175–208.

126. See C. John Sommerville, *The News Revolution in England: Cultural Dynamics of Daily Information* (New York: Oxford, 1996) on the importance of periodicity to the rise of the newspaper.

127. John Brewer, *The Pleasures of the Imagination: English Culture in the Eighteenth Century* (New York: Farrar, Straus and Giroux, 1997), 35.

128. *Salisbury Journal*, 28 March 1757, quoted in C. Y. Ferdinand, "Selling It to the Provinces: News and Commerce round Eighteenth-century Salisbury," in *Consumption and the World of Goods*, ed. John Brewer and Roy Porter (London: Routledge, 1993), 401.

129. Quoted in J. Paul Hunter, *Before Novels: The Cultural Contexts of Eighteenth Century English Fiction* (New York: Norton, 1990), 174. See also Shields, *Civil Tongues and Polite Letters*, chapt. 3, "Coffeehouse and Tavern," 55–97.

130. See Baxter, *House of Hancock*, 184; Whitehill, *Boston*, 26.

131. John Mein to Samuel Curwen, 12 December 1767, Curwen Manuscripts, American Antiquarian Society; Phillips, *Salem*, 299, 258. Phillips has Orne paying ten guineas but the original records indicate his contribution at fifteen Guineas.

132. "The Covenant Articles of the Social Library," 31 March 1760, Social Library Records; Phillips, *Salem*, 258. In Great Britain, over 100 social libraries had been formed by the end of the eighteenth century. Commercial circulating libraries were even more popular; London had 112, and 268 had been organized in the provinces before 1800. James Raven, *Judging New Wealth: Popular Publishing and Responses to Commerce in England, 1750–1800* (Oxford: Clarendon Press, 1992), 54 n. 39.

133. Timothy Orne Library account, Orne Papers; charge book, Social Library Records.

134. The trend in setting up social libraries began in Liverpool in 1758, extended to Manchester in 1765, Bristol in 1774, Hull in 1775, and Newcastle in 1784. Raven, *Judging New Wealth*, 128, 166, 188, 129. See also R. G. Wilson, *Gentlemen Merchants: The Merchant Community in Leeds, 1700–1830* (Manchester: Manchester University Press, 1971).

135. Phillips, *Salem*, 142; Journal of the House of Representatives, 17 March 1784, quoted in Rowe, *Diary*, 330.

Chapter 5. A Return to Homespun

1. John Adams, *Diary and Autobiography of John Adams*, vol. 1: *Diary 1755–1770*, ed. L. H. Butterfield (Cambridge, Mass.: Harvard University Press, 1961), 294. On taverns as an important site for the development of revolutionary ideas and actions, see Peter Thompson, *Rum Punch and Revolution: Taverngoing & Public Life in Eighteenth-Century Philadelphia* (Philadelphia: University of Pennsylvania Press, 1999).

2. I am indebted to Robert Calhoon for help in contextualizing Adams's visits. See Peter Shaw, *The Character of John Adams* (Chapel Hill: University of North Carolina Press, 1976), 109–12 198–200. See also Page Smith, *John Adams*, vol. 1, *1735–1784* (Garden City, N.Y.: Doubleday, 1962).

3. Adams, *Diary*, 1:294.

4. John W. Tyler, *Smugglers and Patriots: Boston Merchants and the Advent of the American Revolution* (Boston: Northeastern University Press, 1986), 117, 127.

5. Ibid., 30.

6. Boylston Sr. had purchased an elegant home on School Street, already styled as the "Mansion House," from Jacob Wendell. Carrie Rebora, Paul Staiti, Erica E. Hirshler, Theodore E. Stebbins Jr., and Carol Troyen, *John Singleton Copley in America* (New York: Metropolitan Museum of Art, 1995), 224.

7. Paul Staiti, "Character and Class," in Rebora, *Copley in America*, 53–54. Staiti expresses the role of portraiture in eighteenth-century Boston most eloquently, noting that the paintings had the "power to calibrate social position in graphic ways that were legible to a community." They "helped to constitute class in Boston." He reinforces the importance of material goods in shaping group and individual identity, stating that "all forms of visual display in eighteenth-century British North America were bearers of

identity and class definition." This society, Staiti asserts, "loved objects and facts and numbers and money." See also Richard L. Bushman, *The Refinement of America: Persons, Houses, Cities* (New York: Knopf, 1992), 402–11.

8. Rebora, *Copley in America*, 228–29.

9. The robe or gown is named after the Banyas, an Indian caste whose members were the preeminent merchants in northern and central India and "commanded a large part of Indian commerce." Irfan Habib, "Merchant Communities in Precolonial India," in *The Rise of Merchant Empires: Long-Distance Trade in the Early Modern World, 1350–1750*, ed. James D. Tracy (Cambridge: Cambridge University Press, 1990), 385, 379–96; Staiti, "Character and Class," 54; personal communication with John Fairbanks, Museum of Fine Arts, Boston; K. N. Chaudhuri, *The Trading World of Asia and the English East India Company, 1660–1760* (Cambridge: Cambridge University Press, 1978), 137.

10. Staiti notes that in many of Copley's portraits, professional identity is subsumed to consumer identity where lavish material goods are the essence of the picture. The portraits "represent a class position via consumer objects." Staiti, "Character and Class," 68.

11. Rebora, *Copley in America*, 228–29; Tyler, *Smugglers and Patriots*, passim.

12. William Pencak, *War, Politics, and Revolution in Provincial Massachusetts* (Boston: Northeastern University Press, 1981), 171, 221; Gary B. Nash, *The Urban Crucible: Social Change, Political Consciousness, and the Origins of the American Revolution* (Cambridge, Mass.: Harvard University Press, 1979), 281; Edmund Morgan, "The Puritan Ethic and the American Revolution," *William and Mary Quarterly*, 3d. ser., vol. 24 no. 1 (January 1967): 82. According to Tyler, the merchants were divided from the beginning of the second non-importation movement in late 1767. Tyler, *Smugglers and Patriots*, 167–68.

13. Tyler, *Smugglers and Patriots*, 128, 137, 163, 250; Arthur Meier Schlesinger, *The Colonial Merchants and the American Revolution, 1763–1776* (New York: Unger, 1917), 40–42. On rising prices see Schlesinger, *Colonial Merchants*, 586–90. For information on John Hancock's poor business practices and failed ventures see W. T. Baxter, *The House of Hancock: Business in Boston, 1724–1775* (Cambridge, Mass.: Harvard University Press, 1945) passim.

14. Nash, *Urban Crucible*, 335; G. B. Warden, *Boston, 1689–1776* (Boston: Little, Brown, 1970), 226, 300; Mary Beth Norton, *Liberty's Daughters: The Revolutionary Experience of American Women, 1750–1800* 2d ed. (Ithaca: Cornell University Press, 1996), 166; [Samuel Quincy] to [Robert Treat Paine], 2 February 1756, quoted in Norton, *Liberty's Daughters*, 8.

15. Adams, *Diary*, 1:294–95. See Tyler, *Smugglers and Patriots*, 156.

16. Schlesinger, *Colonial Merchants*, 40–42; Tyler, *Smugglers and Patriots*, 110–11.

17. John Rowe, *Letters and Diary of John Rowe, Boston Merchant, 1759–1762, 1764–1779* (Boston: W. B. Clarke, 1903), 88–89. For a venomous account of this episode, see Andrew Oliver's brother Peter's description in eds., Douglass Adair and John A. Schutz, *Peter Oliver's Origin and Progress of the American Rebellion: A Tory View*, (San Marino, Calif.: The Huntington Library, 1963), 53–54. Benjamin Lynde, Jr. of Salem noted in his diary that "a mob beset his house destroyed a building and ruined glasses etc." Lynde also described a mob that "rose again and beset" Lieutenant Governor Hutchinson's house and destroyed furniture, books, etc., to the value of twenty-three thousand pounds Massachussets money. Benjamin Lynde Jr., *The Diaries of Benjamin Lynde and of Benjamin Lynde, Jr.* (Boston: Privately printed, 1880), 190.

18. Mrs. Mary (Vail) Holyoke, *The Holyoke Diaries, 1709–1856* (Salem: The Essex Institute, 1911), 65; Benjamin Lynde Jr., *Diary*, 191; Adams, *Diary*, 1:312; Rowe, *Diary*, 95–96, 126, 130.

19. Rowe, *Diary*, 211–12; *Essex Gazette*, 20–27 December 1768; Rowe, *Diary*, 184.

20. Rowe, *Diary*, 88–89.

21. Benjamin Lynde Jr., *Diary*, 203; Holyoke, *Diaries, 1709–1856*, 83, 88; James Duncan Phillips, *Salem in the Eighteenth Century* (Salem, Mass.: Essex Institute, 1969), 323.

22. Rowe, *Diary*, 269–71. Alison Olson agrees that after the Boston Port Act, it became "virtually impossible for members [of the merchant group] to remain neutral." Alison Gilbert Olson, *Making the Empire Work: London and American Interest Groups 1690–1790* (Cambridge, Mass.: Harvard University Press, 1992), 167, 171.

23. Richard D. Brown, *Revolutionary Politics in Massachusetts: The Boston Committee of*

Correspondence and the Towns, 1772–1774 (New York: Norton, 1970), 188– 89; Rowe, *Diary*, 270, 273.

24. Rowe, *Diary*, 274; Warden, *Boston*, 296.

25. Brown, *Revolutionary Politics*, 195–97; Rowe, *Diary*, 275–77. For a detailed discussion of the newspaper essays printed by both sides see Tyler, *Smugglers and Patriots*, 219–23. Warden says that Rowe and John Amory led the opposition to the Solemn League and Covenant. If so, it is not evident in Rowe's actions. Warden, *Boston*, 294.

26. Schlesinger, *Colonial Merchants*, 40–42; Tyler, *Smugglers and Patriots*, 226; Brown, *Revolutionary Politics*, 198–99.

27. Rowe, *Diary*, 261, 271, 277–78, 280, 287, 299. On signatories to the address to Gage, see the Table of Boston Merchants in the appendix to Tyler, *Smugglers and Patriots*, 253–77. Benjamin Pickman, *The Diary and Letters of Benjamin Pickman* (Newport, R.I.: Wayside Press, 1928), 15, 20–22 et passim. (The bulk of Pickman's diary consists of entries made and letters written while he was in England.) *Boston News Letter*, 15 March 1775; builder's contract, Timothy Orne Papers, Phillips Library, Peabody Essex Museum.

28. Rowe, *Diary*, 300, 302.

29. J. G. A. Pocock, *Virtue, Commerce, and History: Essays on Political Thought and History, Chiefly in the Eighteenth Century* (Cambridge: Cambridge University Press, 1985), 70, 115; Rowe *Diary*, 301–4; Benjamin Lynde Jr., *Diary*, 206.

30. Bernard Bailyn, *The Ideological Origins of the American Revolution*, enl ed. (1967: Cambridge, Mass.: Harvard University Press, 1992), 94–143. See T. H. Breen, " 'Baubles of Britain': The American and Consumer Revolutions of the Eighteenth Century," *Past and Present* (1988): 73–104, reprinted in *Of Consuming Interests: The Style of Life in the Eighteenth Century* ed. Cary Carson, Ronald Hoffman, and Peter J. Albert (Charlottesville: University Press of Virginia, 1994.) My work is deeply indebted to the studies of Anglo-American consumer culture by T. H. Breen.

31. Schlesinger, *Colonial Merchants*, 27, 295. For a detailed discussion of the importation of Country Party ideology and the complicated origins of this phrase note Bailyn, *Ideological Origins*, 36, 137.

32. Quoted in Breen, " 'Baubles of Britain,' " 467; Adams quoted in Nash, *Urban Crucible*, 297; Rebora, *Copley in America*, 228.

33. Rowe, *Diary*, 152–53, 155; Pencak, *War, Politics, and Revolution*, 163–64; Tyler, *Smugglers and Patriots*, 167–68; Nash, *Urban Crucible*, 354; Schlesinger, *Colonial Merchants*, 91.

34. Schlesinger, *Colonial Merchants*, 63; Breen, " 'Baubles of Britain,' " 473, 469; On how generational differences influenced the choice for Loyalism or Patriotism, see Pencak, *War, Politics, and Revolution*, 201–29. On the turn to New England goods see Margaret Ellen Newell, *From Dependency to Independence: Economic Revolution in Colonial New England* (Ithaca: Cornell University Press, 1998), 291–94.

35. David Hackett Fischer, *Paul Revere's Ride* (New York: Oxford University Press, 1994), 20–22; Pauline Maier, *From Resistance to Revolution: Colonial Radicals and the Development of American Opposition to Britain, 1765–1776* (New York: Norton, 1991), 169–70; Warden, *Boston*, 187, 189, 194–95; Hillsborough to North American governors, 21 April 1768, quoted in Maier, *Resistance to Revolution*, 170; Rowe, *Diary*, 167, 168, 171–72, 175; Warden indicates that the Redcoats marched with loaded weapons. See also the Revere print of British soldiers disembarking at Long Wharf and marching down King Street to the center of town. John Adams discusses the Rescinders in his *Diary*, 1:355–56; Paul Revere, Museum of Fine Arts, Boston, shown in Fischer, *Paul Revere's Ride*, 23.

36. This brief summary of Wilkes's political career has been compiled from accounts in Paul Langford, *A Polite and Commercial People: England 1727–1783* (Oxford: Clarendon Press, 1989), 377–79; Maier, *Resistance to Revolution*, 161–78, 256–63. The most lucid explanation of Wilkes's connection with American politics is found in Maier.

37. Maier, *Resistance to Revolution*, 170, 204. The phrase "novel sort of political controversy" is from Langford, *Polite and Commercial People*, 358, 357–64; John Brewer, "Commercialization of Politics," in Neil McKendrick, John Brewer, and J. H. Plumb

The Birth of a Consumer Society: the Commercialization of Eighteenth-Century England, (Bloomington: Indiana University Press, 1982), 201, 232–33, 237–40.

38. *Boston Gazette,* 21 August 1769; Adams, *Diary,* 1:341.

39. On merchant families in Boston see Tyler, *Patriots and Smugglers,* appendix; Holyoke, *Diaries,* 54.

40. Broadside, 1 December 1773 (Boston, 1773); Rowe, *Diary,* 256, 258; Dirk Hoerder, *Crowd Action in Revolutionary Massachusetts, 1765–1780* (New York: Academic Press, 1977), 260–61, 263; Oliver, *Origin and Progress,* 102.

41. Adams, *Diary,* 3:85–86; Warden, *Boston,* 284; Hoerder, *Crowd Action,* 263–64; Rowe, *Diary,* 258; Oliver, *Origin and Progress,* 102.

42. Oliver, *Origin and Progress,* 103. Like a carnival, the Tea Party can be read as an inversion ritual that critiqued "high" culture. As such, "it marks the suspension of all hierarchical rank" and a "temporary liberation from the prevailing truth of the established order." Therefore it is a moment of change and renewal, which in this case proved progressive, not temporary. M. M. Bakhtin, *Rabelais and his World,* trans. H. Iswolsky (Cambridge, Mass.: MIT Press, 1968), 109, quoted in Peter Stallybrass and Allon White, *The Politics and Poetics of Transgression* (Ithaca: Cornell University Press, 1986), 7.

43. Holyoke, *Diaries,* 86–88; Pickman, *Diary and Letters,* 154–56.

44. *Essex Gazette,* 21–28 September 1773; Louisa Dresser, "The Orne Portraits by Joseph Badger," *Worcester Art Museum Bulletin* vol. 1 no. 2 (February 1972): 12.

45. Richard Brown says of this event, "The people of Worcester performed a pageant of popular sovereignty" when they required court-appointed officials to walk through the crowd while reading a pledge to ignore parliamentary acts. Brown, *Revolutionary Politics,* 217. He estimates the crowd at six thousand while Calhoon uses the figure two thousand.

46. For an expanded account of the crowd action in Worcester that day, see Robert McCluer Calhoon, *The Loyalists in Revolutionary America, 1760–1781* (New York: Harcourt Brace Jovanovich, 1973), 275–76.

47. Oliver, *Origin and Progress,* 153. Samuel Paine to William Paine, 22 June 1775, quoted in Calhoon, *Loyalists in Revolutionary America,* 276. See also Brown, *Revolutionary Politics,* 217.

48. Dresser, "Orne Portraits," 15; Mary Holyoke, *Diary,* 112.

49. Mary Holyoke, *Diary,* 86, 87–89, 113; Pickman, *Diary and Letters,* 154–55, 159, 160, 166; James Duncan Phillips, *Salem in the Eighteenth Century,* (Salem, Mass.: Essex Institute, 1969), 384–85, 388; Rowe, *Diary,* 273; Mary Beth Norton, *The British-Americans: The Loyalist Exiles in England, 1774–1789* (Boston: Little, Brown, 1972), 76–79.

50. Norton says that this firm began in 1756 as Lane and Booth, but documentary evidence shows prior incarnations of the firm as Lane & Caswell as early as 1744. Members of the firm entertained Pickman twelve times during the month of June 1783, perhaps hoping to reestablish commercial goodwill now that the war had ended. Merchant house and shipping correspondence, Orne Papers; Pickman, *Diary and Letters,* 89–93, 158–59, 162–63.

51. Pickman, *Diary and Letters,* 102–104, 107; Norton, *British-Americans,* 77–79, 86, 101; On class consciousness see Oliver, *Origin and Progress,* 27, 29, 63, 65.

52. For a merchant who prospered as a privateer and then entered the China trade, see the papers of Timothy Orne's cousin, William. William Orne Papers in the Orne Family Papers, Phillips Library, Peabody Essex Museum. Phillips, *Salem,* 390–91, 401, 426, 397; Benjamin Lynde, Jr., *Diary,* 207–8.

Epilogue

1. See Robert F. Dalzell, Jr., *Enterprising Elite: The Boston Associates and the World They Made* (Cambridge, Mass.: Harvard University Press, 1987) and James Duncan Phillips, *Salem in the Eighteenth Century* (Salem, Mass.: Essex Institute, 1969).
2. Quoted in Robert A. Gross, "From Citizens to Subjects: The Formalization of Authority in Post-Revolutionary Massachusetts," in *People and Power: Rights, Citizenship, and Violence*, ed. Loretta Valtz Mannucci (Milan: Istituto di Studi Storici, Università degli Studi di Milano, 1992).
3. Ibid.
4. Dalzell, *Enterprising Elite*, 122, 26–73, 87–88, 83, 94–98, 109–11, 161. See also Peter Dobkin Hall, "What the Merchants Did with Their Money: Charitable and Testamentary Trusts in Massachusetts, 1780–1880," in *Entrepreneurs: The Boston Business Community, 1700–1850*, ed. Conrad Edick Wright and Katheryn P. Viens (Boston: Massachusetts Historical Society, 1997).
5. For Lawrence's earlier years as clerk to a Boston mercantile house and his first efforts at his own business, see William R. Lawrence, ed., *Extracts from the Diary and Correspondence of the late Amos Lawrence* (Boston: Gould and Lincoln, 1856), 29–36; Dalzell, *Enterprising Elite*, 148; Lawrence, *Diary and Correspondence*, 182, 197, 213–15; Carrie Rebora, "Copley and Art History: The Study of America's First Old Master," in *John Singleton Copley in America* by Carrie Rebora, Paul Starti, Erica E. Hirshlor, Theodore E. Stebbins Jr., and Carol Troyen (New York: Metropolitian Museum of Art, 1995), 4–5, 228.
6. Dalzell, *Enterprising Elite*, 148.
7. Adams, *Diary*, 1:294.
8. On demand for English goods at all levels see T. H. Breen, "An Empire of Goods: the Anglicization of Colonial America, 1690–1776," *Journal of British Studies* vol. 25 no. 4 (October 1986), 467–99.
9. Richard L. Bushman maintains that "gentility did its part in advancing capitalism. A large market for consumer goods was a prerequisite for industrialization." Bushman, *Refinement of America*, 406–7.
10. See Richard Bushman, *From Puritan to Yankee: Character and the Social Order in Connecticut, 1690–1765* (Cambridge, Mass.: Harvard University Press, 1967).

Index

Accounts, 21, 77–78, 126–27, 129, 149; of Philip English, 67–69; of Andrew Faneuil, 120; importance of, 21, 129; of Timothy Orne, 126–29; and wealth, 129

Adams, John, 133, 147–49, 155–56, 159, 163–64, 173

Adams, Samuel, 151, 155–56, 159

Addison, Joseph, 76, 142

Adventure. *See* Trading ventures

Advertisements, 89–90

Africa, 2, 41, 80–81, 124

Alehouses, 52–53, 56, 95, 114; culture of, 52–54, 56. *See also* Taverns

Ambivalence: about consumer culture, 100–101; about foreign trade, 134; about gentility, 93–96, 108

America, 1, 2, 71–72, 96, 101, 103; colonial, 1, 2; housing in, 115–16

American identity, 13, 146, 148, 158–59, 165, 169, 171, 175

American revolution, 125, 146, 147–69

Amsterdam, 11, 27, 78, 121, 135

Ancient and Honorable Artillery Company, 113

Anderson, Benedict, 80

Andros, Sir Edmund, 58–59, 65

Anglican Church, 35, 45–46, 59, 64, 66, 68, 91, 95, 105–6, 119–20; members of, 35, 45–46, 52, 58, 64, 67–68, 73, 86, 91–92, 94–96, 119

Anglo-America, 4, 14, 17, 72, 75, 78, 80, 98; cultural change in, 137; elites of, 87–88, 100, 132, 143–44, 153, 158–59, 165; ports of, 28; shared culture of, 153, 158, 165, 175; urban centers of, 90; urban renaissance of, 117

Anglo-Americans, 5, 8, 119

Anglo-French trade, 46–47

Annapolis, Md., 109

Anti-French feeling, 65, 70. *See also* French dogs

Antinomian crisis, 36

Appleton family, 170, 175

Apprentices, 49–51, 70, 135; and apprenticeships, 22, 24

Apthorp, Charles, 113

Aristocracy, 75, 96, 99, 108

Aristocrats: customs and values of, 4, 72, 96, 99, 107; and West End (London), 114

Artisans, 17, 27, 31, 33, 56, 86, 99, 103, 108, 128, 134–35, 148, 155, 168; impoverished, 128, 134; products of, 34; skill of, 22

Artists, 114, 122–23. *See also* Copley, John Singleton; Smibert, John

Asia, 3, 80, 100, 170; fabric from, 100, 112; imports from, 112, 117–18; trade with, 100

Assemblies, 83, 90, 110, 133, 142–43, 153–54; in Boston, 110; and public sphere, 142–43; in Salem, 110, 153–54

Assembly rooms or buildings, 110, 173; in Salem, 110, 116, 133; in York (England), 110

Assize of Bread, 103–4

Atlantic World, 1–2, 8–10, 22, 32–33, 37, 41, 47–51, 71, 78, 82

Atlantic Ocean, 2, 3, 159, 174; trade across, 27; trading network across, 22. *See also* Transatlantic trade

Attorneys, 110, 113

Authority, 127–28; commercial and cultural, 141

Azores, 48, 57

Bach, Johann Sebastian, 110

Bailyn, Bernard, 23, 25

Baldin, Mrs., 51

Balls, 106, 133, 154

213

Lightning Source UK Ltd.
Milton Keynes UK
UKHW010703201220
375546UK00008B/288/J

9 780801 438554